IMAGES
of America

WEST NEWBURY

I0807672

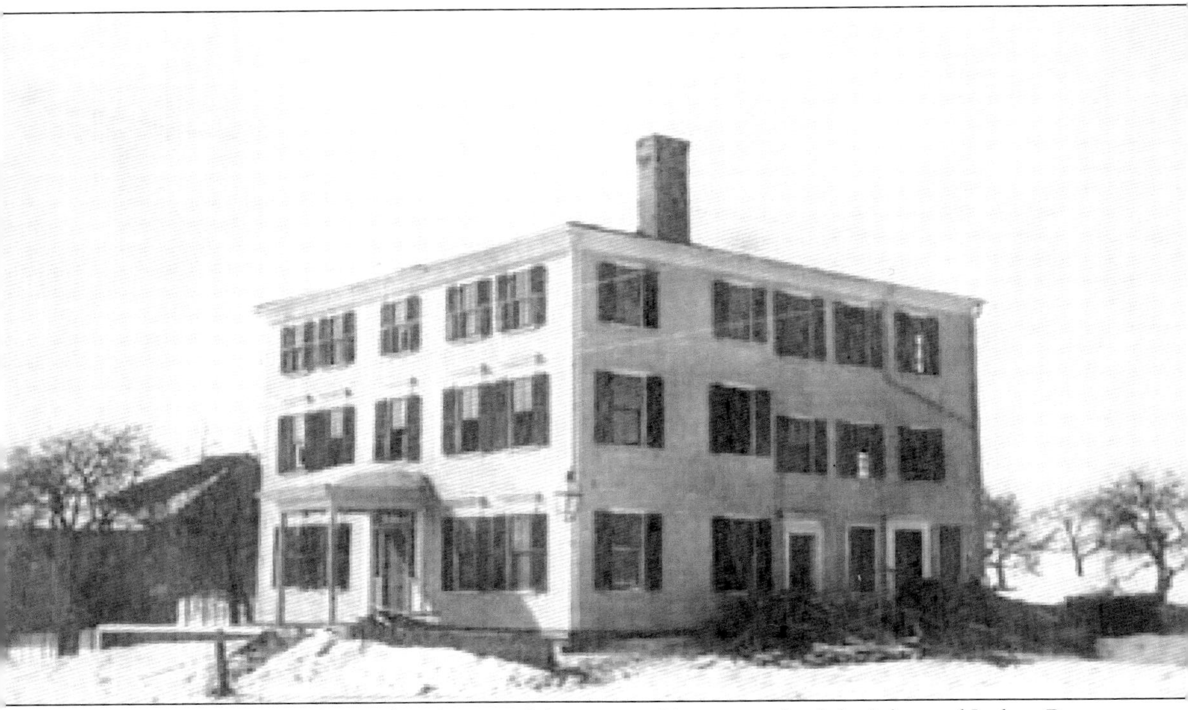

The Hotel Albion, located at the site of the present library, was built by John and Joshua Brewster during the first years of the 19th century. About 1886, it began use as a hotel. Disapproving of alleged illegal activities there, the Emery sisters purchased the property, tore down the building, and gave the property to the town for a library in 1937. (Courtesy of Elinor Spofford.)

On the Cover: The original bridge at this location, between West Newbury and Rocks Village in Haverhill, was built in 1795 and washed out in a spring freshet in 1818. The replacement bridge was built in 1828. It was 900 feet long, 22 feet wide, and was supported by four stone piers and two abutments. It was built entirely of plank except for the floor timbers. (Courtesy of the West Newbury Historical Society.)

IMAGES
of America

WEST NEWBURY

Susan Poore Follansbee and
Jane Wallace Wild

ARCADIA
PUBLISHING

Copyright © 2011 by Susan Poore Follansbee and Jane Wallace Wild
ISBN 978-0-7385-7642-8

Published by Arcadia Publishing
Charleston, South Carolina

Printed in the United States of America

Library of Congress Control Number: 2011926574

For all general information, please contact Arcadia Publishing:
Telephone 843-853-2070
Fax 843-853-0044
E-mail sales@arcadiapublishing.com
For customer service and orders:
Toll-Free 1-888-313-2665

Visit us on the Internet at www.arcadiapublishing.com

This volume is dedicated to Steve Cashman, who did not live to see this book completed but gave us his unwavering support and enthusiasm.

Contents

ACKNOWLEDGMENTS

This volume would not have been possible without the contributions of the following people and institutions, who have generously made their collections available: Cynthia Adams, Rachel Adams, Della Armstrong, Doris Bailey-Jones, Sandra Berkenbush, Scott Berkenbush, William Daley, Warren Dixon, Raymond "Rock" Dower, Elaine Cooney Drolet, Charles Fowler, Donald Fowler, Peter Haack, Barbara Hain, Zella Haskell, Donald Laing, Nancy Elwell Lewis, Acha Moseley Lord, John McGrath, Bruce Merrill, Emily Poore, Jeannette Poore, John Poore, Theresa Poore, Richard Preble, Kim Sharpe, Elinor Spofford, Emilie Steele, John Thurlow, Valerie Tipton, Jacqueline Willis, Laurel Grange, the Grand Army of the Republic Memorial Library in West Newbury, the Newburyport Archival Center at the Newburyport Public Library, the Special Collections Department of the Haverhill Public Library, the Governor's Academy Archives, the *Newburyport Daily News*, the West Newbury Historical Society, the Historical Society of Old Newbury, and the West Newbury Historical Commission.

We would also like to thank our consultants Robert Richard, for his knowledge regarding old cars, and Heather Hull-Colby, for her expertise about horses and carriages. We acknowledge with gratitude the collections and writings of the late Elizabeth Thompson, which supplied many details, as well as newspaper articles by Adelaide Janes, Stephen Cashman, and others.

In addition, we are grateful to Dorothy Cavanaugh, Adelaide Janes, and Katherine M. Gove for reading the manuscript and making suggestions. We would also like to thank our families for their encouragement and patience, especially our husbands, Gordon Follansbee and Robert Wild.

INTRODUCTION

In 1634, men and women on the ship Mary and John arrived in Ipswich from England, intent on settling in the New World. After wintering in Ipswich, they sailed north and landed on the north shore of what is now the Parker River. Here, they began their settlement, which they named Newbury. Soon after, more ships arrived bringing sheep and cattle. Although this stock-raising experiment failed, the settlers remained, and the settlement prospered. As the population grew and land near the river became scarce, some people moved to the west of the Artichoke River, to the "upper woods." The town granted large parcels of land in this area: 300 acres to Edward Rawson in 1644; 80 acres to John Emery in 1659; and 103 acres to Francis Browne—all near the Artichoke River. In 1663, Capt. William Gerrish was granted 260 acres at the Groveland line, and what was then referred to as the "first division of lots" occurred in 1686, parceling out the remaining land between the Bradford Road (later Main Street) and the Merrimack River, from that of Emery to that of Gerrish. John Emery established a gristmill at the mouth of the Artichoke River, and Joseph Pike constructed a dam and sawmill at the mouth of the Indian River. The remainder of what eventually became West Newbury was granted to more settlers in five subsequent divisions of land.

With travel limited to foot or horseback, settlers in this part of the town found it a hardship to attend church, and attendance was required of all residents. After many years of petitioning the town to allow them to separate from the original community, permission was granted in 1693 and the Second Parish of Newbury was established. This separation eventually resulted in a new town, West Newbury, incorporated in 1819. When settlers moving further west found the location of this new church a hardship, the Fourth Parish of Newbury was established.

Relations between the settlers and the Indians appeared to be amicable. Great Tom, an Indian, sold the property on Indian Hill to the town in 1650 for three pounds. There are only two reports of troubles, with one child being killed and nine persons captured in an Indian raid on the Brown farm at 135 Turkey Hill Road in 1695. One girl hid, then ran to spread the alarm. All the captives were eventually rescued, although some later died from the stress of the ordeal. The other incident involved Hananiah Ordway, who lived from 1665 to 1758. He shot and killed an Indian whom he observed skulking around his "garrison" house on Indian Hill at the intersection of Garden Street.

Local industries included shoe making, which began with farmers making shoes for their families in little shops on their farms. Several shoe factories sprang up and thrived for a time; the last, J. Durgin & Sons, closed and moved to Haverhill in 1889. Fortunately for the shoe factory workers, public transportation to Haverhill began in 1886.

During the Battle of Bennington, a Hession soldier and comb maker named William Cleland was captured and quartered in West Newbury. Cleland joined Enoch Noyes, who had been making coarse combs and buttons by hand near 127 Main Street. By the 1830s and 1840s, there were 32 comb shops in town, including the Somerby C. Noyes Company at 320 Main Street and others on

Pleasant Street and Harrison Avenue. As the comb industry expanded throughout the country, it declined in West Newbury. The last comb shop in town, S.C. Noyes & Co., closed in 1904.

Other industries flourished in West Newbury for a time. There were carriage businesses on Pipestave Hill, the Training Field, and Rogers Street. There was a tannery on Whetstone Street, a brickyard near the Groveland line, a short-lived cigar-making business, and straw bonnets were made by housewives on Crane Neck Hill. Dairy farms, orchards, poultry farms, and truck gardens flourished; Cherry Hill Nurseries was internationally known for its peonies and trees. A large stand of oak trees stood on Pipestave Hill, and they were used to make barrel or "pipe" staves. Larger trees were cut and sold for masts to the shipbuilders of Newburyport. Ships docked at a wharf at the foot of Whetstone Street brought raw materials for shoes and combs.

Notable residents include Cornelius Conway Felton, a West Newbury native and president of Harvard College. Other well-known residents included E. Moody Boynton, inventor of the monorail railroad and a crosscut saw, concert tenor Roland Hayes, and Julian D. Steele, the first commissioner of the Massachusetts Department of Commerce and Development. For a time, beloved children's book author Virginia Lee Burton lived at Chestnut Hill Farm, and while there wrote *Mike Mulligan and His Steam Shovel.* When she could not think of an ending to her book, then 12-year-old Dickie Birkenbush [sic] suggested turning the steam shovel into a furnace.

According to Joshua Coffin in his book *A Sketch of the History of Newbury, Newburyport, and West Newbury,* John Kelly Sr. was given permission in 1694 to keep a ferry over the Merrimack River just upstream from the location of Rocks Bridge. Later, John Swett Jr. was licensed to keep a ferry there. The first Rocks Bridge opened for business on November 26, 1795. Consisting of four arches, a draw, and supported by five piers and two abutments, at 1,000 feet long it was the longest bridge over the Merrimack River. The second Rocks Bridge was constructed in 1828, after the first was swept away by ice in 1818. This bridge had a covered drawbridge and six covered spans, which were gradually replaced by steel spans between 1894 and 1914.

In 1819, West Newbury separated from Newbury. The town, first named Parsons, was renamed West Newbury in 1820, with 1,279 residents reported in the census the same year. The population increased to 2,087 in 1865 and decreased to a low of 1,405 in 1904. West Newbury's population began to increase in the 1950s after Interstate 95 opened up the possibility of commuting to Boston. Farming, once a mainstay, declined with the conversion of farmland to homes, and the population steadily increased to 4,549 by 2010.

The town is known as a picturesque residential community and home to Christmas tree farms. Residents, many of whom work from home, remain involved in the town as they did so long ago. Recreational areas and open space abound where there was once farmland. We have tried to capture the essence of the town in photographs of the last century, knowing that space would not permit printing them all. We are fortunate in the abundance of photographs that still exist of those earlier days. Some of the people pictured here you may have known, others you may only have heard of, or they may be strangers to you, but they all have a story. Many of the buildings will be recognizable and West Newbury, thankfully, is still beautiful and welcoming. It is beneficial to all to look back at what it was like in earlier days. (The information in this introduction came mainly from *History of Newbury, Mass., 1635–1902* by John J. Currier.)

One

Rivers
On and Over the Water

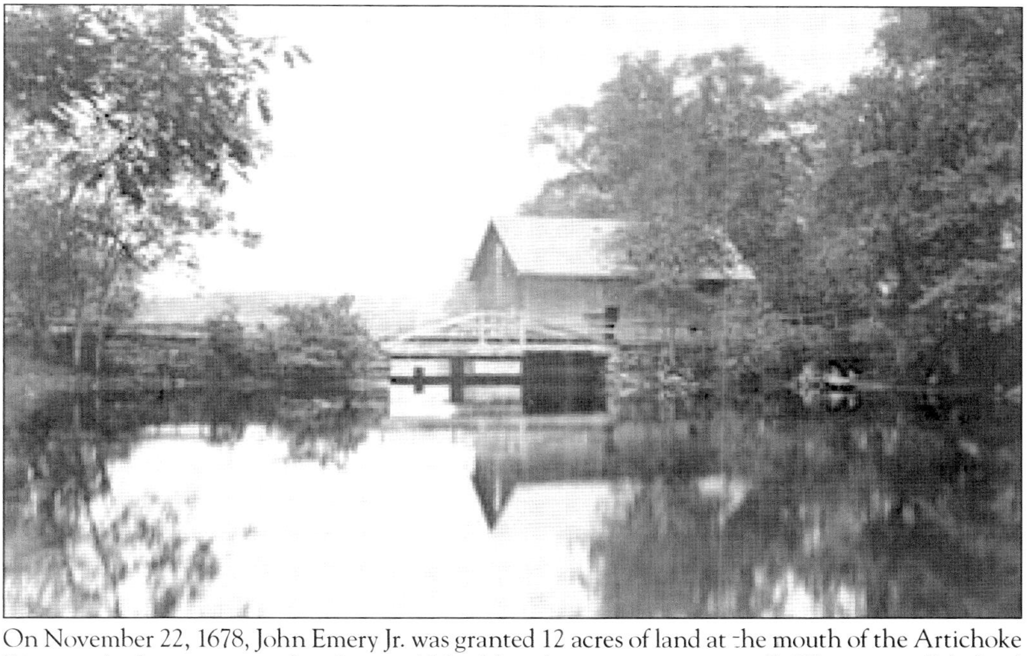

On November 22, 1678, John Emery Jr. was granted 12 acres of land at the mouth of the Artichoke River with the provision that he would build and maintain a gristmill. The gristmill helped "the Inhabitants of the town to have their corn ground according to their Turnes before any of another town," according to *Ould Newbury* by John J. Currier. (Courtesy of the West Newbury Historical Society.)

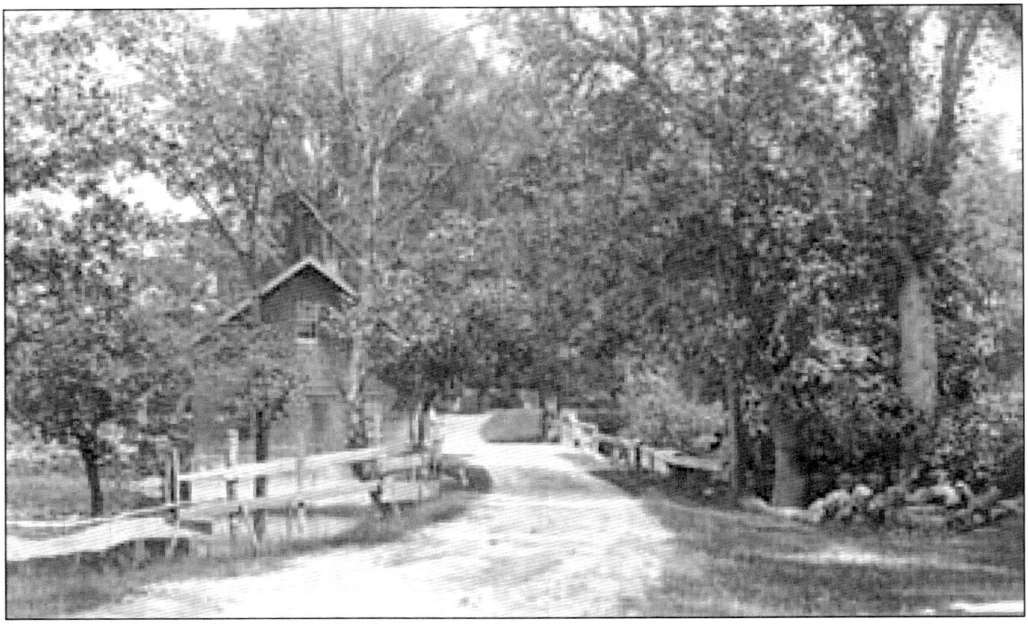

John Emery's mill was sold out of the family in 1761, and about 60 years later, Samuel Curson of Newburyport purchased the mill, along with a house and barn on the Newburyport side of the bridge. In 1908, a concrete dam was built here. (Courtesy of the West Newbury Historical Society.)

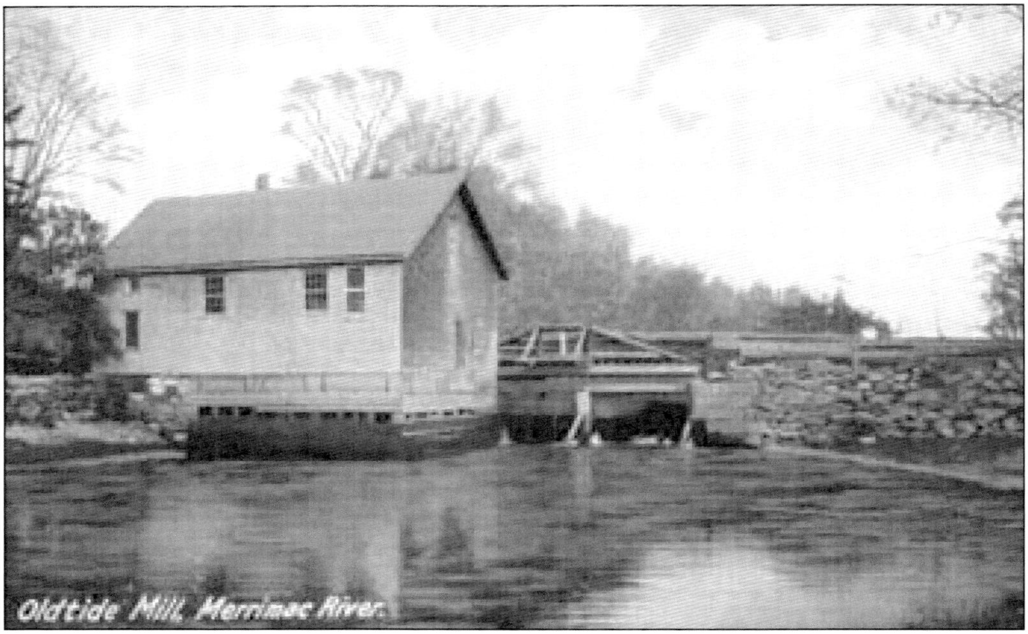

Artists and photographers have long been attracted to the picturesque beauty of Curzon Mill, as it is now known, and its surroundings. This image is unusual in that it shows the mill from below the dam. The bridge is no longer open to automobiles. (Photograph by H.C. Leighton Co.; courtesy of Rock Dower.)

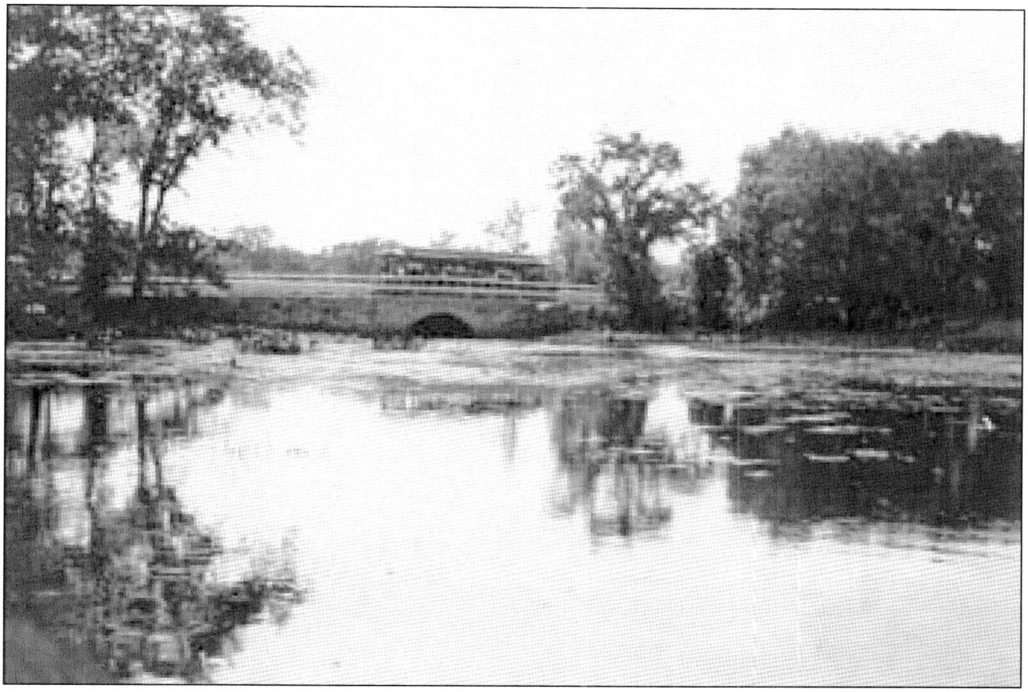

Trolleys went along Main Street, between Haverhill and Newburyport, from 1895 until the 1930s. A bridge over the Artichoke River at the Bradford Road, later known as Main Street, is shown on the 1729 map of West Newbury. It is uncertain whether the bridge pictured here is the original one, but there has been a bridge at that location ever since. In 1972, the bridge was replaced with a more-modern highway bridge, the curve in the road was straightened, and the road was widened at that time. (Above, courtesy of the Newburyport Archival Center at the Newburyport Public Library; below, courtesy of the West Newbury Historical Society.)

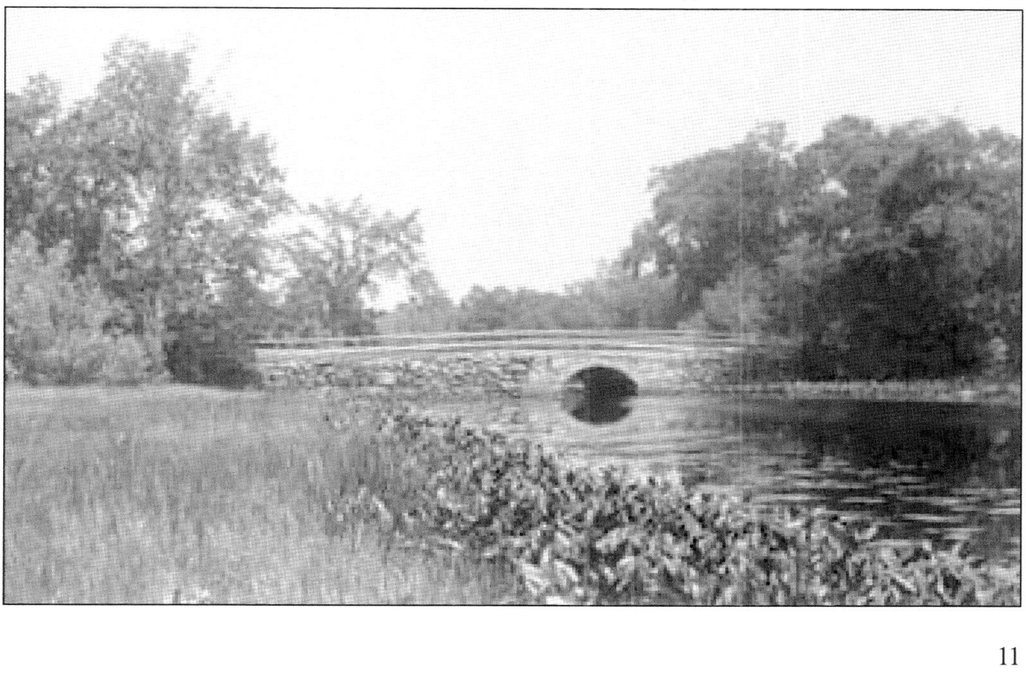

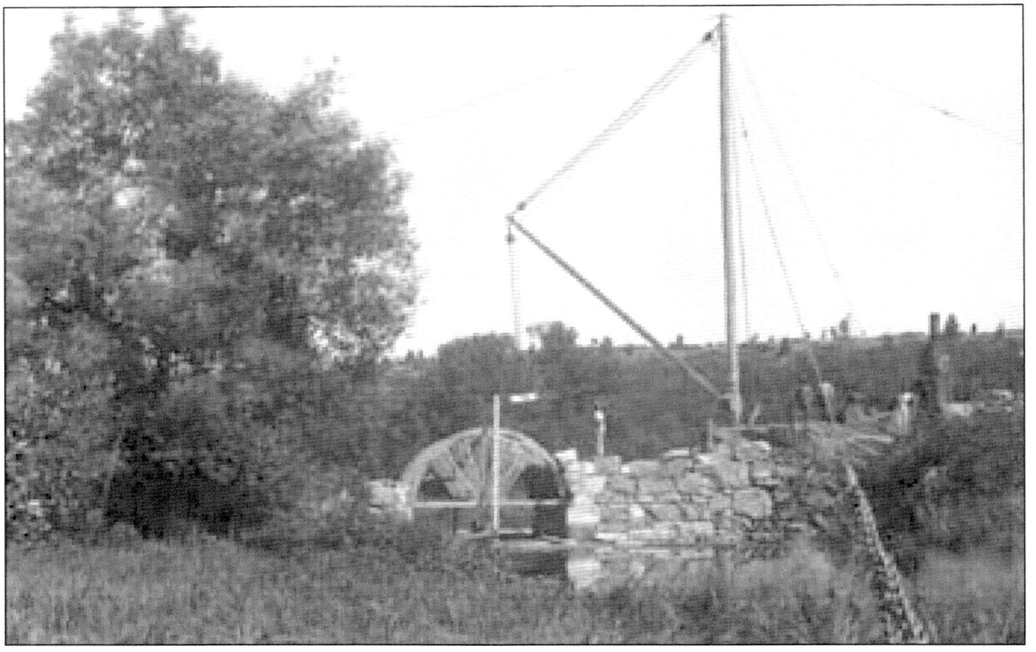

This bridge over the Artichoke River on Middle Street, called Plummer Spring Road in Newburyport, was built in 1891. This unusual photograph by John White Winder, a well-known Newburyport photographer of the time, shows the method used to create the arched bridge. (Part of the John White Winder collection housed at the Governor's Academy Archives, Byfield, Massachusetts. Reprinted with the permission of the Governor's Academy.)

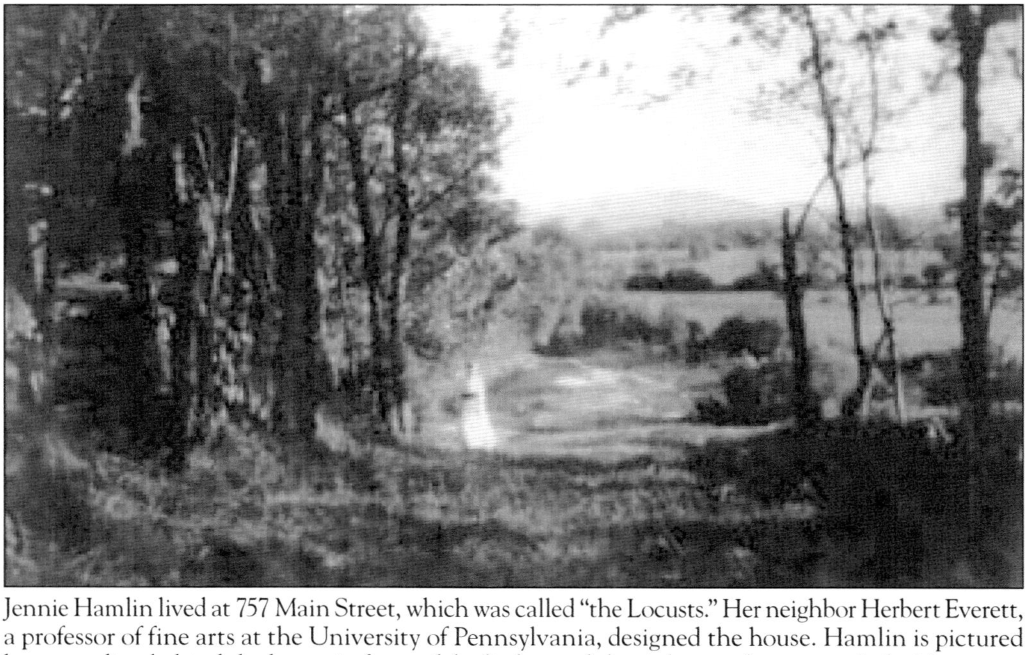

Jennie Hamlin lived at 757 Main Street, which was called "the Locusts." Her neighbor Herbert Everett, a professor of fine arts at the University of Pennsylvania, designed the house. Hamlin is pictured here standing behind the house in front of the little pond that is known by some as Lake Henrietta. Indian Hill is seen in the distance to the south. (Courtesy of Susan Poore Follansbee.)

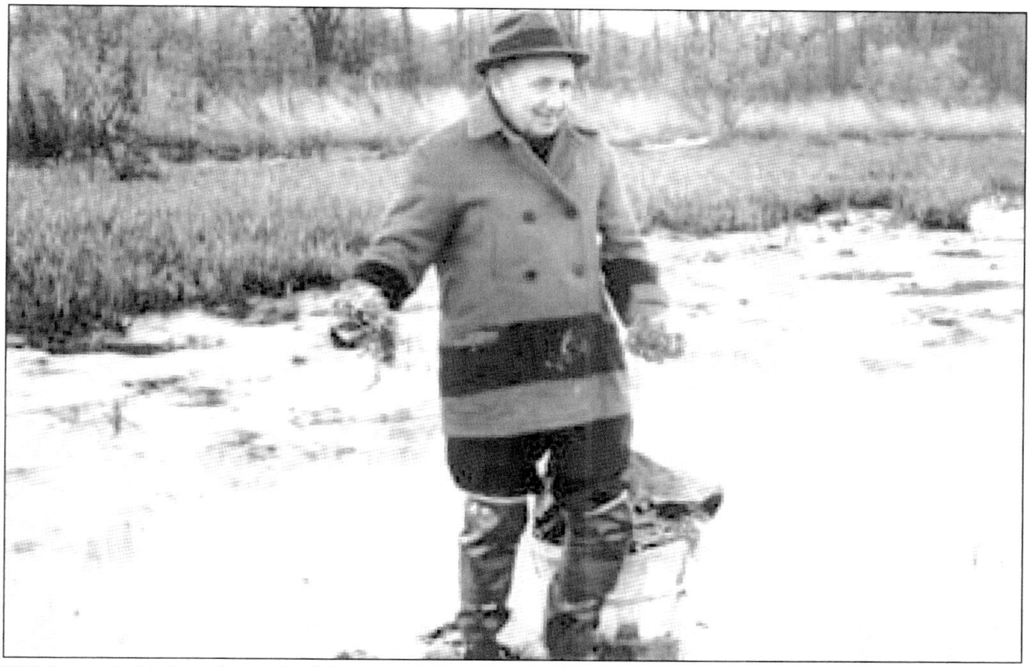

Wild rice fields lay along the Merrimack River near the foot of Coffin Street, offering both food and nesting places for annual migrations of waterfowl and shorebirds. This is a popular bird-watching area. Volunteers, such as Joseph McAuliffe, shown here, planted the fields many years ago. (Courtesy of Susan Poore Follansbee.)

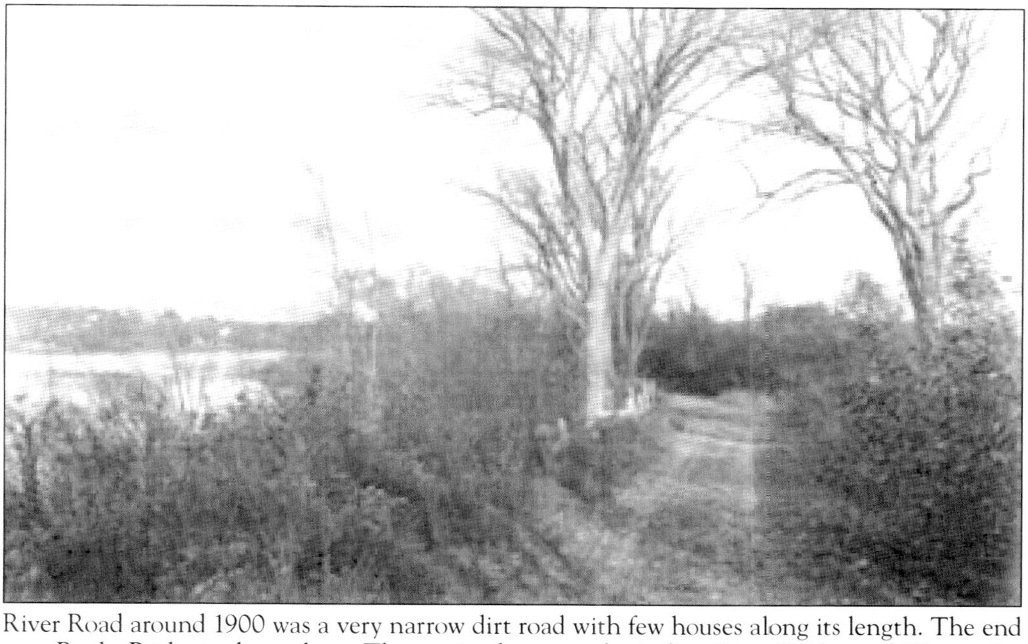

River Road around 1900 was a very narrow dirt road with few houses along its length. The end near Rocks Bridge is shown here. The section between the Indian River Bridge and Way to the River at the other end was abandoned around 1985. (Photograph by William E. Sharples; courtesy of John McGrath.)

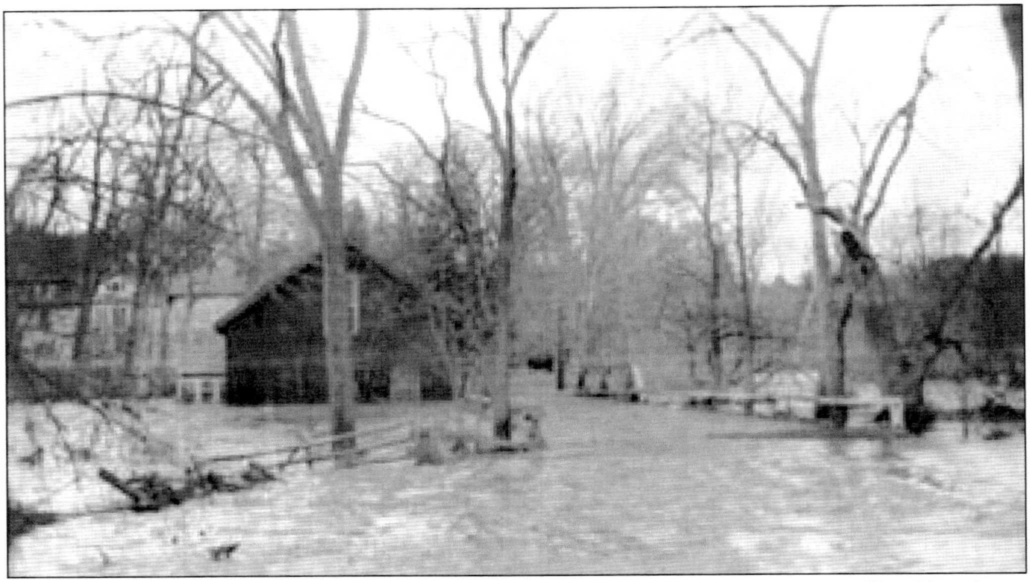

During the spring flood of 1936, the Merrimack River crested at 30 feet above flood height in Haverhill. At its crest, the river flowed backwards into the Artichoke River. Curzon Mill is shown here on March 22, 1936, two days after the highest water. Notice the water line above the window; at its highest, the water covered the handrail of the bridge. (Courtesy of Susan Poore Follansbee.)

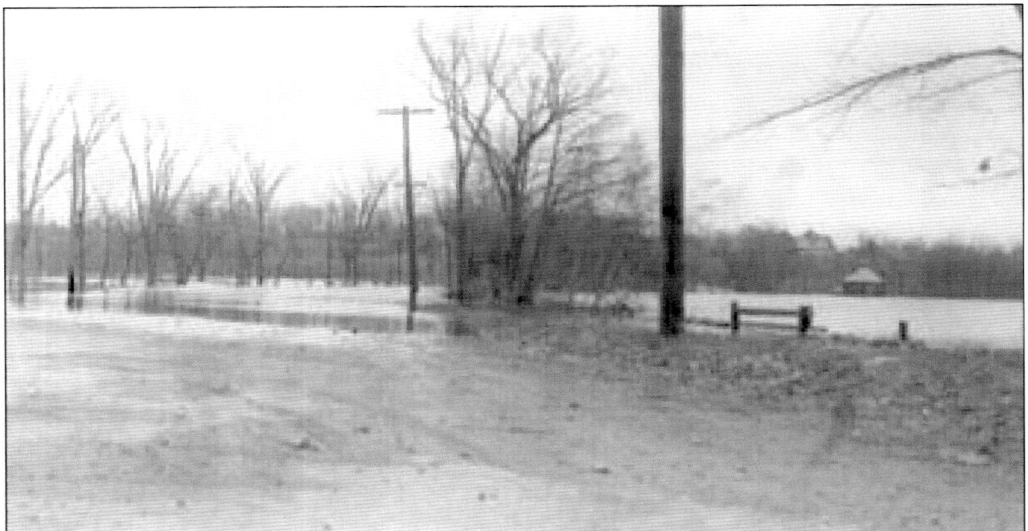

On March 22, 1936, Main Street was blocked at the Artichoke River by floodwaters, as was the road by Curzon Mill. The Middle Street, Rogers Street, and Pikes Bridge Road Bridges were also under water. Looking toward the Artichoke Bridge, Sawyer's Hill in Newburyport is seen in the distance. This photograph was taken from the vicinity of the current West Newbury Water Department Building. (Courtesy of Susan Poore Follansbee.)

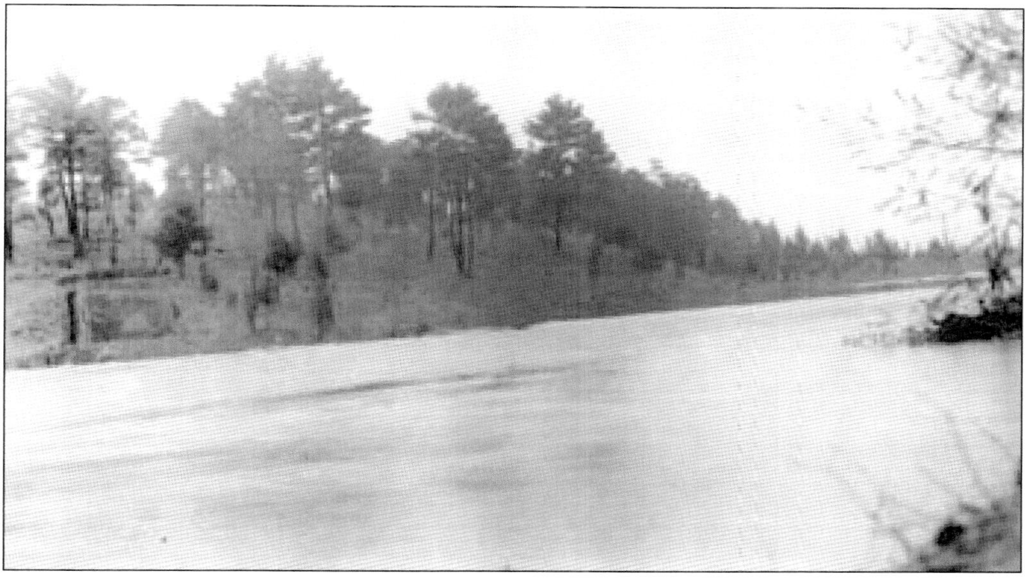

On March 22, 1936, two days after high water, the dam just below Middle Street was completely covered, as shown in the picture above, and the Merrimack River flowed up into the entire Artichoke River reservoir. Notice the high water line just above the door on the pump house. According to the *Newburyport Daily News*, Newburyport could only be reached from West Newbury by way of Byfield and Governor Dummer Academy. On April 26, 1936, about 35 days after the above picture was taken, the photograph below was captured from approximately the same spot. The Merrimack River had receded several feet by then but was still above flood height. Pictured are Mary and Howard Poore. (Both, courtesy of Susan Poore Follansbee.)

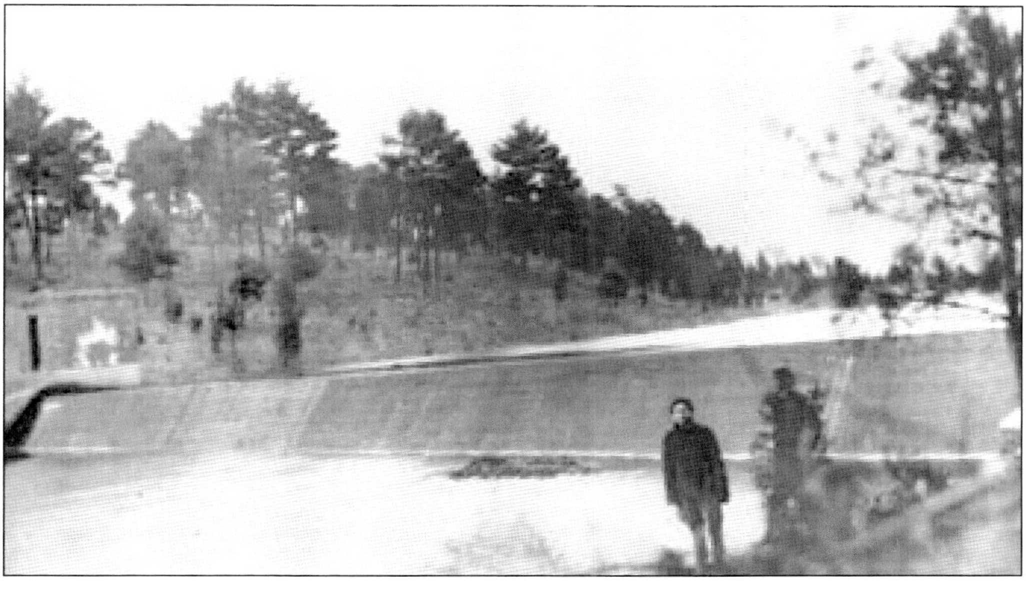

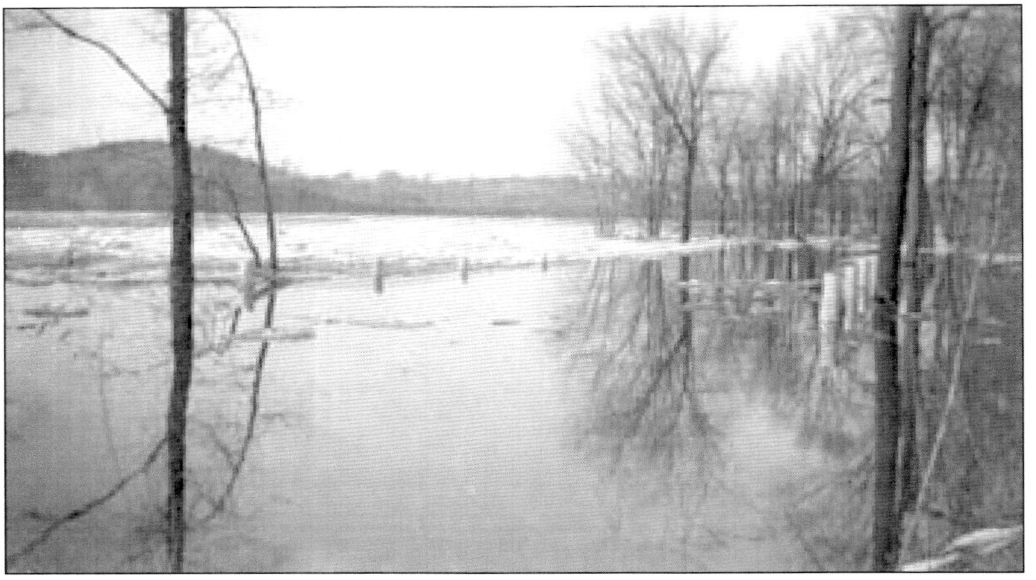

The March 1936 flood also caused problems in the vicinity of Rocks Bridge. River Road was totally under water near Worth's Lane, as was the end of Bridge and Church Streets. In Groveland, flooding was worse, and the bridge roadbed was totally underwater with debris piling up against the bridge. (Courtesy of the West Newbury Historical Society.)

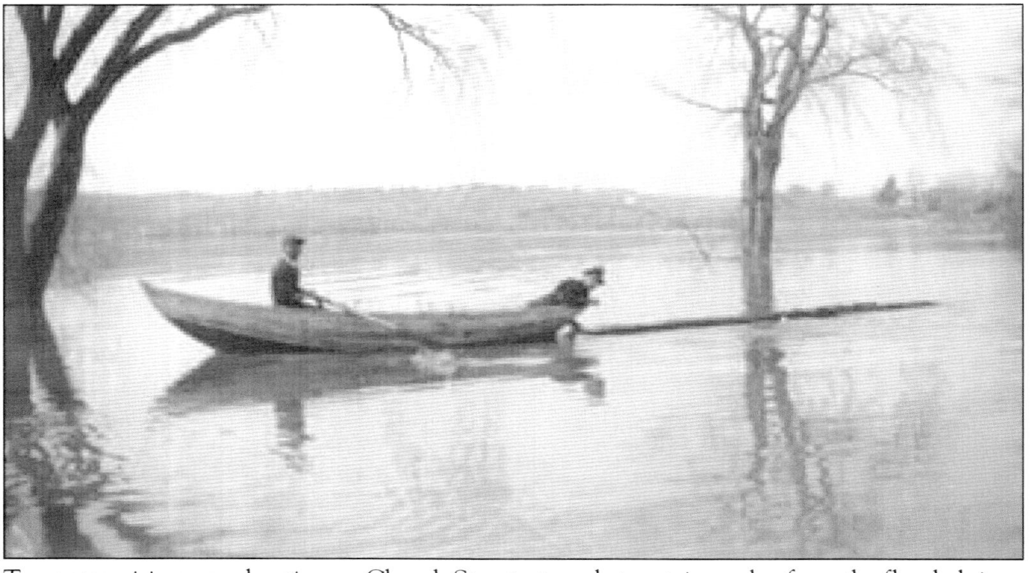

Two enterprising men, boating on Church Street, struggle to retrieve a log from the flooded river. Rocks Bridge is in the distance, and its roadbed is nearly, but not quite, covered by the flood. Church Street, Bridge Street, Ferry Lane, and River Road were all impassible due to the high waters. (Courtesy of the West Newbury Historical Society.)

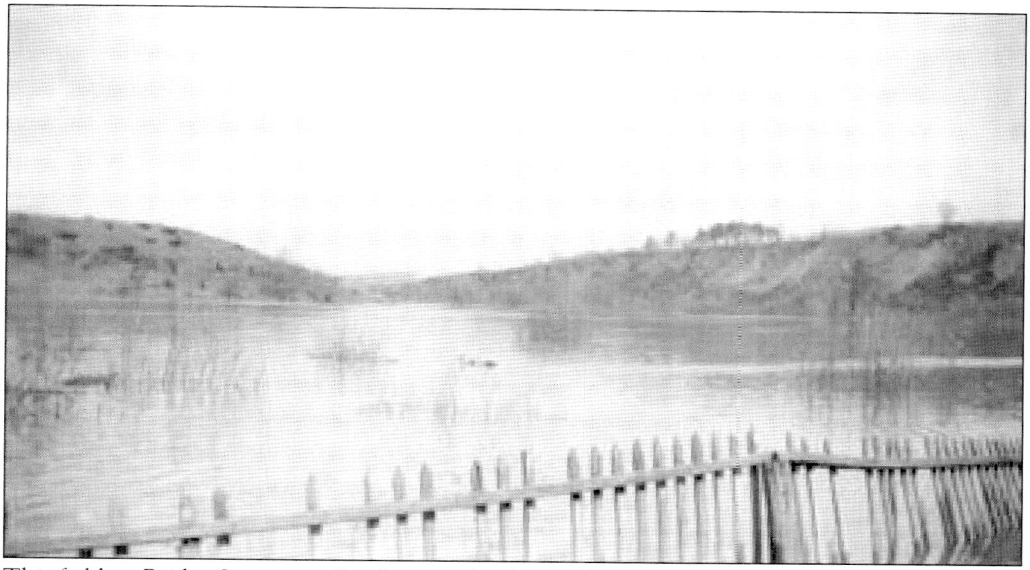

This field on Bridge Street was flooded to a depth of 10 feet. The water went from the river across Church and Bridge Streets, around the high land at the end of River Road, and back across River Road to the river. River Road residents were cut off from the rest of the town unless they traveled by boat or walked across lots. (Courtesy of the West Newbury Historical Society.)

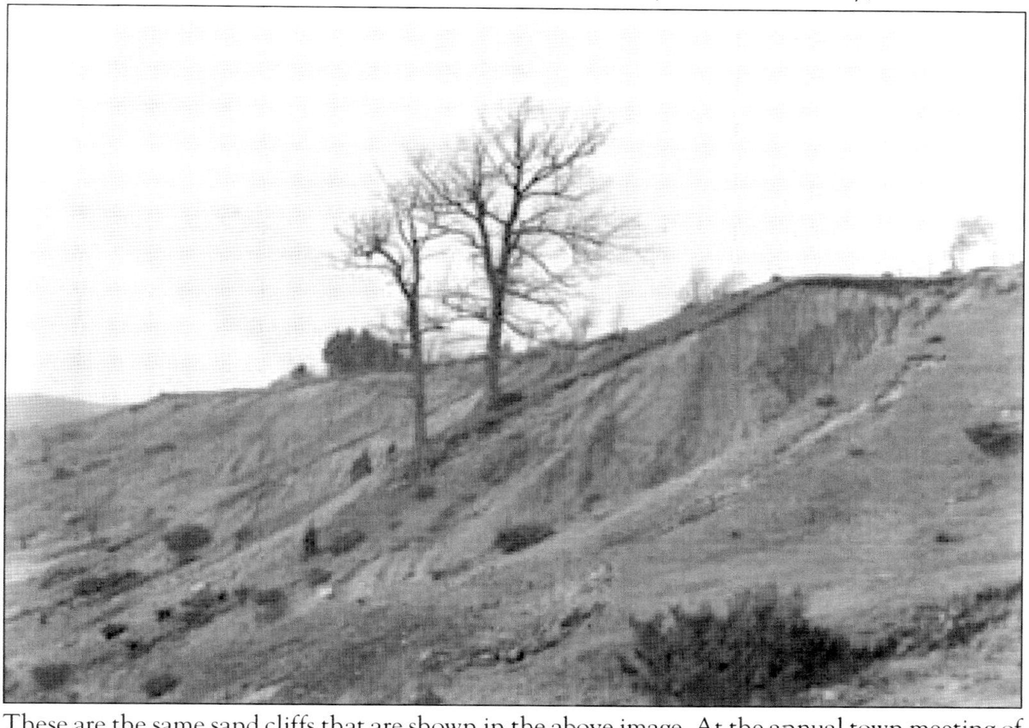

These are the same sand cliffs that are shown in the above image. At the annual town meeting of March 2, 1868, it was voted to discontinue the road between the end of Bailey's Lane and Worth's Lane. This was because the road was continuing to cave in and land repairs were proving costly and dangerous. (Photograph by William E. Sharples; courtesy of John McGrath.)

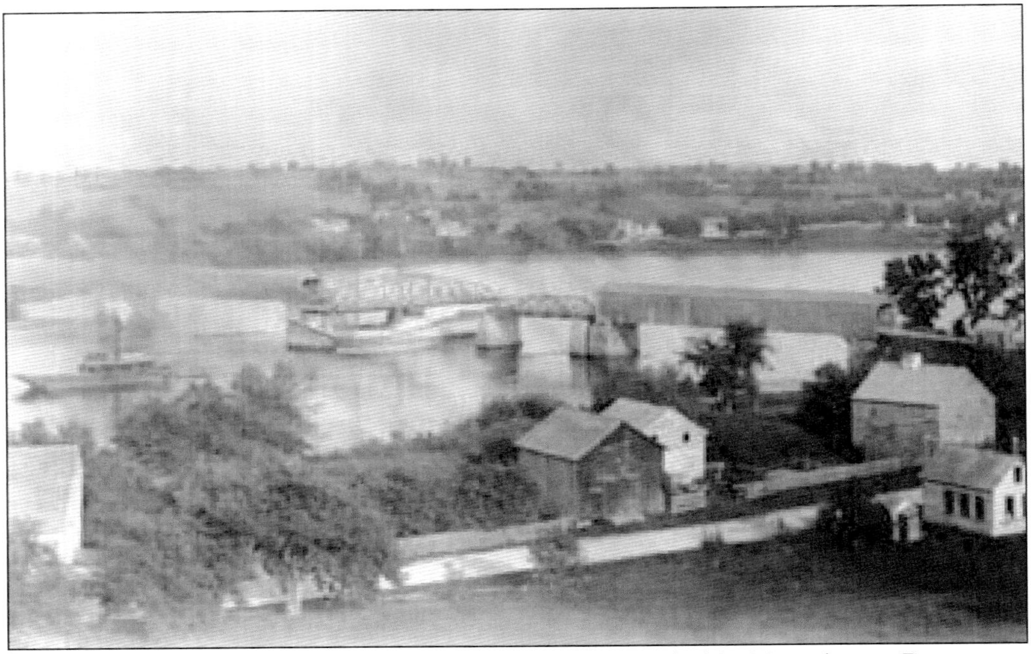

Rocks Bridge contains the oldest moveable span under the control of the Massachusetts Department of Transportation. In 1982, it was said to be one of only two hand-operated draws in this part of the state. Looking toward West Newbury, this picture was taken before 1894, which was when the Haverhill end was replaced with an iron span from Rocks Village. (Courtesy of the Trustees of the Haverhill Public Library, Special Collections Department.)

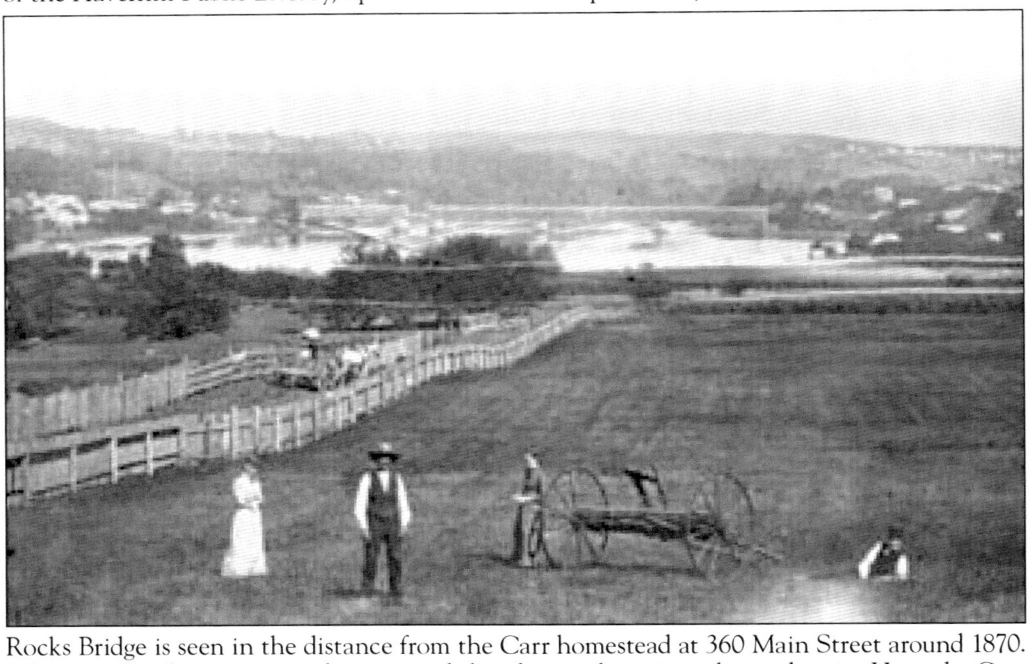

Rocks Bridge is seen in the distance from the Carr homestead at 360 Main Street around 1870. A horse pulls a hay wagon in the center while a dump rake waits to be used again. Here, the Carr family poses for a picture. (Courtesy of the West Newbury Historical Society.)

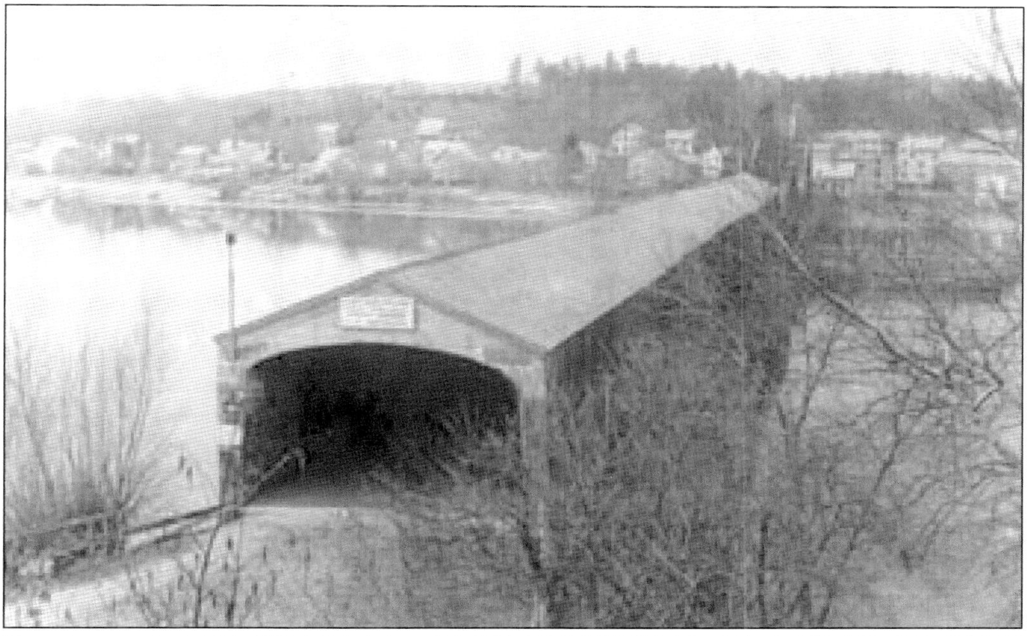

The sign reads, "HEAVY LOADS or DRIVING FASTER THAN A WALK, STRICTLY FORBIDDEN, per order County Commissioners." Rocks Bridge is seen here from the West Newbury side with Rocks Village in the background. The picture was taken after 1894, which was when the covered section on the Haverhill end was removed. (Courtesy of the Trustees of the Haverhill Public Library, Special Collections Department.)

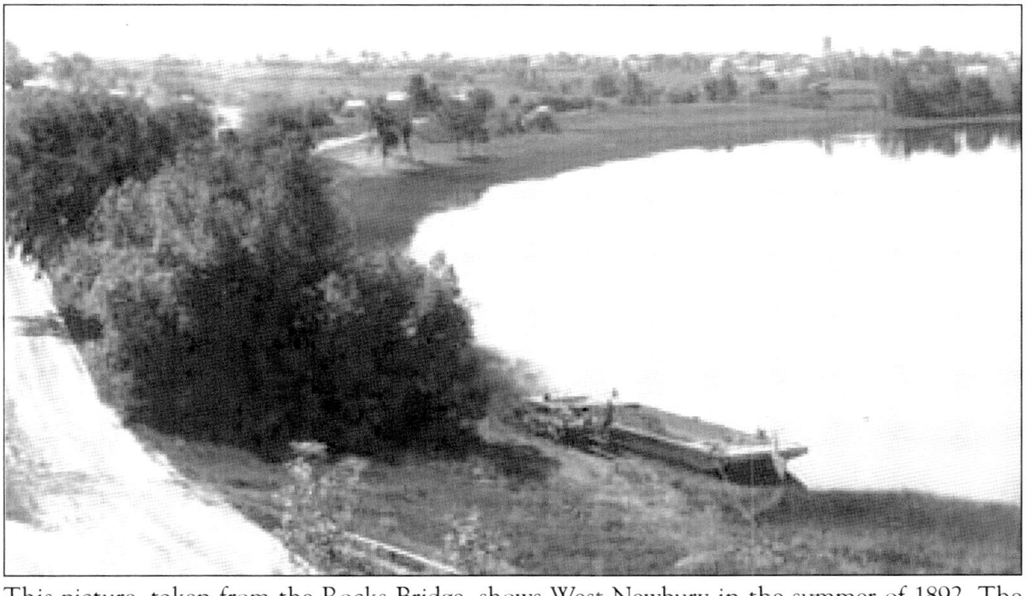

This picture, taken from the Rocks Bridge, shows West Newbury in the summer of 1892. The steeples of the Second Congregational and St. Ann's Churches are visible at the right, and Meetinghouse Hill is in the far distance. In the foreground, a team of horses is pulled up to a gundalow filled with coal. (Photograph by Charles Osgood; courtesy of the Trustees of the Haverhill Public Library, Special Collections Department.)

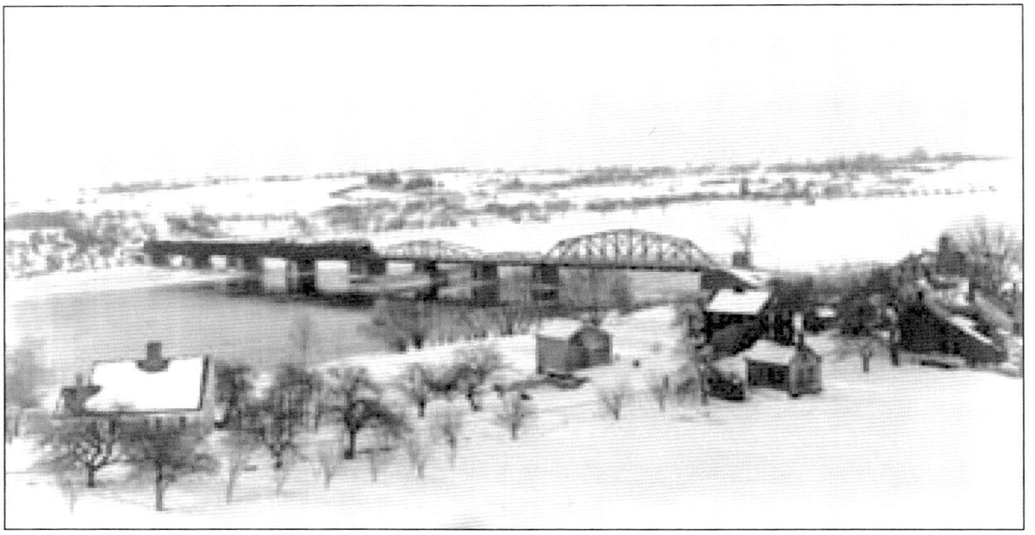

Rocks Bridge is pictured in winter looking from Rocks Village toward West Newbury. Although tolls were abolished in 1868, the tollhouse remains just to the right of the bridge. The fenced-in area in the center background is Bridge Street Cemetery. (Photograph by William E. Sharples; courtesy of John McGrath.)

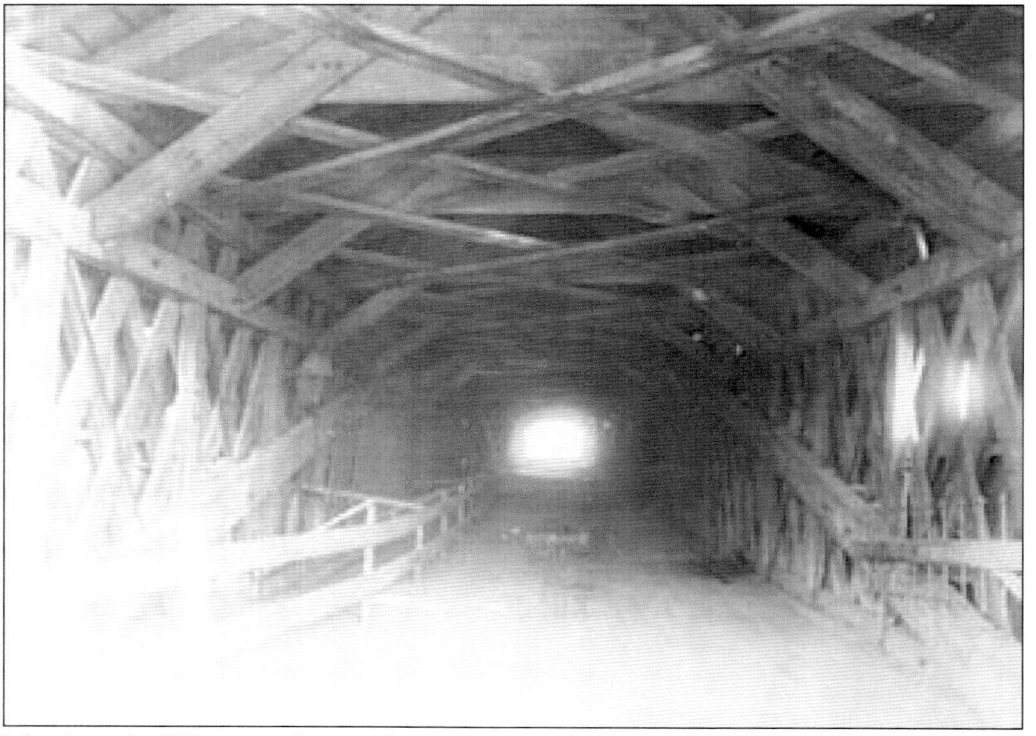

John Greenleaf Whittier, a famous 19th-century poet from Haverhill, mentioned the bridge in his poem "The Countess" as follows: "To the dark tunnel of the bridge, the street comes straggling down." This view inside Rocks Bridge shows the bracing and the "light at the end of the tunnel." (Courtesy of the Trustees of the Haverhill Public Library, Special Collections Department.)

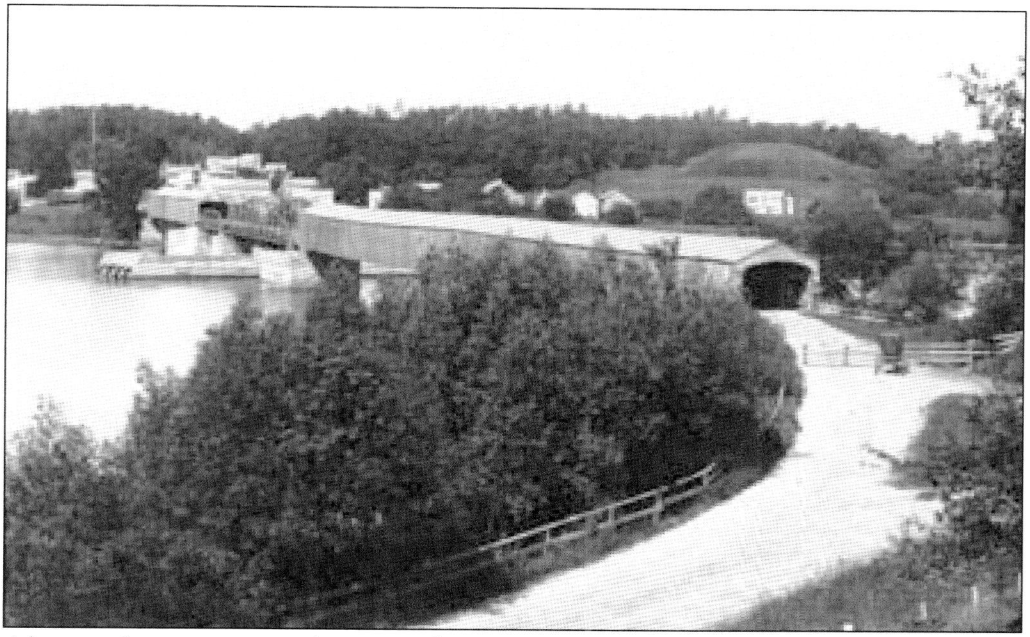

A horse and carriage waits at the gate on the West Newbury end. Tolls were abolished in 1868 when toll bridges became public highways by act of the Massachusetts General Court. At that time, the county commissioners awarded the stockholders of Rocks Bridge 30¢ on a dollar for their shares. (Courtesy of the Trustees of the Haverhill Public Library, Special Collections Department.)

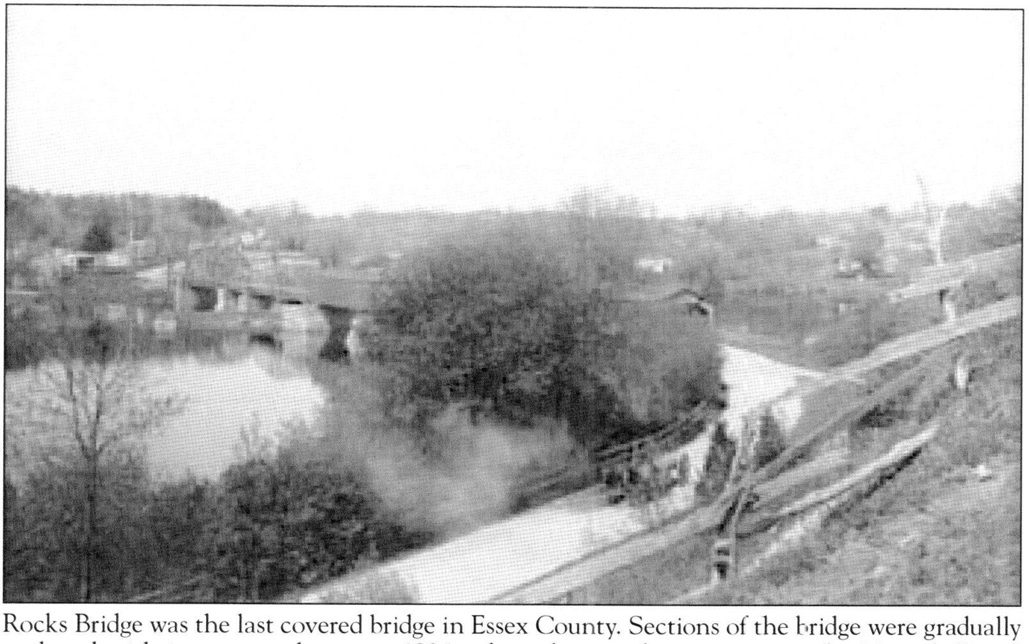

Rocks Bridge was the last covered bridge in Essex County. Sections of the bridge were gradually replaced with iron spans between 1894, when the wooden section on the Haverhill end was removed, and 1914, when the wooden section on the West Newbury end was removed. (Photograph by G.W.W. Bartlett; courtesy of the Trustees of the Haverhill Public Library, Special Collections Department.)

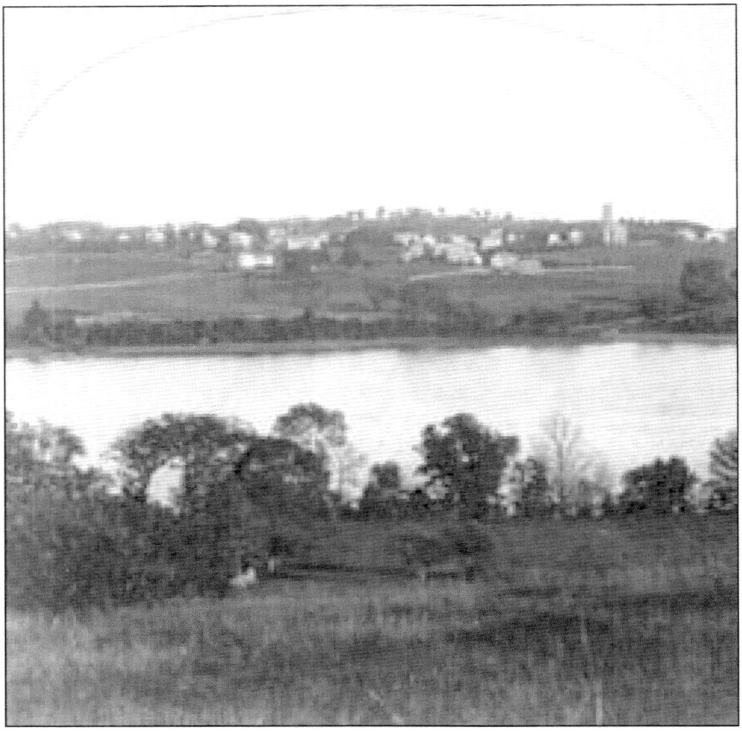

This stereopticon slide is of West Newbury village looking across the Merrimack River from East Haverhill. The steeple of the Congregational church is visible at the right but not the steeple of the Catholic church, which was built in 1878. (Stereopticon slide by O.H. Copeland, New Market, New Hampshire; courtesy of Valerie Tipton.)

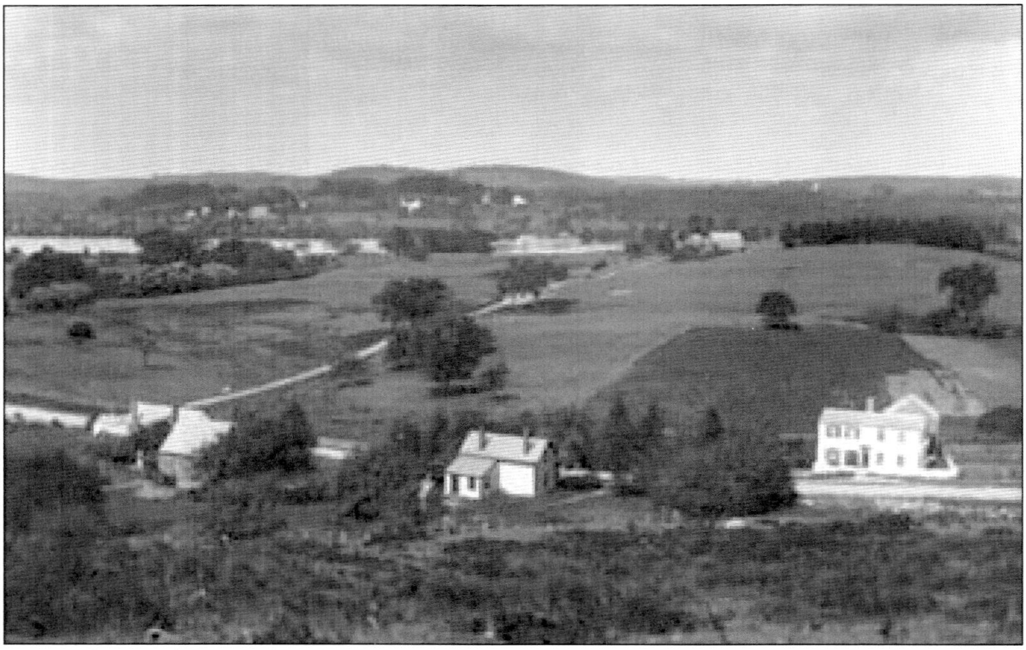

Pictured from the top of Brake Hill, the steamer *Merrimack* is traveling downstream toward Newburyport. Farm Lane leads from Main Street to the Jaques farm, later known as Chestnut Hill Farm. The field to the left of Farm Lane is now the location of Pentucket Senior High School. (Courtesy of Warren Dixon.)

Two

AGRICULTURE
A BYGONE LIFESTYLE

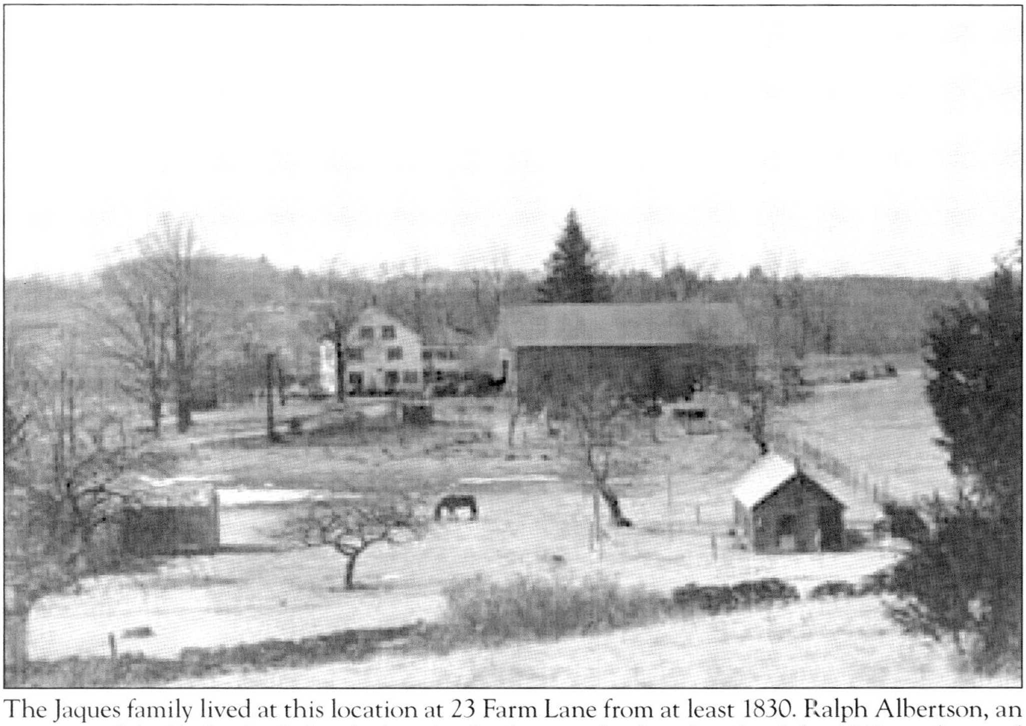

The Jaques family lived at this location at 23 Farm Lane from at least 1830. Ralph Albertson, an ancestor of the Berkenbush family, bought the farm in the first decade of the 1900s and named it Chestnut Hill Farm for its chestnut trees, which Romulus Jaques had planted there. (Courtesy of Sandra Berkenbush.)

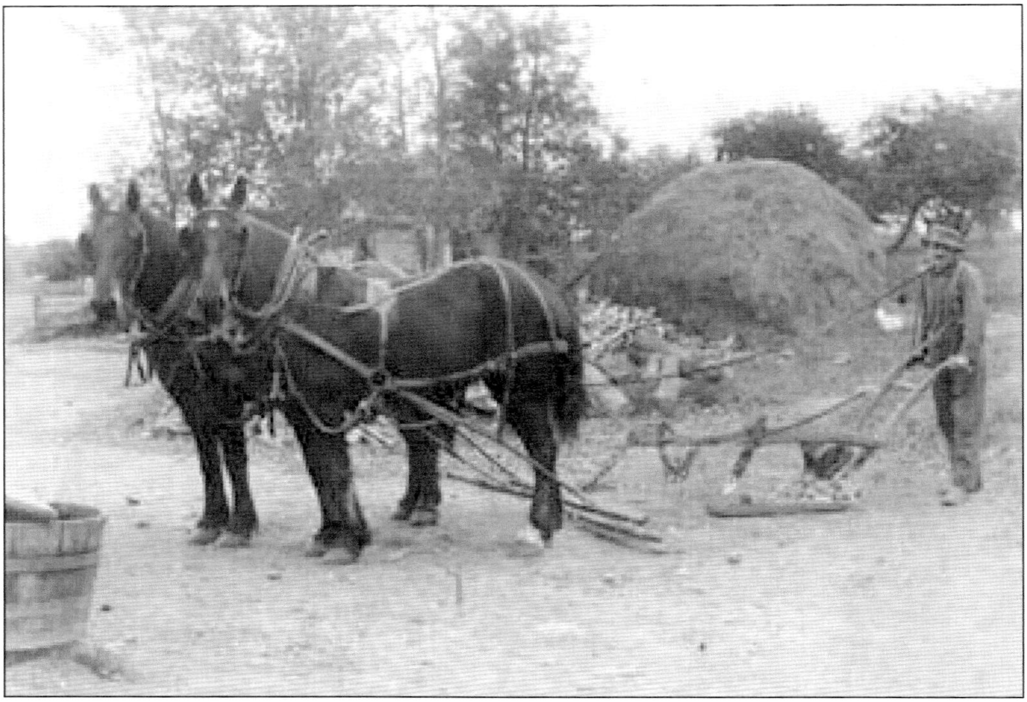

Romulus Preston Jaques, a lifelong West Newbury resident who lived on Stewart Street, prepares to plow with his two horses. Jaques, with his hands busy holding the plow, has wrapped the reins around his body so he can guide the horses, although the horses may be voice trained and not need the reins. (Courtesy of the West Newbury Historical Society.)

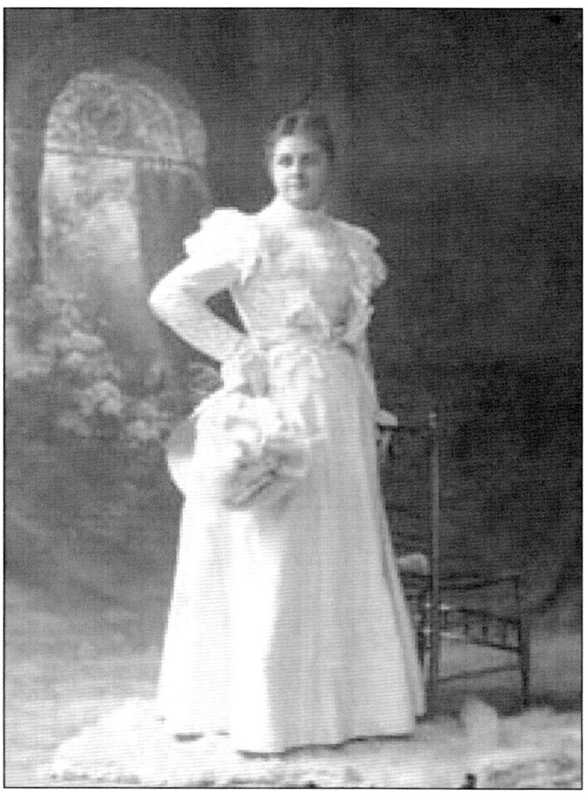

According to town reports, Eva Sprague Flook taught at No. 2 School from 1902 to 1906 and then substituted at Nos. 3 and 9 and at Central School. The wife of Lewis Flook, she was widowed at age 56 when her husband fell from his hayloft. Here, the fashionable Eva is dressed up for some event in 1898, prior to her marriage. (Courtesy of the West Newbury Historical Society.)

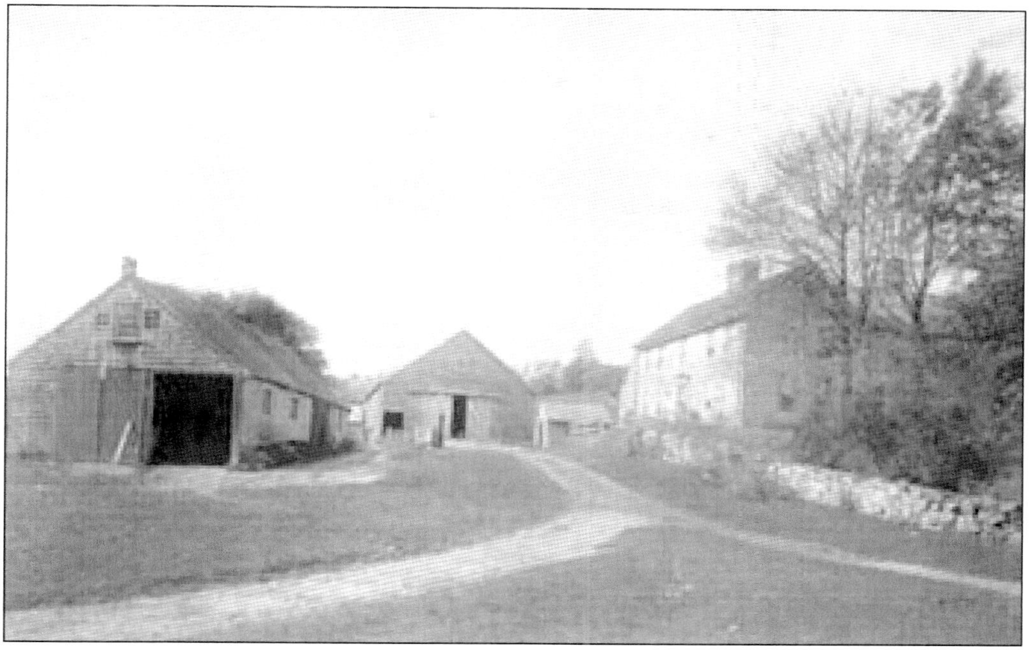

The two Flook farms are shown on the West Newbury maps of 1872 and 1884, one at the foot of the back side of Crane Neck Hill and one slightly beyond it on the corner of Brown Island Road. The farm shown above is the Lewis Flook farm. Pictured below is Lewis Flook with his horse and milk wagon, which says "G.L. Flook & Son" above the door. The Flooks were the first in the area to raise strawberries and ship them to Boston by way of the Byfield railroad depot. (Above, courtesy of Sandra Berkenbush; below, courtesy of the West Newbury Historical Society.)

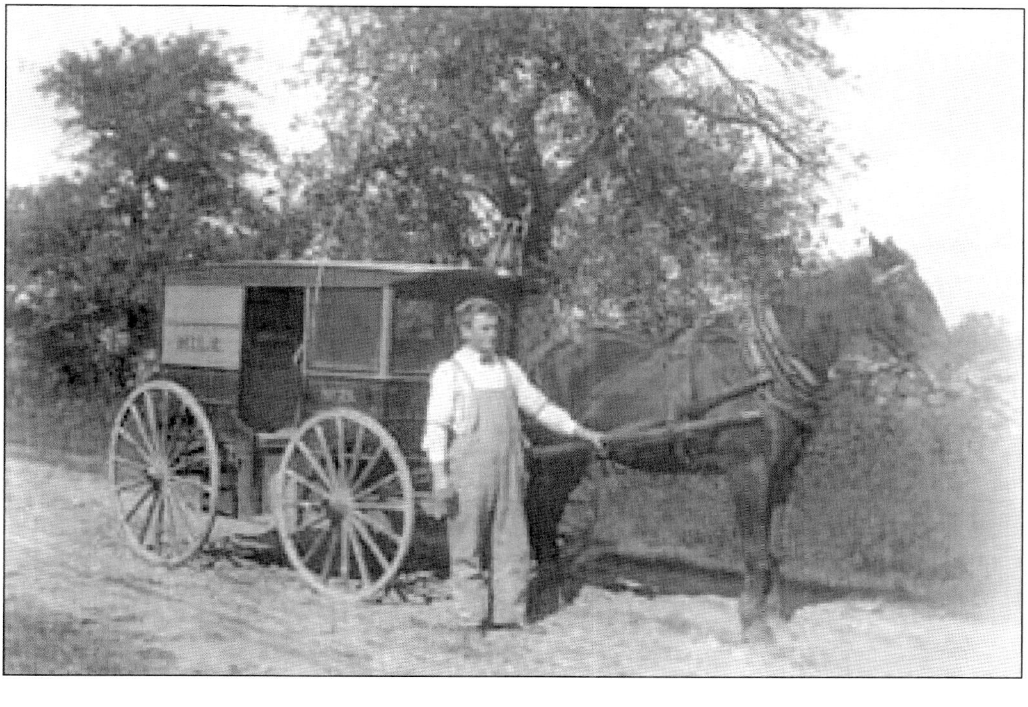

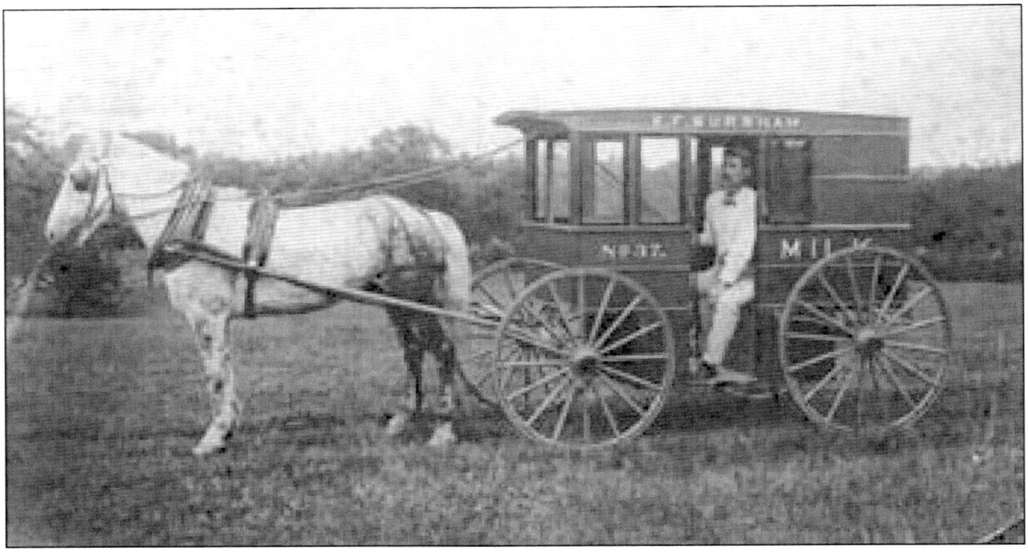

Benjamin Franklin Burnham moved to West Newbury from New Hampshire sometime prior to 1895 when his first child, Elmer Burnham, was born. The family lived in the garrison house at 154 Main Street. Burnham was a farmer, running a milk delivery route in West Newbury and Haverhill. (Courtesy of William Daley.)

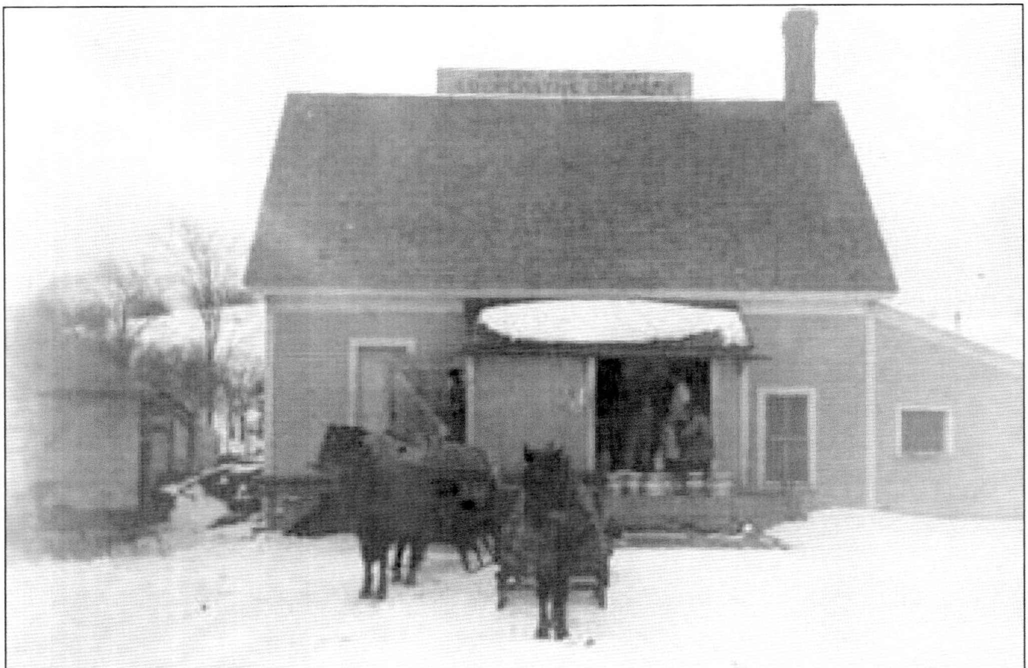

The West Newbury Cooperative Creamery, located at 961 Main Street, was in business for several years around 1900. On July 17, 1905, the building burned to the ground, and in 1909, the stockholders voted to dispose of the entire plant, including land, buildings, and machinery. The Emery sisters of Emery Lane bought the land and erected a house there for their employee Daniel Lyons. (Courtesy of the West Newbury Historical Commission.)

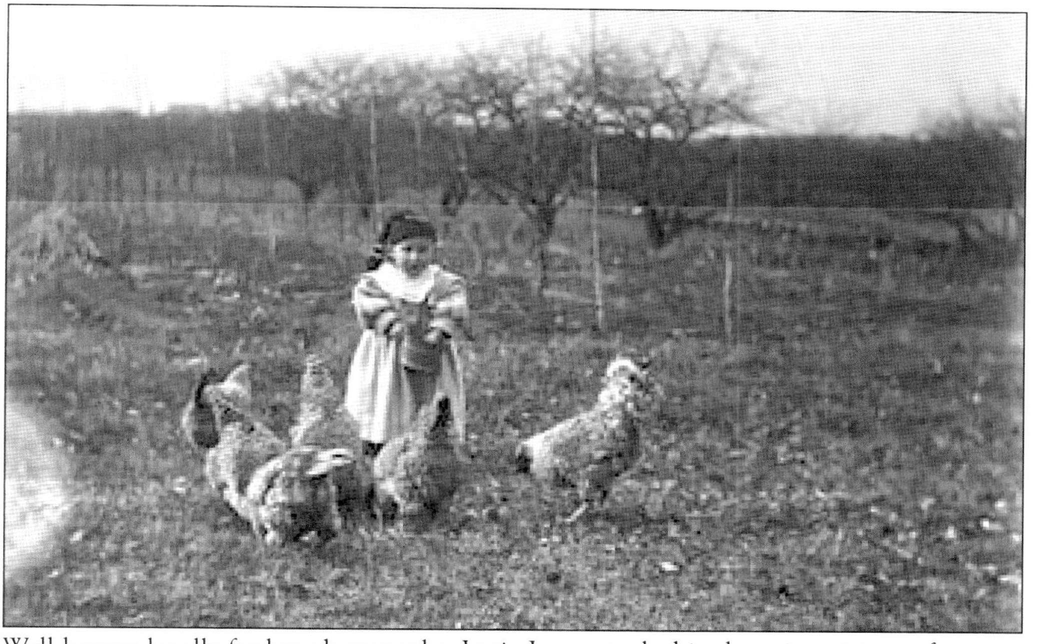

Well known locally for her photographs, Jessie Jaques took this charming picture of a sweet child, possibly a younger relative. Except for the name of the photographer, very little is known regarding this picture, except that children were taught at a very early age the responsibilities that living on a family farm entailed. Everyone pitched in to help. (Photograph by Jessie Jaques; courtesy of Donald Laing.)

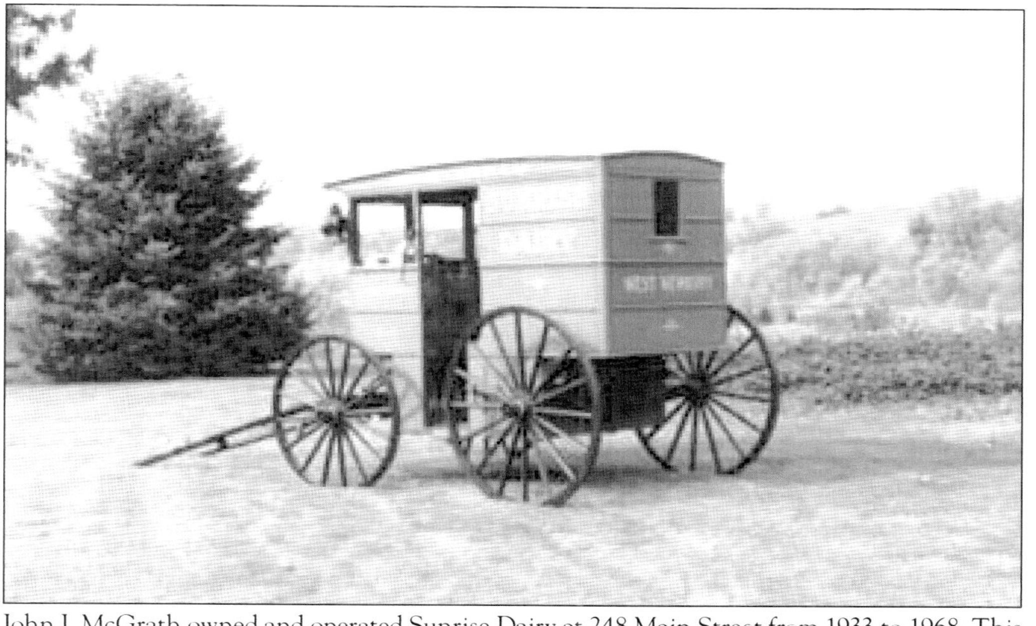

John J. McGrath owned and operated Sunrise Dairy at 248 Main Street from 1933 to 1968. This vehicle, with only one step from the ground, was built and patented by John R. Powers of Earville, New York. It was so popular with milkmen that 400 wagons were built and sold in 1892 alone. (Courtesy of John McGrath.)

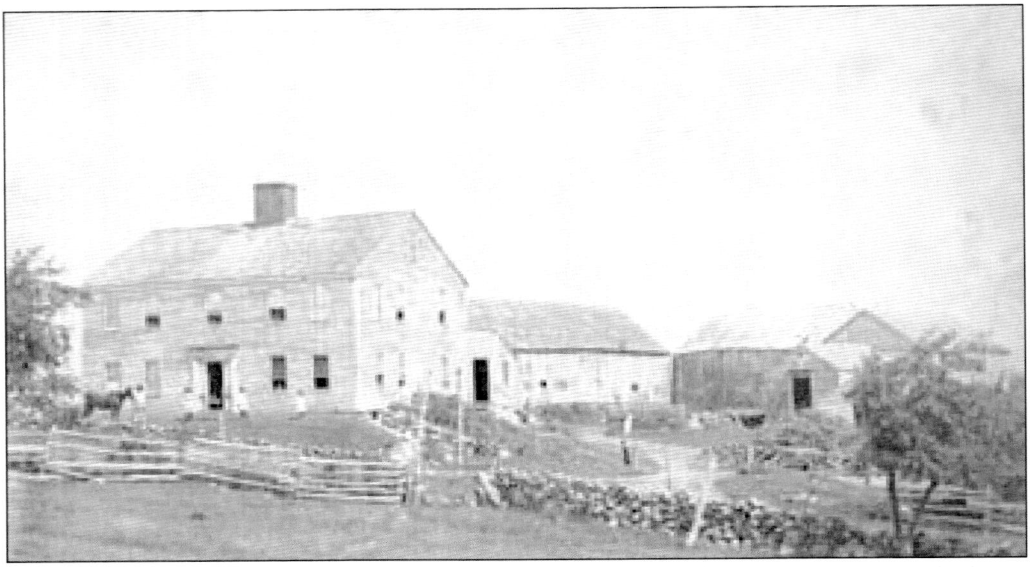

The Illsley farm on Illsley Hill is shown in this 1886 picture, with family members and a horse gathered around the front door. Before the Illsleys, Solomon Holman lived at this location, and the road was called Holman's Lane. The house was dismantled in the 1950s and moved to Argilla Road in Ipswich; it is not known whether the house was reassembled. (Courtesy of the Historical Society of Old Newbury.)

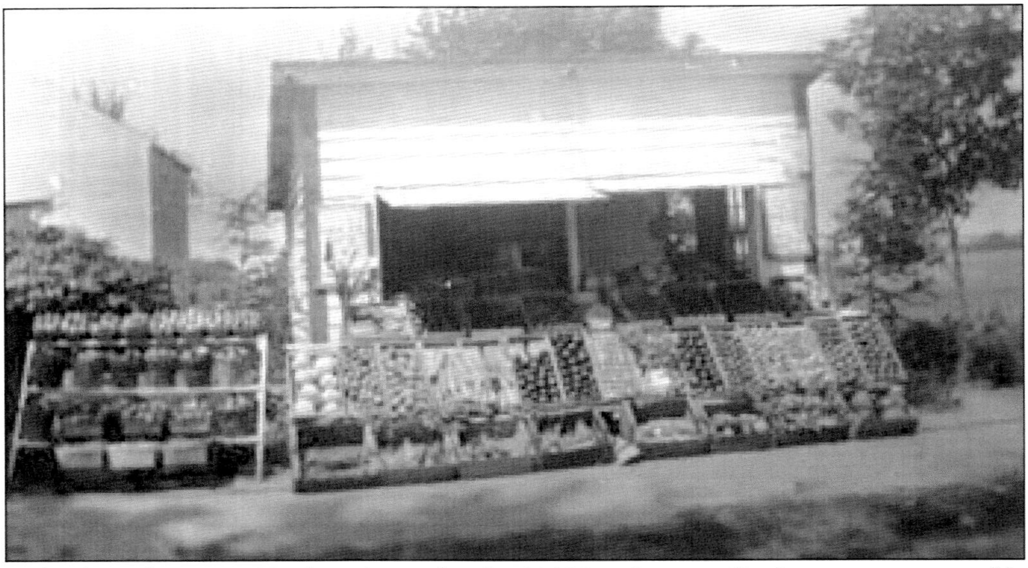

Richard Knight, a West Newbury farmer, lived at 836 Main Street and had an extensive vegetable garden. His roadside farm stand, shown above, was a showpiece of beautiful vegetables and gladioli. He had a fish delivery route. Knight was instrumental in organizing the Garden Street fire station and was one of the last survivors of the Haydn Brown steamer days. (Courtesy of the West Newbury Historical Society.)

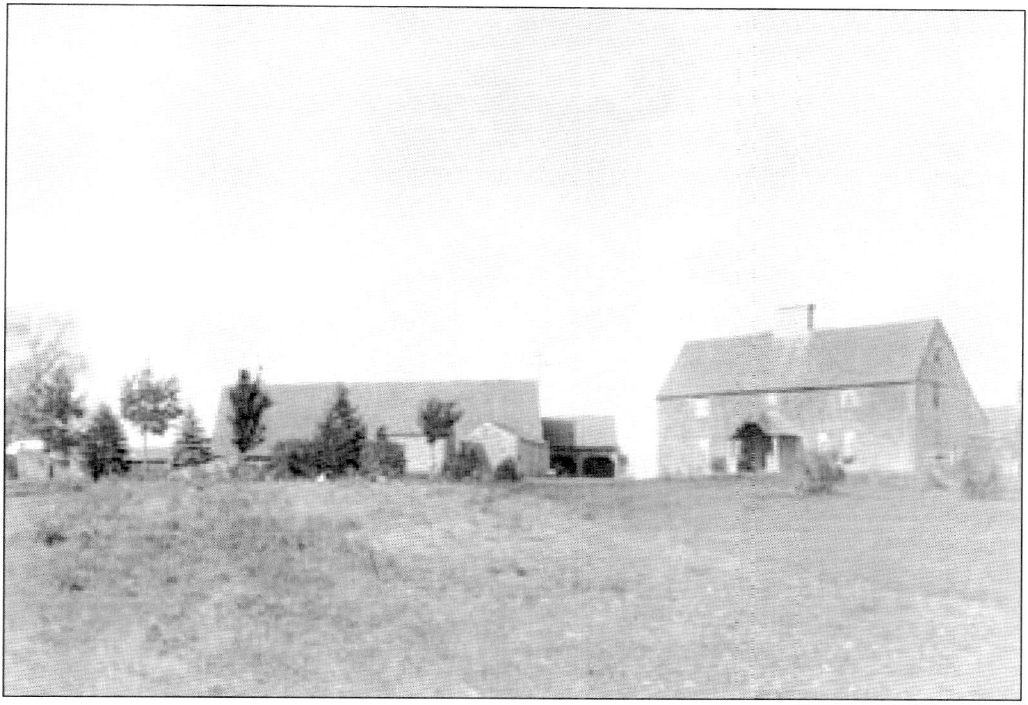

According to Sarah Anna Emery in her *Reminiscences of a Nonagenarian*, farmers living on Crane Neck Hill watched the smoke from the Battle of Bunker Hill from this spot. The house shown here at 175 Crane Neck Street was built about 1709. It is the former location of Orcland Farms, which was famous for its Morgan horses. (Courtesy of Zella Haskell.)

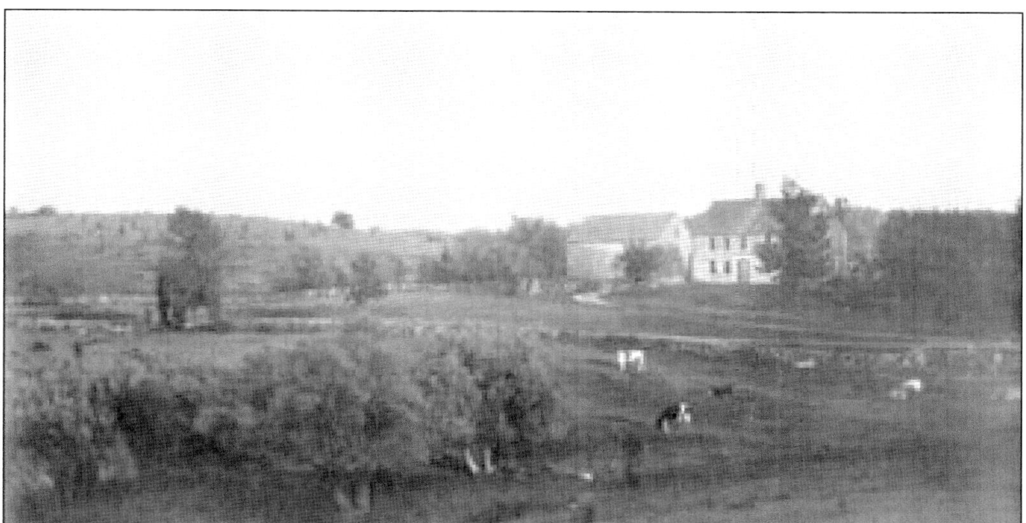

This farm at 23 Archelaus Place was home to the Hills family from 1830 until the mid-1900s. As with most West Newbury farms, cows and chickens were raised for milk and eggs. A fire destroyed the house and barn in the 1950s. Members of the Hills family also built the houses at 407 and 479 Main Street. (Courtesy of Jeannette Poore.)

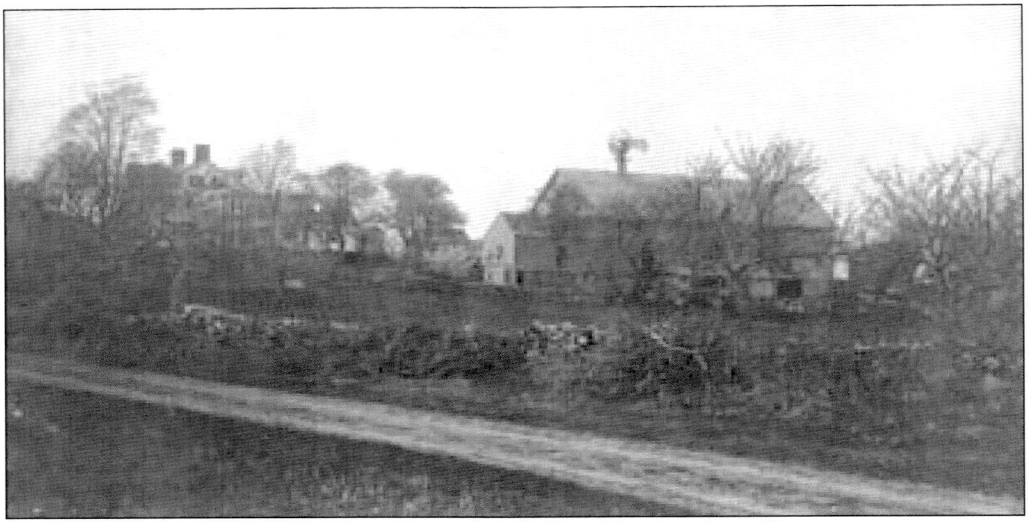

This farm, which was located at about 25 Turkey Hill Road, is listed on an 1830 map as D. Sawyer. Sometime after 1884, Granville Goodrich bought it; after his death in 1918, his son-in-law Carroll Ordway took over running the farm. Although the house burned down in 1979, the extensive stone walls and stone-walled well are still standing. (Courtesy of John Thurlow.)

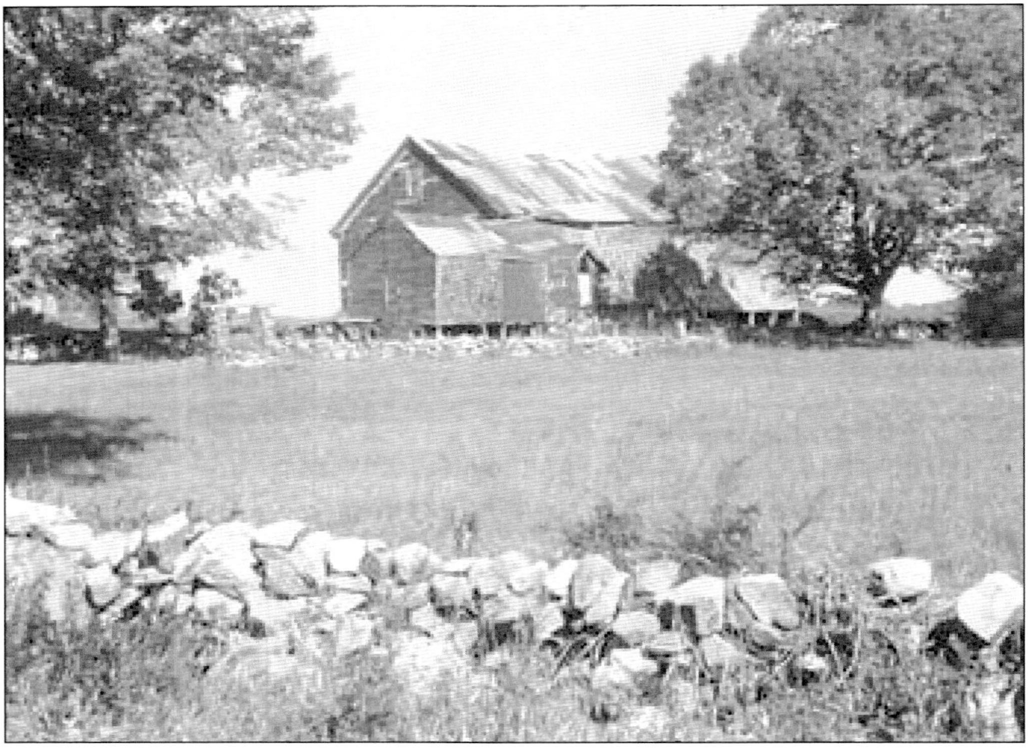

This is the same barn as in the above picture, taken about 1950. Carroll Ordway, whose wife was a daughter of Granville Goodrich, used the barn for many years. Being a frugal farmer, he patched the roof with odd lots of shingles; although unintended, this was a visual aid to low-flying pilots. (Courtesy of Susan Poore Follansbee.)

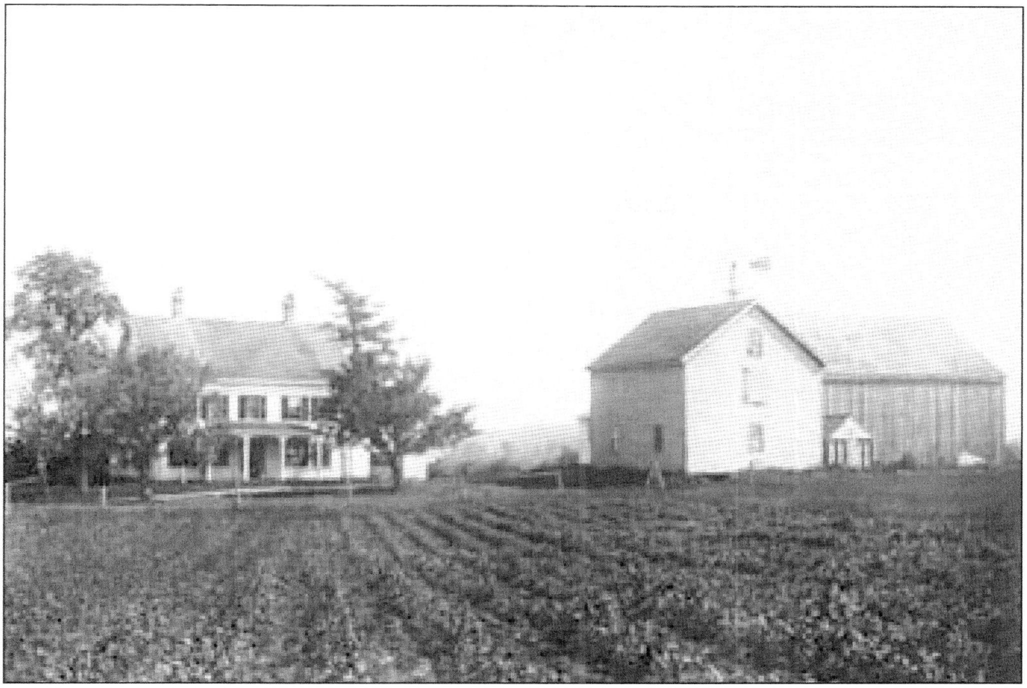

In 1820, Ebenezer Poore bought 68 acres off Garden Street, where he built his house and barn, at what is now 14 Poores Lane. His son Moses Hall Poore added onto the house, and its size doubled. Ebenezer's descendants have lived in this house up to the present time. In 1943, lightning struck the barn, totally destroying it along with the livestock. (Courtesy of Emily Poore.)

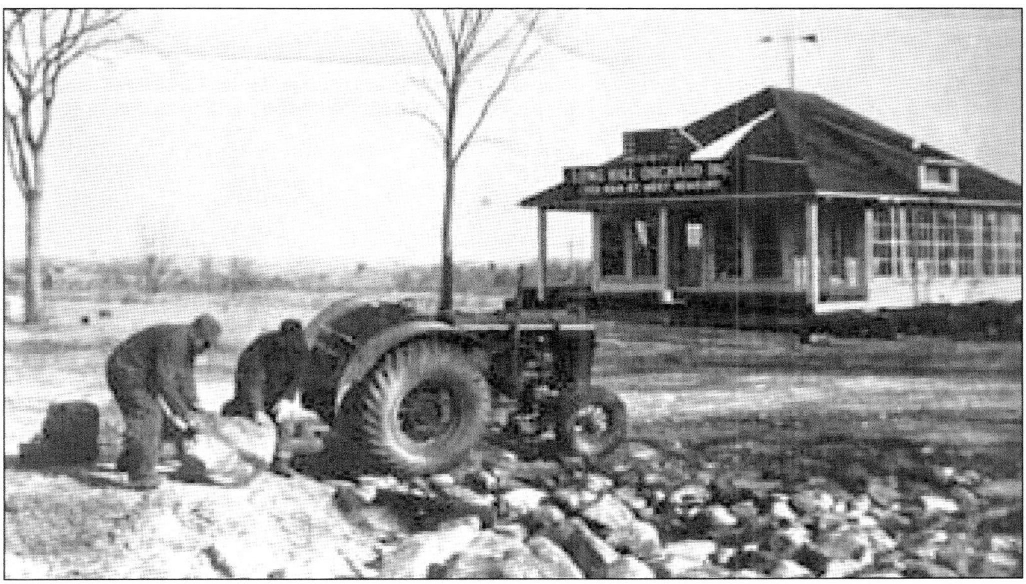

Long Hill Orchard was founded in 1915, and the retail store is pictured here on February 3, 1934. The first owner had a red wooden crow on his roof that honored his pet crow. The store began by selling apples and cider, later adding other products. An ice cream stand was added a few years ago. The farm now offers Community Supported Agriculture (CSA). (Courtesy of Cynthia Adams.)

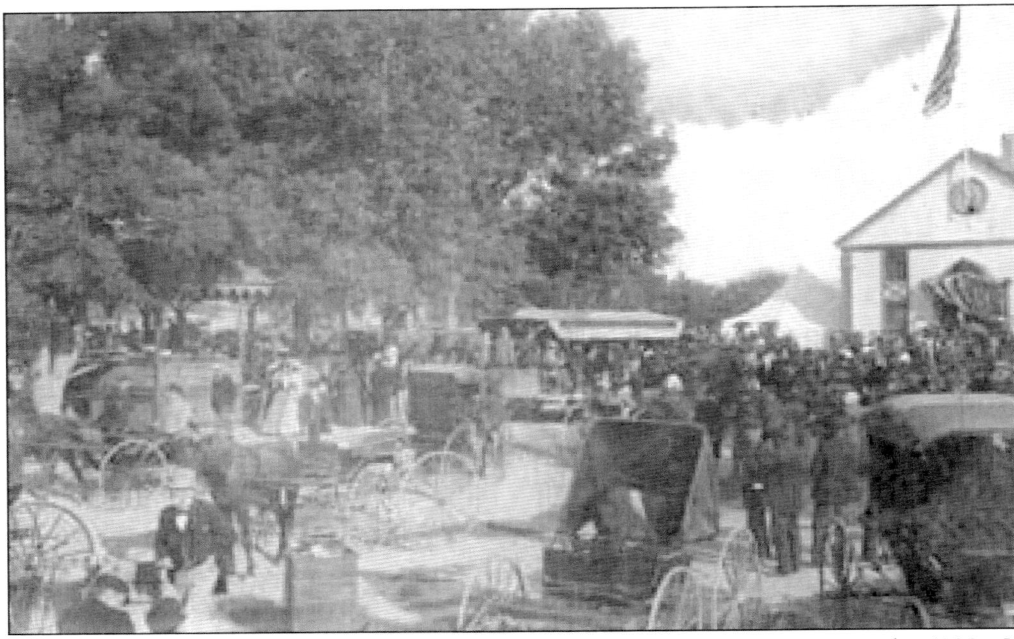

The West Newbury Farmers Club was an important and active organization in the 1800s. Its annual fair on the Training Field brought forth wonderful displays of prize fruits, flowers, grains, vegetables, farm animals, and various forms of needlework. There were trials of draft horses and oxen, plowing matches, bicycle and running races, a band concert, a parade, dinner, and speeches. (Courtesy of the West Newbury Historical Society.)

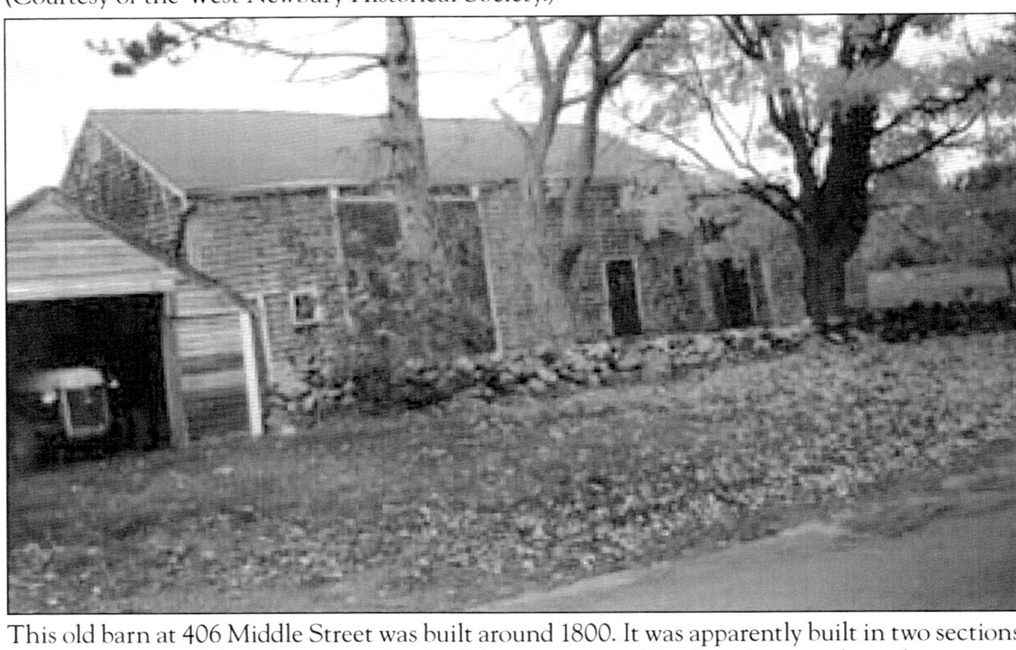

This old barn at 406 Middle Street was built around 1800. It was apparently built in two sections: the framing is doubled about two-thirds of the way across. The last door on the right goes to a modern addition. The little shed on the left houses a 1949 Ford tractor. The barn was dismantled in 2003 for eventual erection at a different location. (Courtesy of Susan Poore Follansbee.)

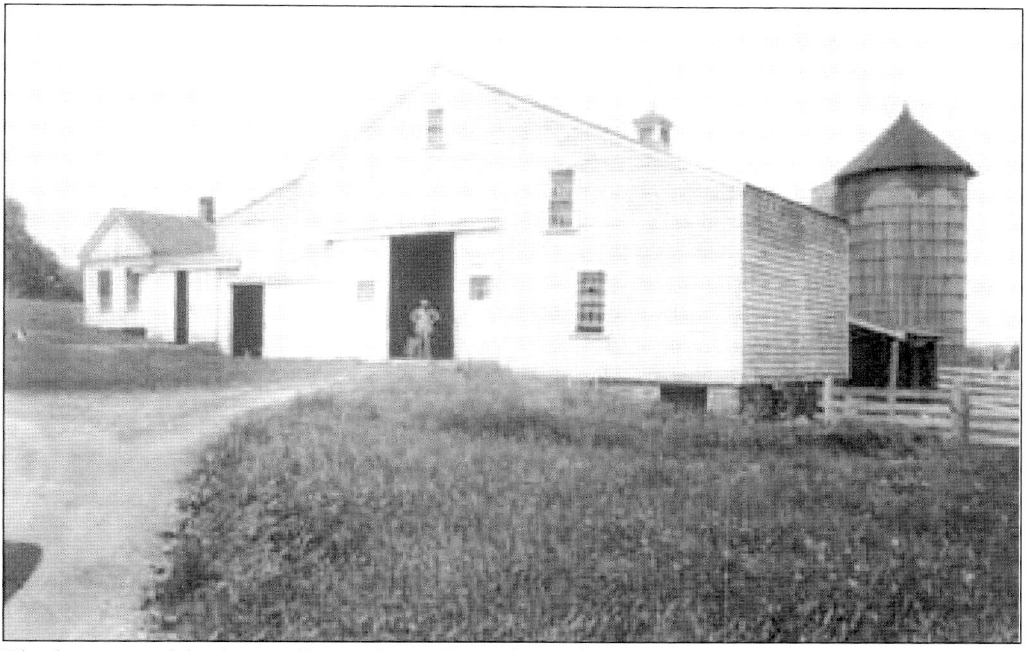

The front part of this barn at Brown Spring Farm, located at 866 Main Street, is the original; sections at the back and sides and the silo were added later. The original house, owned by C.B. Gardner on an 1872 map, was probably just to the right of the barn. The little building on the left was once a shoe shop and was later used as a dairy building. (Courtesy of Elaine Cooney Drolet.)

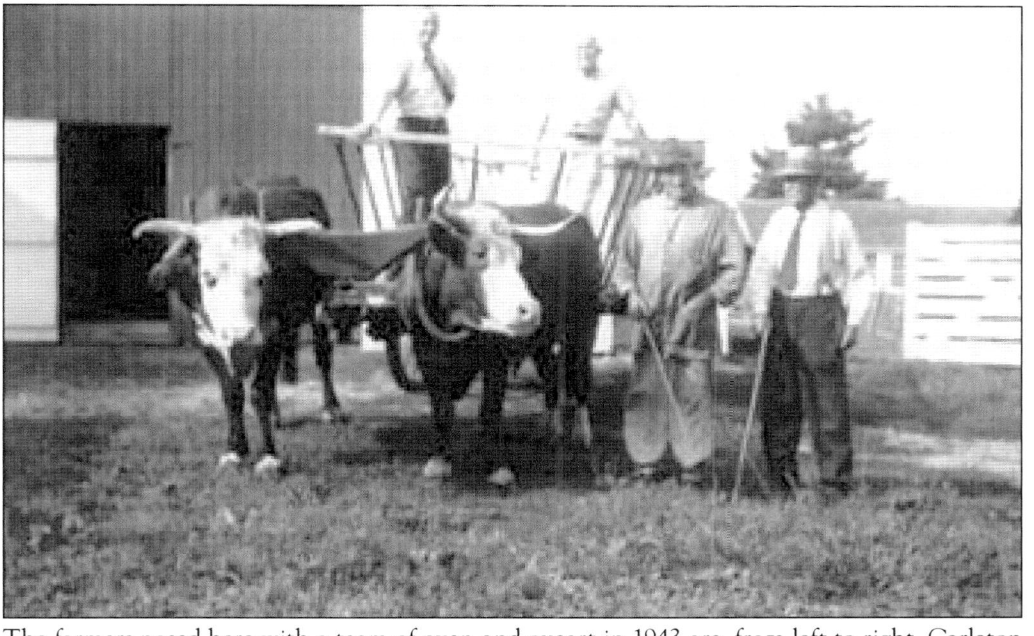

The farmers posed here with a team of oxen and oxcart in 1943 are, from left to right, Carleton Collister; Jeremiah Sullivan; Orace Moulton of Hampton, New Hampshire; and Marcellus James. For many years, oxen were used instead of horses for farm work since they were stronger and able to pull for a longer period of time. (Courtesy of John Thurlow.)

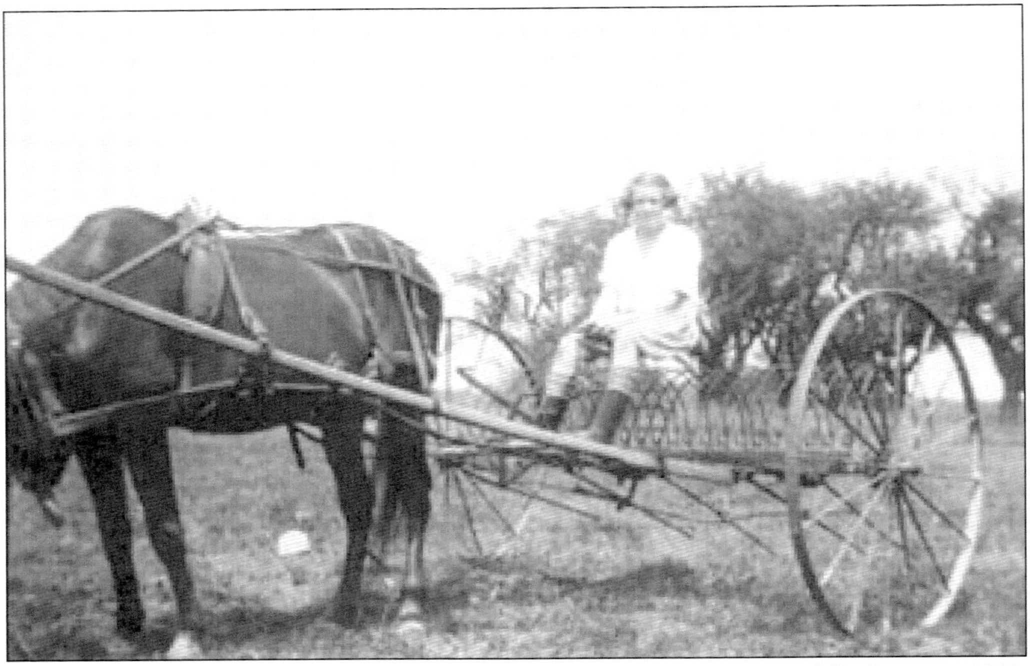

Mary Anderson, age 14, prepares to rake her father's hay field at 406 Middle Street in 1922. Dump rakes, as shown here, were developed in the mid-1800s. The tines of the rake slid along the ground gathering up hay; when it was full, the rider pulled a lever, which raised the tines momentarily, leaving a row of hay ready for pitching onto the hay wagon. (Courtesy of Susan Poore Follansbee.)

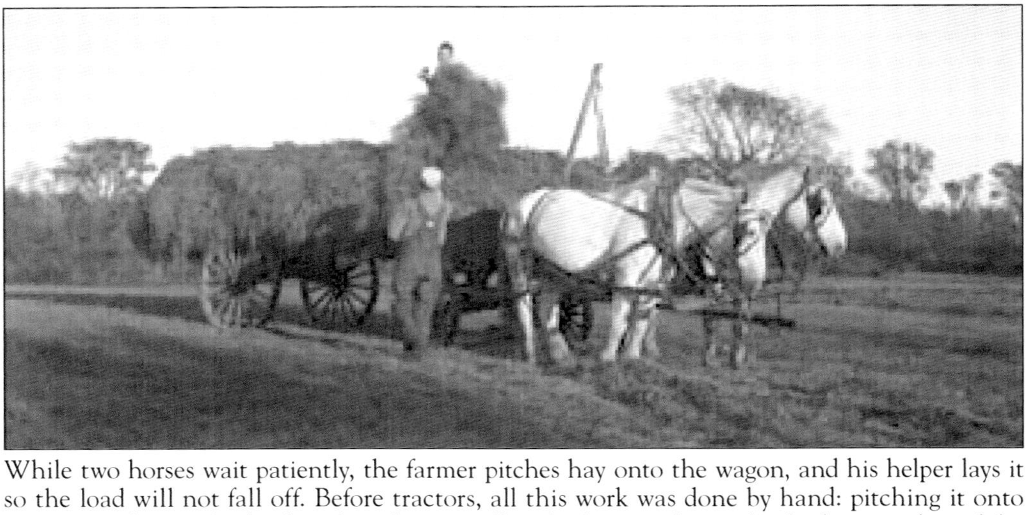

While two horses wait patiently, the farmer pitches hay onto the wagon, and his helper lays it so the load will not fall off. Before tractors, all this work was done by hand: pitching it onto the wagon, laying the load, and pitching it off in the barn and into the farthest reaches of the haymows. (Courtesy of Peter Haack.)

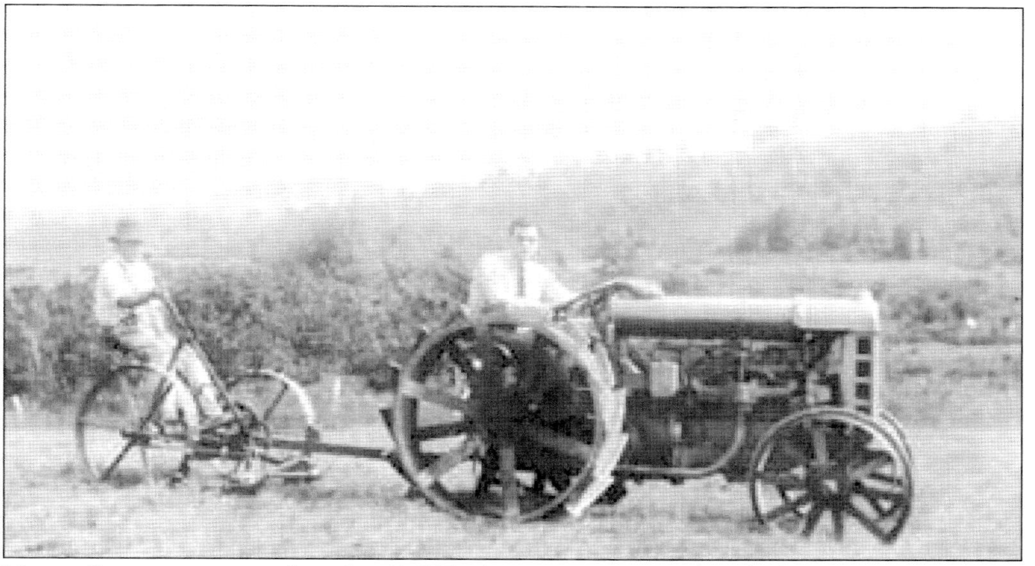

Horace Brown poses seated on this 1917 Fordson tractor; an unidentified person rides the plow. Presumably, Brown would not do farm work in a white shirt and tie and with no hat on. Henry Ford & Sons made Fordsons from 1917 until 1920, when the company merged into the Ford Motor Company. (Courtesy of Elinor Spofford.)

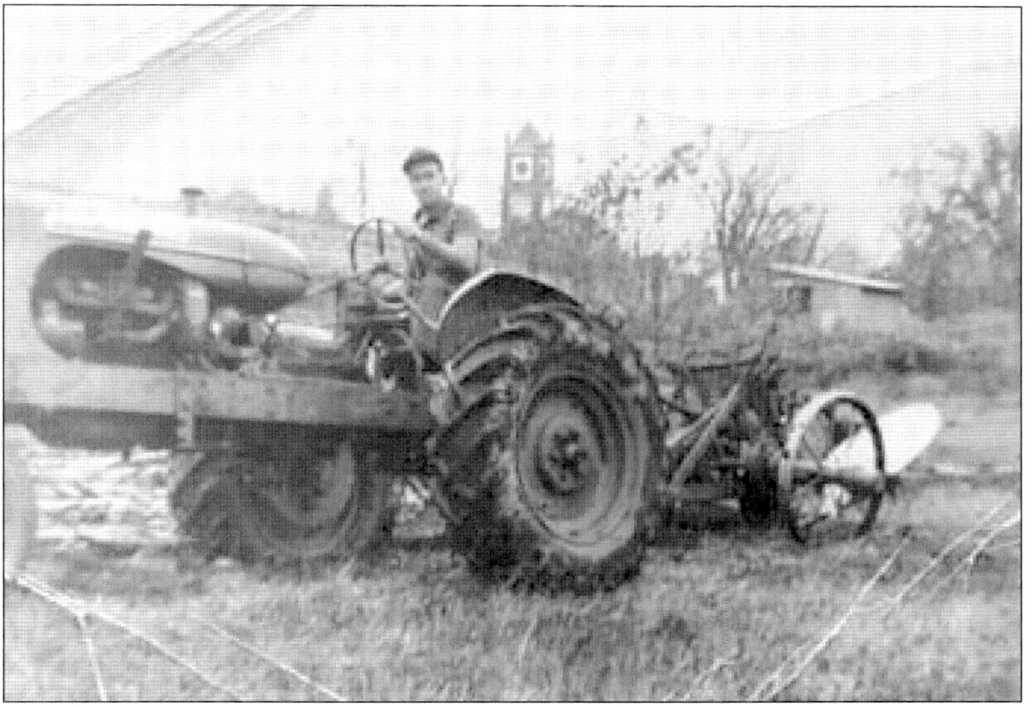

Here, C. Alan "Baldy" Merrill is plowing the field behind 360 Main Street in the early 1940s with his Allis-Chalmers Model WC tractor. Note the steeple of the Second Congregational Church in the background. Allis-Chalmers made tractors beginning in 1914. The Merrill dairy farm was at 28 Baileys Lane. (Courtesy of Bruce Merrill.)

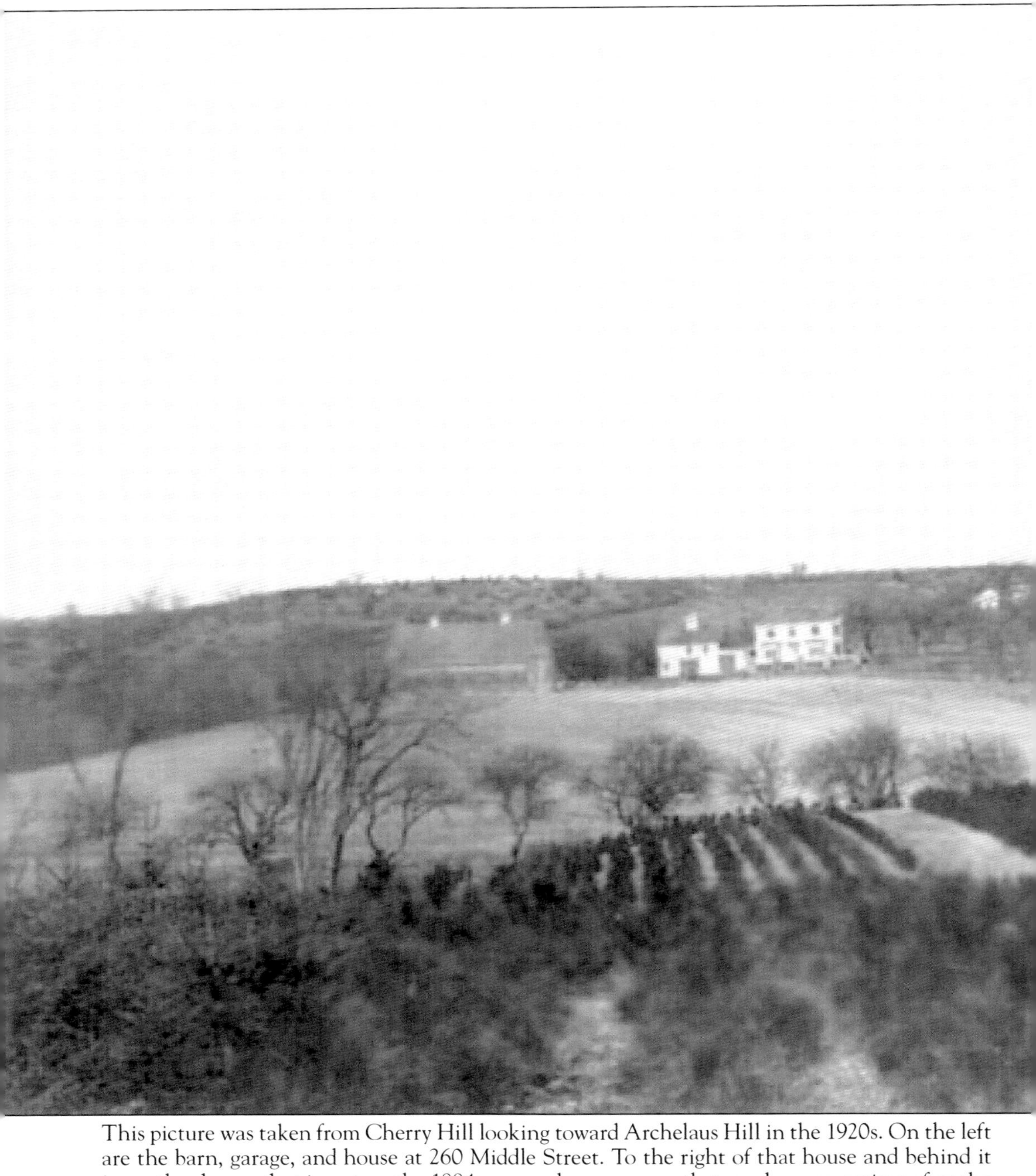

This picture was taken from Cherry Hill looking toward Archelaus Hill in the 1920s. On the left are the barn, garage, and house at 260 Middle Street. To the right of that house and behind it is another house that is not on the 1884 map and was apparently torn down sometime after the photograph was taken. The house on the right is the Captain Stanwood house at 13 Indian Hill

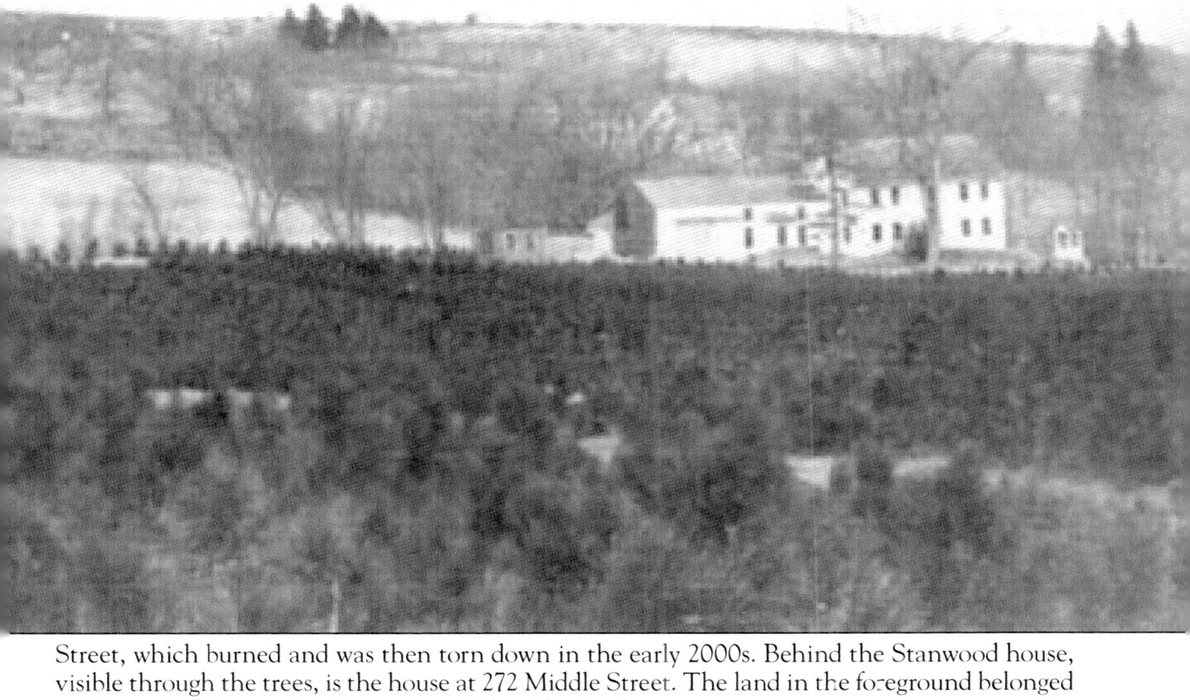

Street, which burned and was then torn down in the early 2000s. Behind the Stanwood house, visible through the trees, is the house at 272 Middle Street. The land in the foreground belonged to Cherry Hill Nurseries. (Courtesy of John Thurlow.)

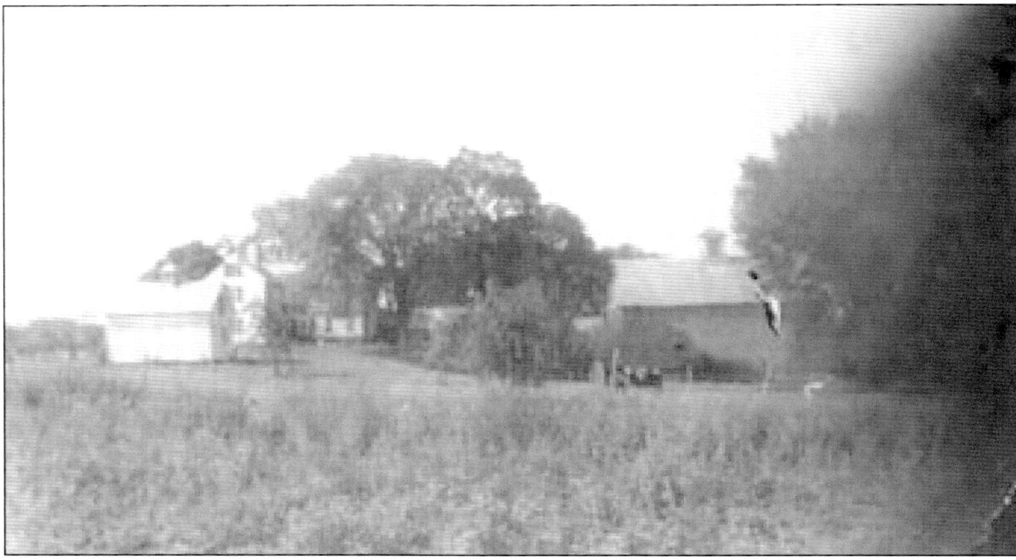

The Dole farm, shown above, was situated at the end of Dole Place along the banks of the Merrimack River. The 1729 map of the West Parish of Newbury shows Captain Greenleafe as the owner; the 1830 map shows the owner to be Dole. The original house was torn down in 1850, and a new one, built then and shown here, has since been torn down. The barn burned in 1959. (Courtesy of Peter Haack.)

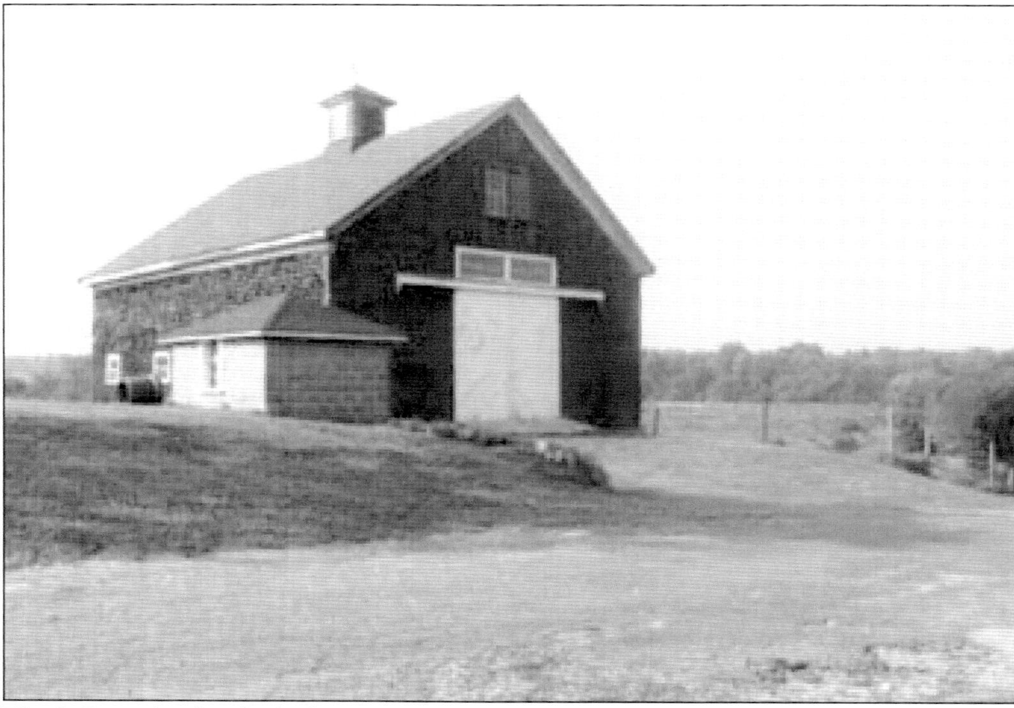

The Sullivan family, who had emigrated from Ireland, was living on Sullivan's Court before 1860. They had a dairy farm here until the 1960s. This barn was built about 1905; it was not the first barn on the site. The small building in front was a milk house. (Courtesy of Della Armstrong.)

Three

West Newbury

The Building of a Community

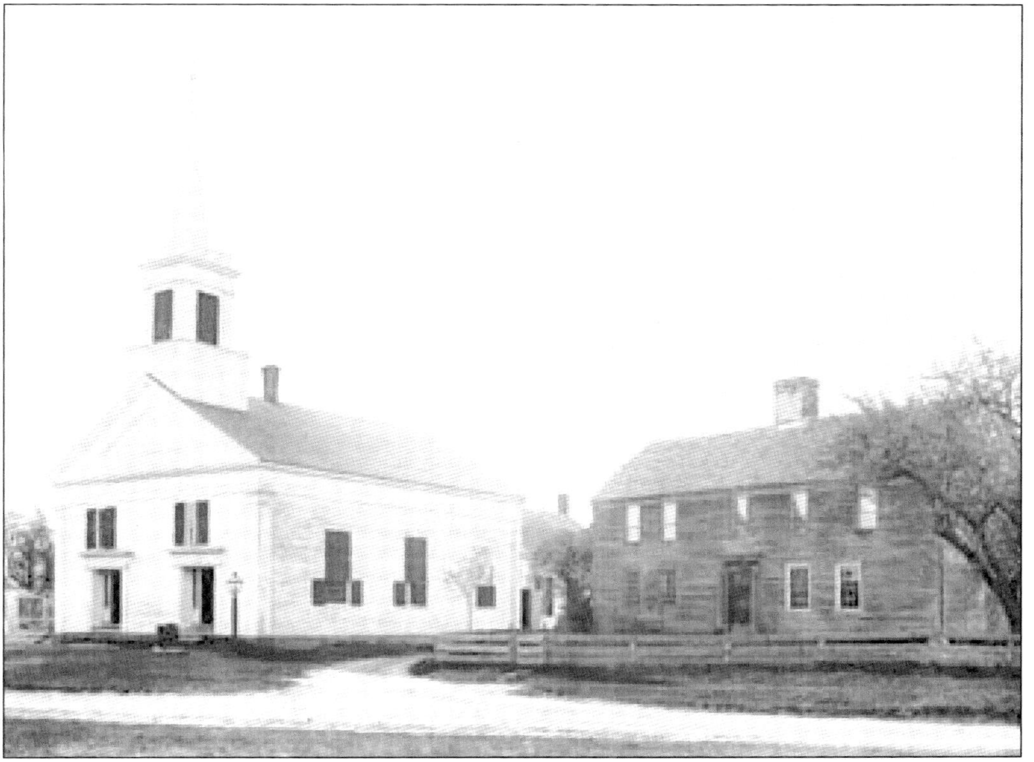

The First Congregational Church, located on the corner of Main Street and Way to the River, was built about 1840. It was the fourth building for the congregation, which was established in 1698 as the Second Parish of Newbury. The building is now a private residence. The Huse-Bailey-Ordway house to the right was built about 1680. (Courtesy of the Newburyport Archival Center at the Newburyport Public Library.)

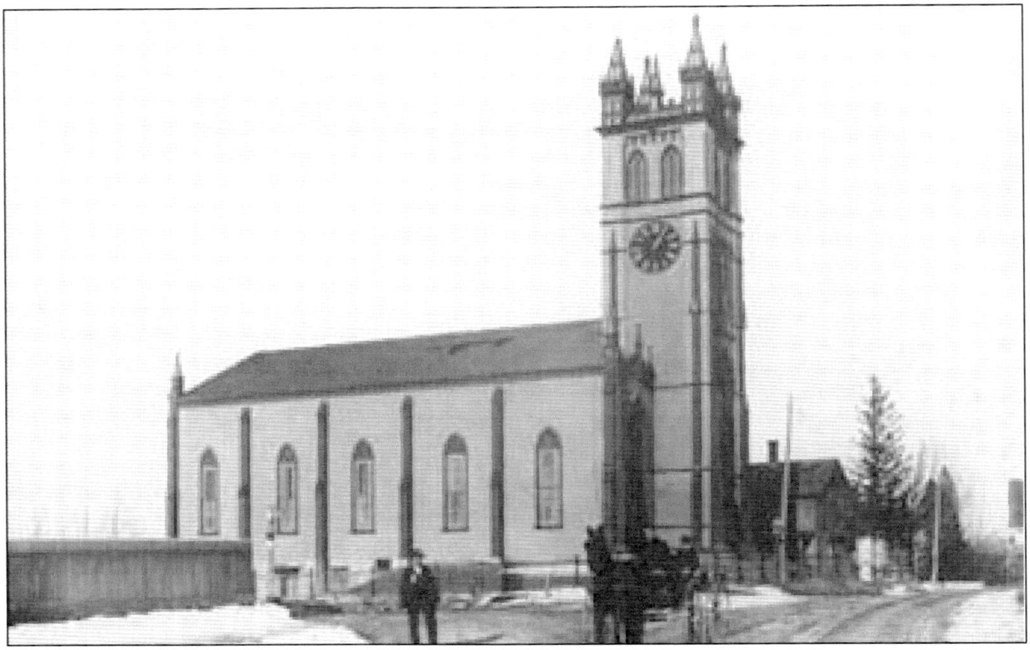

The Second Congregational Church was founded in 1731 and was called, at that time, the Fourth Parish of Newbury. The first building was on Meetinghouse Hill. The church pictured here was built in 1816 on what is now Maple Street and was moved to the corner of Church and Main Streets in 1856 and remodeled. (Courtesy of the West Newbury Historical Society.)

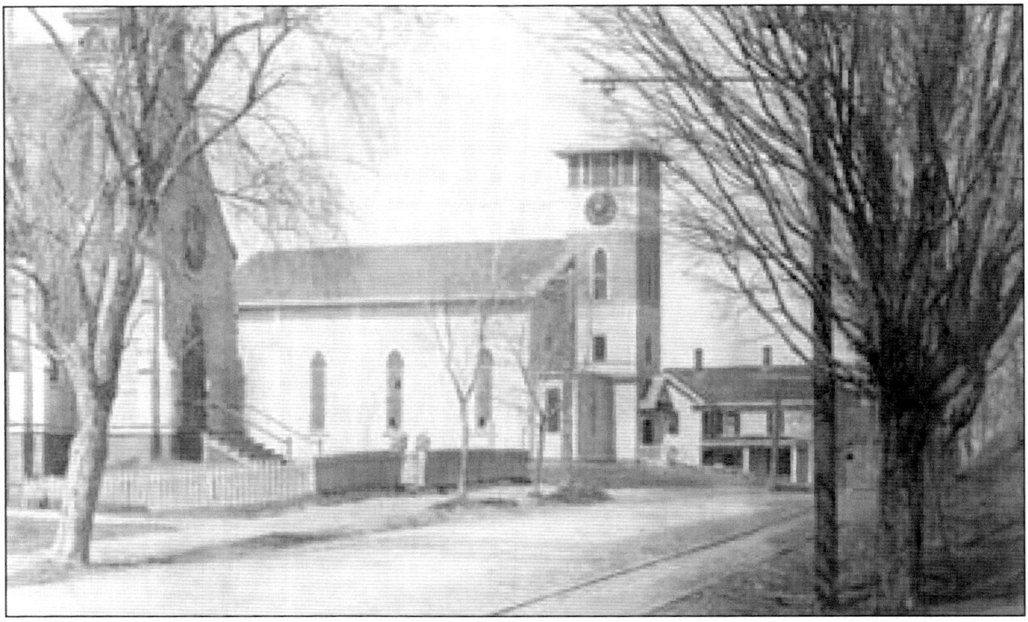

In 1908, the Gothic building of the Second Congregational Church was badly in need of repair, and the church voted to tear down the tower and reduce the size of the building. On April 24, 1909, the evening before the first service was to be held in the new building, shown above, it burned flat to the ground. (Courtesy of the West Newbury Historical Society.)

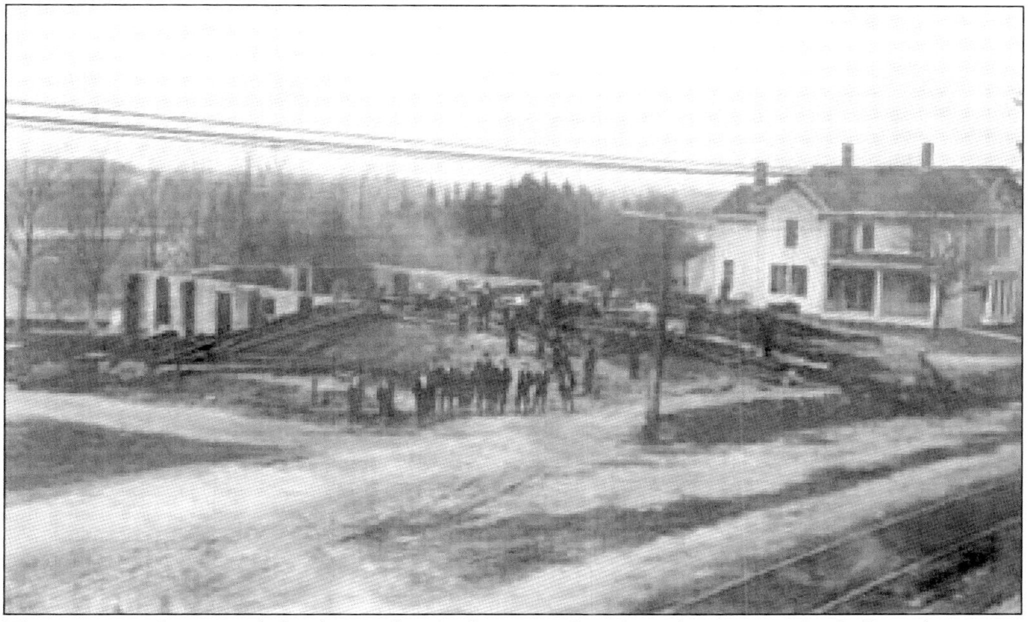

The minister discovered the fire and rushed to give the alarm by ringing the bell in the tower. Flames spread so quickly that he had to break down the locked front door to escape with his life. All that was saved were the communion table and a piano. (Courtesy of Rock Dower.)

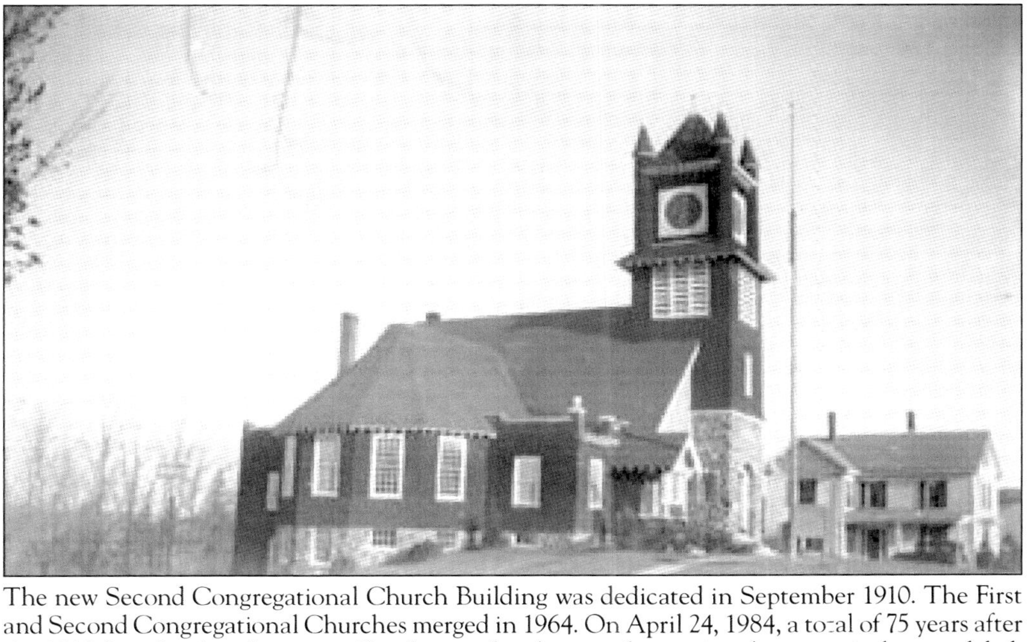

The new Second Congregational Church Building was dedicated in September 1910. The First and Second Congregational Churches merged in 1964. On April 24, 1984, a total of 75 years after the 1909 fire, the church again suffered major fire damage, forcing it to be extensively remodeled. The parsonage, shown to the right, was built in 1857; it was badly burned in 1979 and torn down. (Courtesy of the West Newbury Historical Society.)

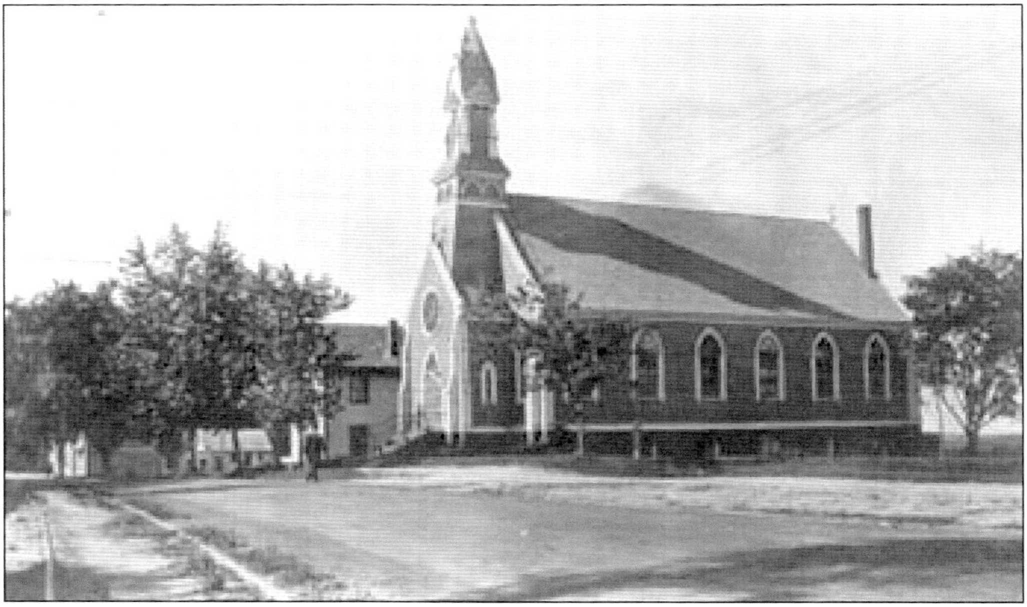

The first Catholic mass was celebrated in West Newbury Town Hall around 1860. Rebecca Heath, owner of a fine dwelling on the corner of Church and Main Streets, sold her property to Father McClure, the parish priest at that time. Parishioners donated money and held fairs to finance building the church, and the first mass at St. Ann's Church was said on Christmas Day 1879. (Courtesy of Joyce Burnham Dixon.)

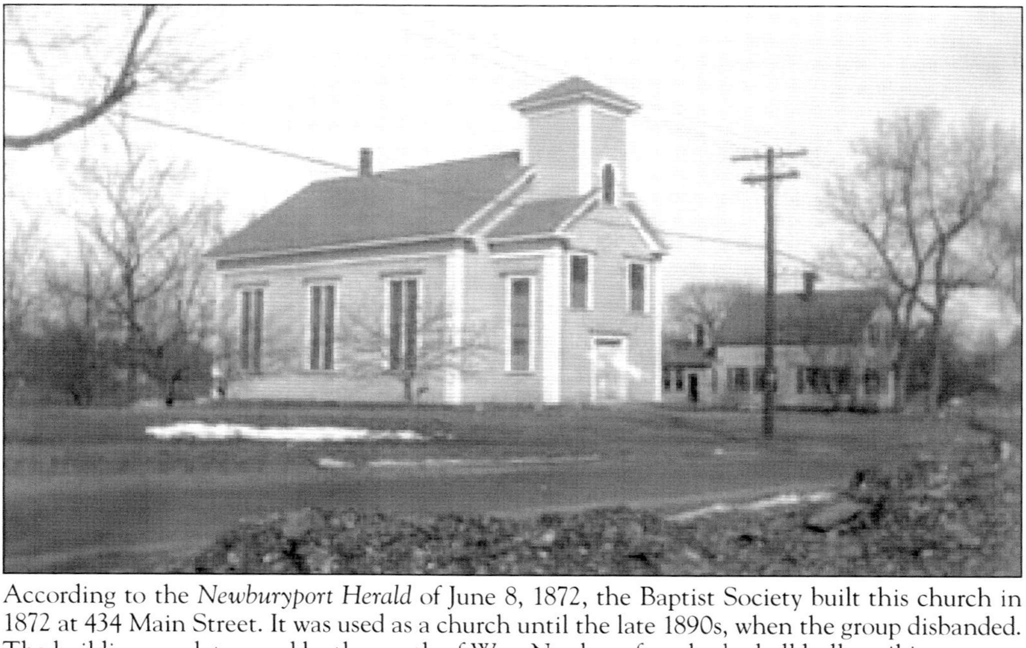

According to the *Newburyport Herald* of June 8, 1872, the Baptist Society built this church in 1872 at 434 Main Street. It was used as a church until the late 1890s, when the group disbanded. The building was later used by the youth of West Newbury for a basketball hall until it was torn down in 1952. (Courtesy of the West Newbury Historical Society.)

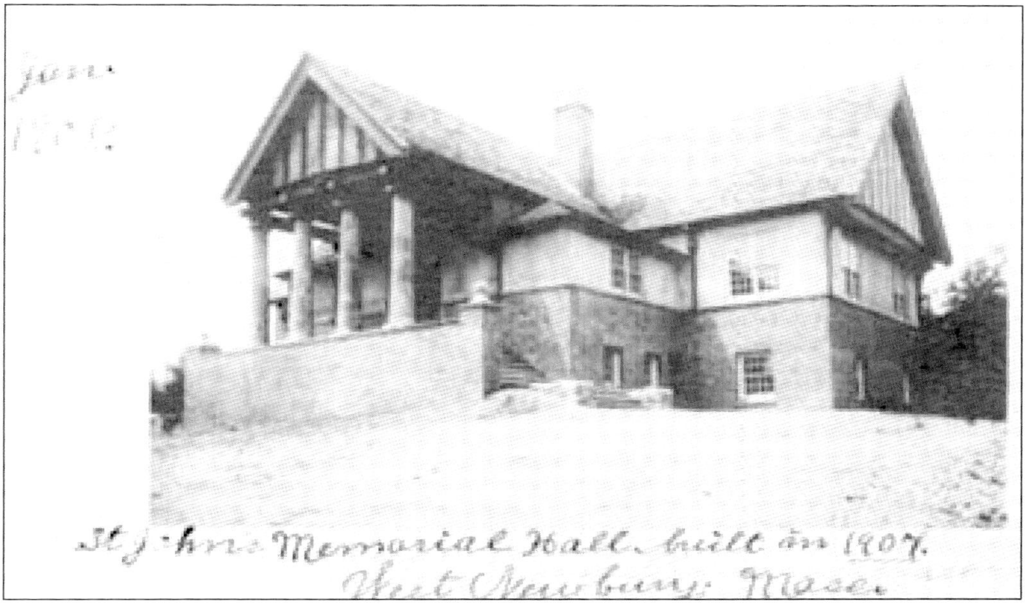

In 1907, St. John's Hall, named for John the Baptist, was built by the Emery sisters to be used as a community hall and for occasional Episcopal services. On November 6, 1910, Rev. Glenn Tilley Morse began holding regular services here, which continued until March 1913, when the church building shown below was completed, and St. John's Hall was then used as a parish hall. (Courtesy of Joyce Burnham Dixon.)

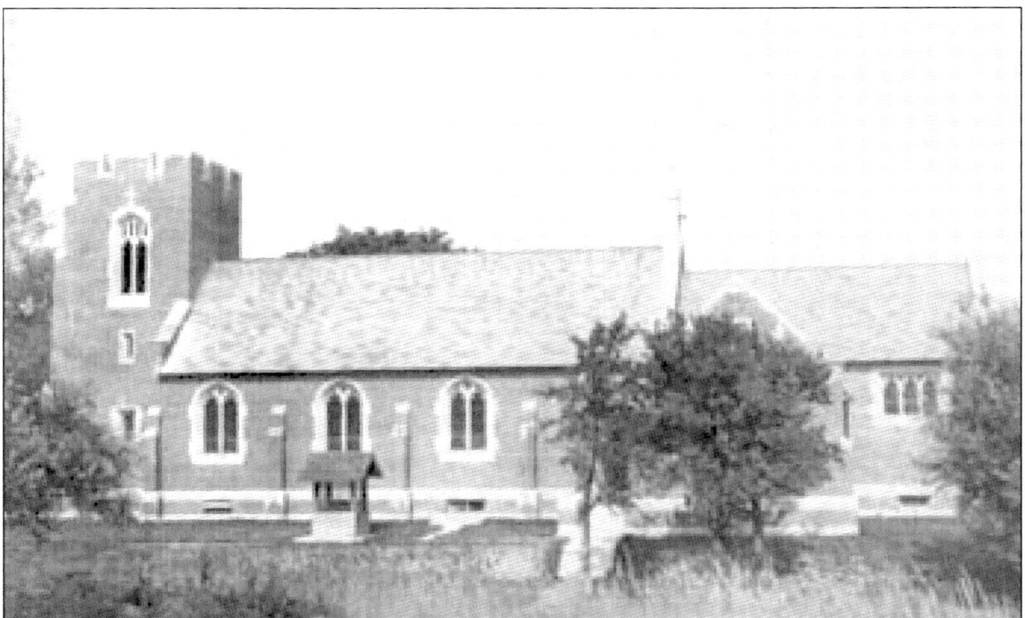

The newest church in West Newbury, All Saints Episcopal Church, was built by the Emery sisters at 885 Main Street on land that they also purchased. The first service was held in the new building on March 22, 1913. The building, a modified form of Perpendicular Gothic, was modeled after St. Nicholas Church in Newbury, England. (Courtesy of Rachel Adams.)

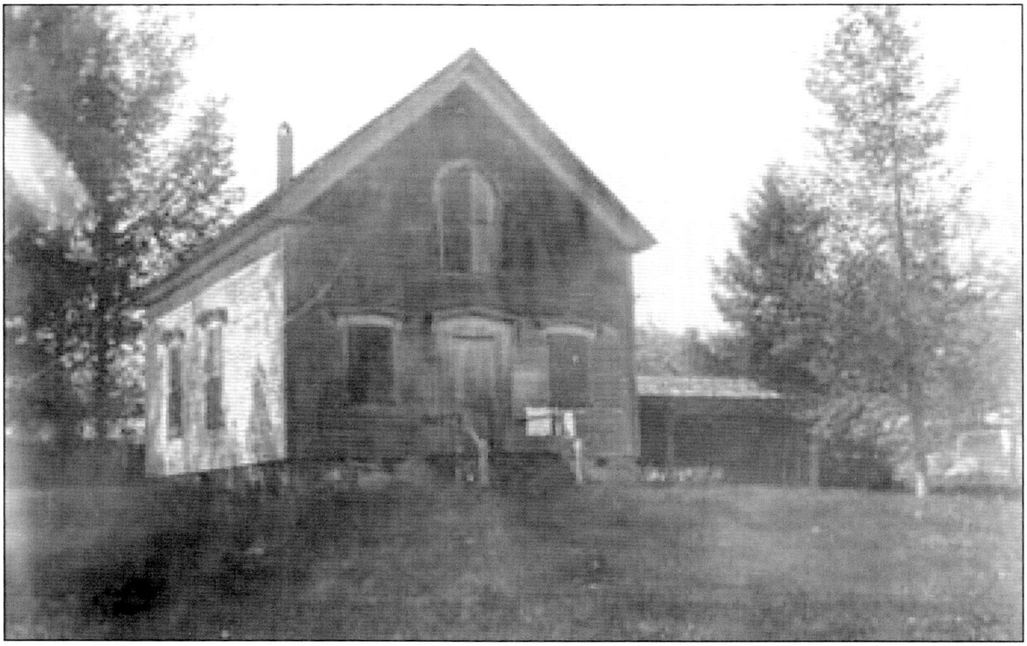

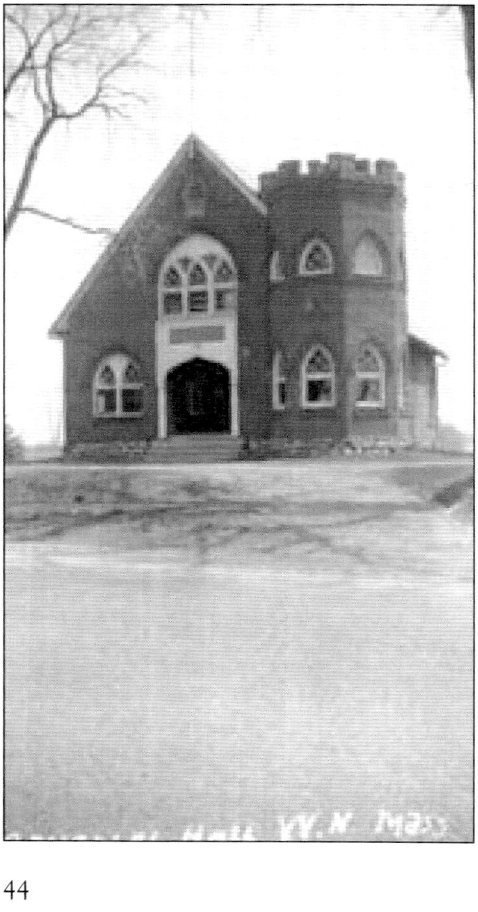

In 1744, a Quaker meetinghouse was built at the corner of Rogers Street and Turkey Hill Road. In 1855, the Quakers bought one acre of land nearby for a burying ground. Eventually, Quakers in West Newbury died out or moved away. In 1917, Wallace Ordway took the building down, using the lumber to build a sunporch on his home at 810 Main Street. (Courtesy of the West Newbury Historical Commission.)

The Charles L. Carr Post, American Legion, at 359 Main Street was built around 1901 using slate from nearby a ledge. It was designed by H.W. Gore Jr., a Braintree architect. Moses Warren Edwards bequeathed $3,000, and Dr. Orin Warren gave the land for the building. The town library was located here from 1927 to 1939, which was when the new library building was completed. (Courtesy of the West Newbury Historical Society.)

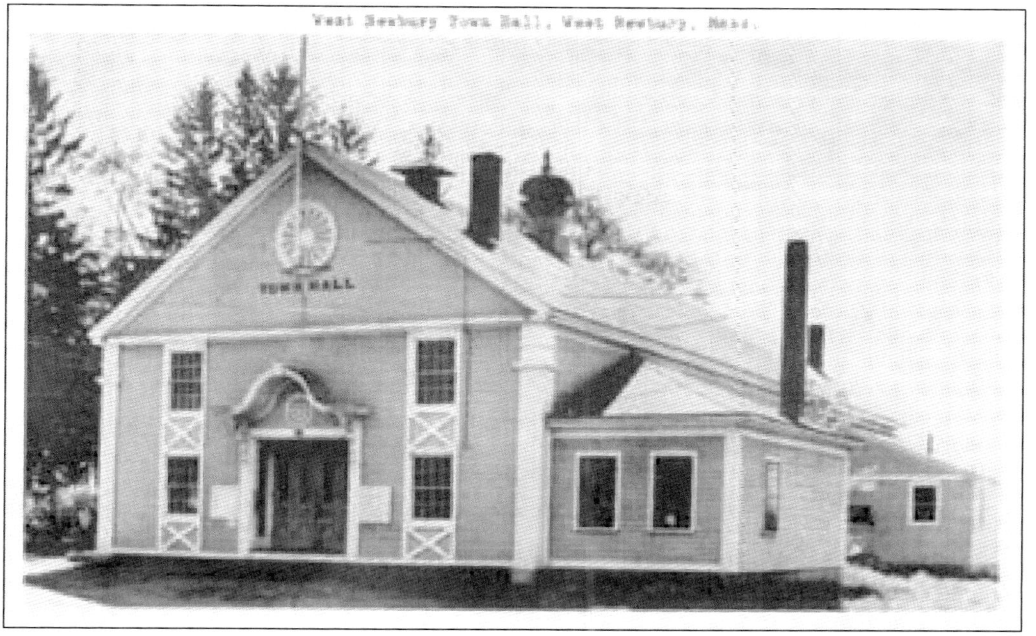

The Colonial Revival–style West Newbury Town Hall was built in 1842 at 491 Main Street on land of Samuel Chase. It was used as an armory in 1852 and during the Civil War. In 1941, Ella A.K. Brown left money to the town, and an addition was built at the rear. Another addition was made in 1968. (Postcard by Fairbanks Card Company; courtesy of Rachel Adams.)

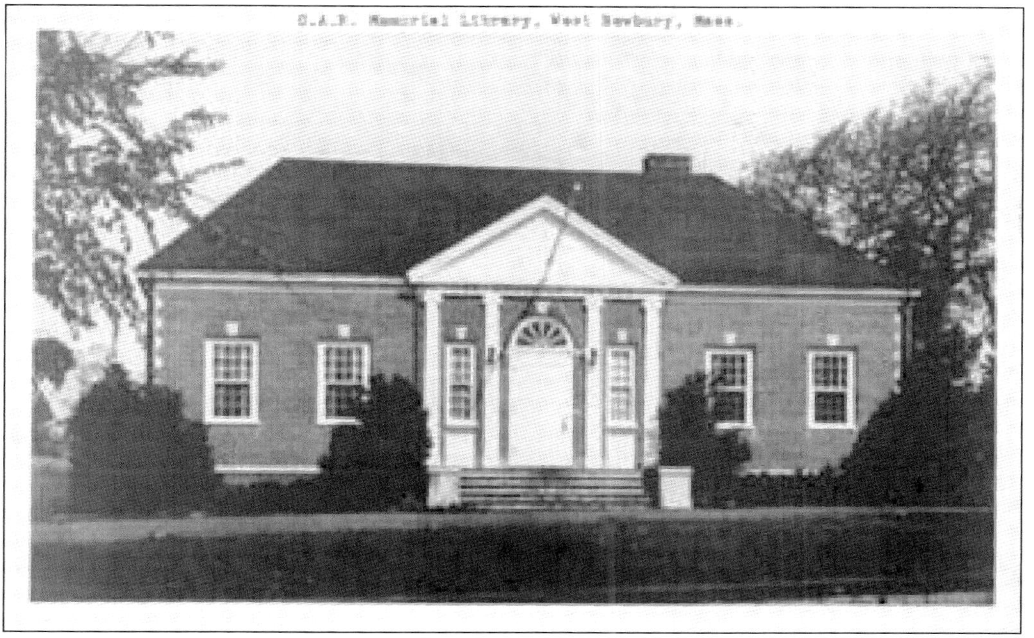

A private library opened in 1875 in a building near the Food Mart and later moved to 32 Maple Street, the corner of Main and Mechanic Streets, and Post Office Square. The first public library was established in the square in 1894; it moved to the legion hall in 1927. Finally, in 1939, a new library building, shown above, was completed at 490 Main Street. (Courtesy of Rock Dower.)

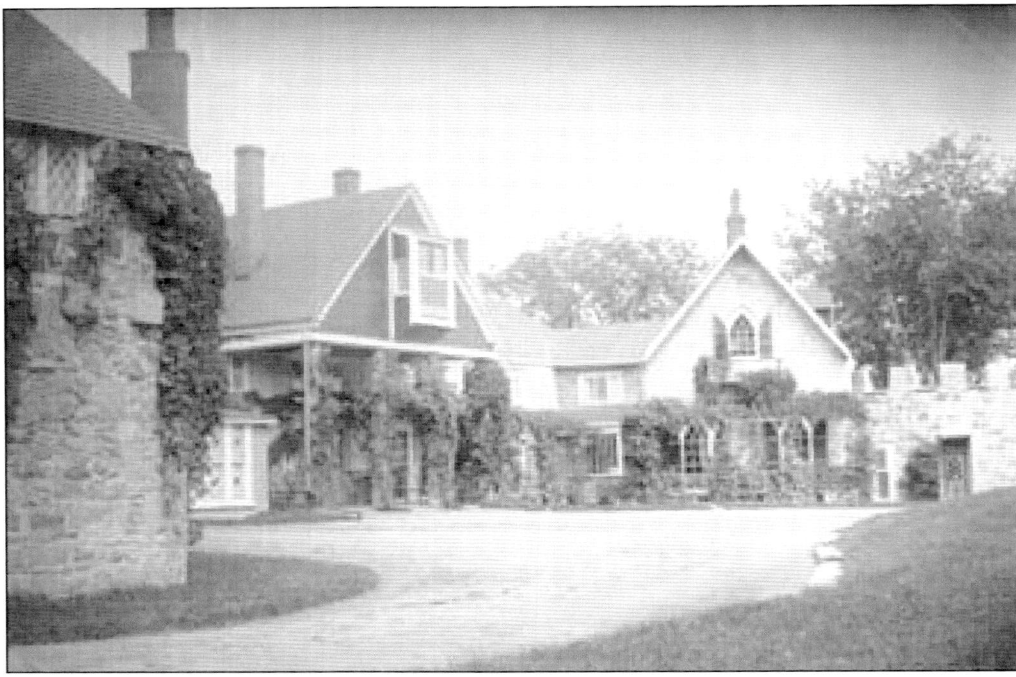

Indian Hill Farm, built around 1880 at 95 Indian Hill Street, was constructed in the style of an old English Manor, being low and rambling and having dormer windows with diamond-shaped leaded panes. It contained 50 rooms and was filled with antiques and collectibles that Maj. "Ben:" Perley Poore had amassed through the years. The castellated wing to the right housed Major Poore's study and library; the wing to the left housed the farm laborers. In 1959, the central part was extensively damaged by fire, which started in an attached barn. Twenty rooms were destroyed. (Above, courtesy of the Newburyport Archival Center at the Newburyport Public Library; below, courtesy of Acha Moseley Lord.)

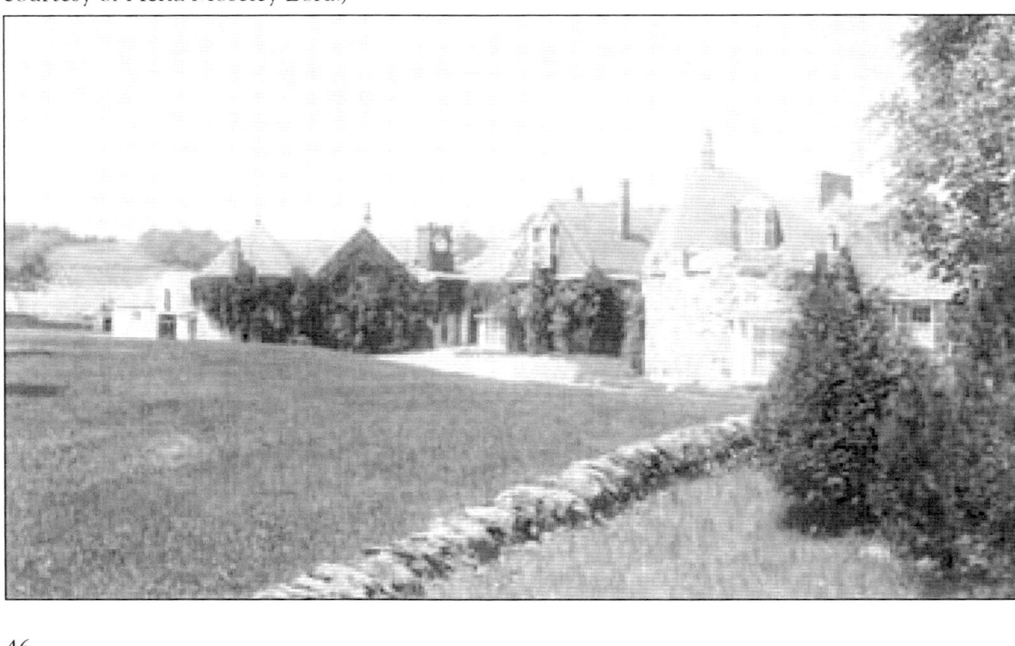

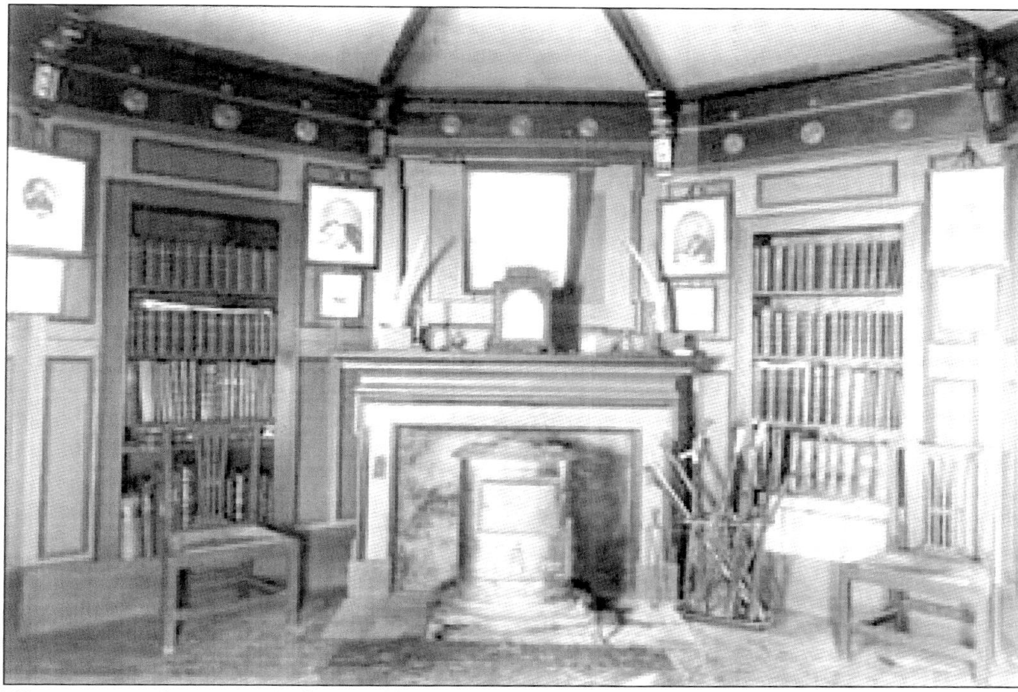

This octagonal room at Indian Hill Farm was Major Poore's library. Poore had an extensive collection of interesting papers, including love letters written by Napoleon and the original letter written by General Washington to his future wife, the widow Custis, asking when their marriage day should be. It has been stated that he had the largest and finest collection of autographs in the country, which consisted of not just the signatures but also many manuscripts of personal value. Notice the collection of canes, some of which had belonged to Presidents Washington and Lincoln and to Brigham Young. In the picture below, Major Poore sits at his front door. (Above, courtesy of Acha Moseley Lord; below, courtesy of Charles Fowler.)

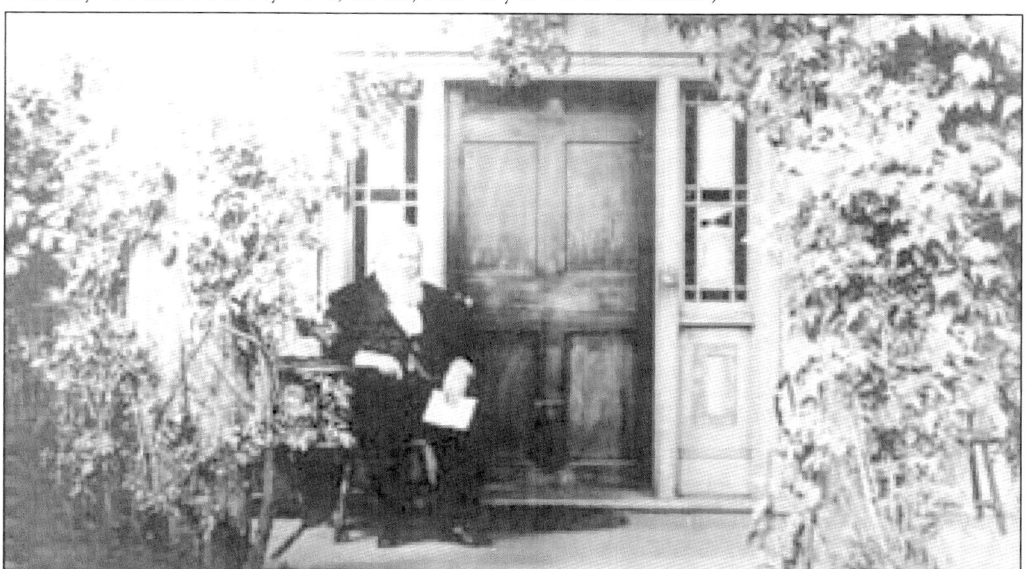

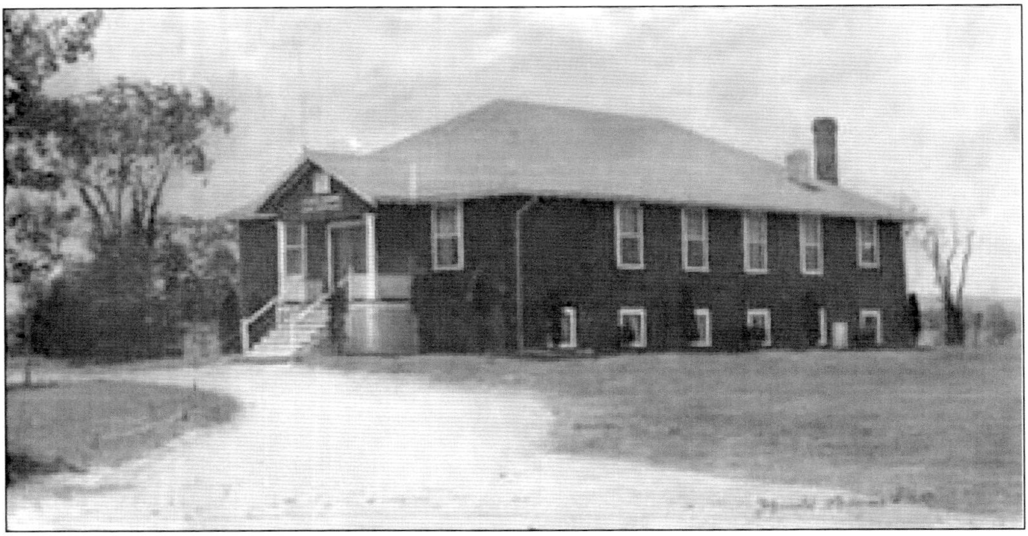

Laurel Grange, organized in 1888, met at 782 Main Street until 1937 when its new hall was built at 21 Garden Street, shown above. The old hall was later sold and moved to 12 Garden Street and is now a residence. Another grange, West Newbury Grange, which met at 320 Main Street, was in existence from 1887 until at least 1925. (Photograph by Harold Adams; courtesy of Laurel Grange.)

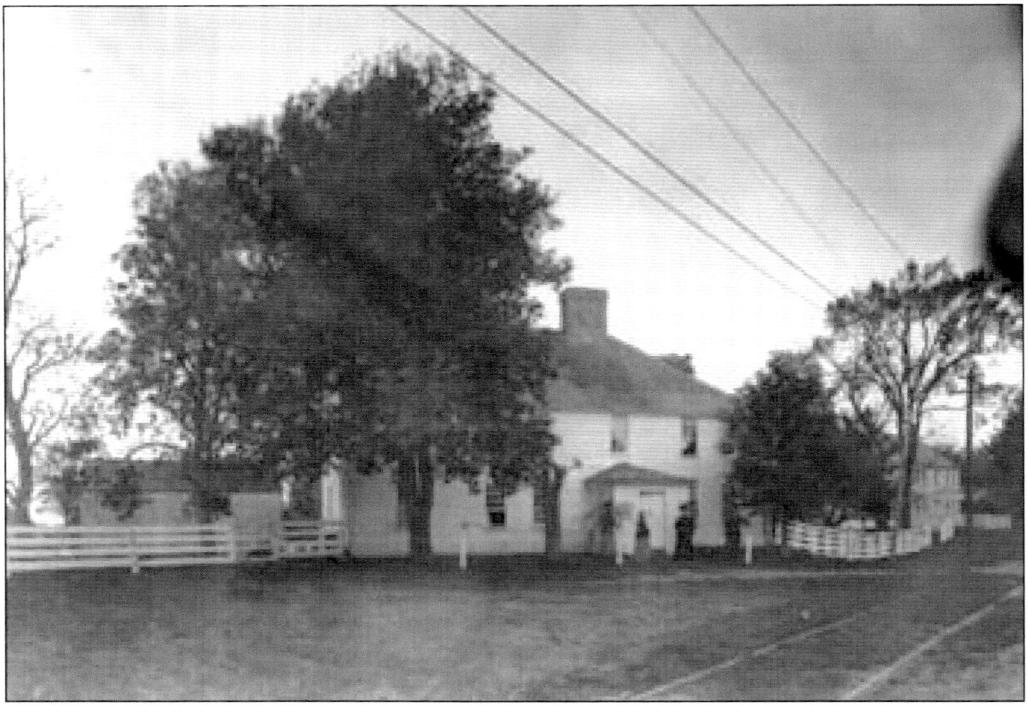

The original part of this house at 803 Main Street was built by Caleb Moody for his bride, Sarah Pierce, in 1658. In 1773, Caleb Moody III added eight rooms across the front. The base of the huge central chimney in the older part of the house is nearly 30 feet across. Moody descendants owned this house until 1937. (Courtesy of the West Newbury Historical Commission.)

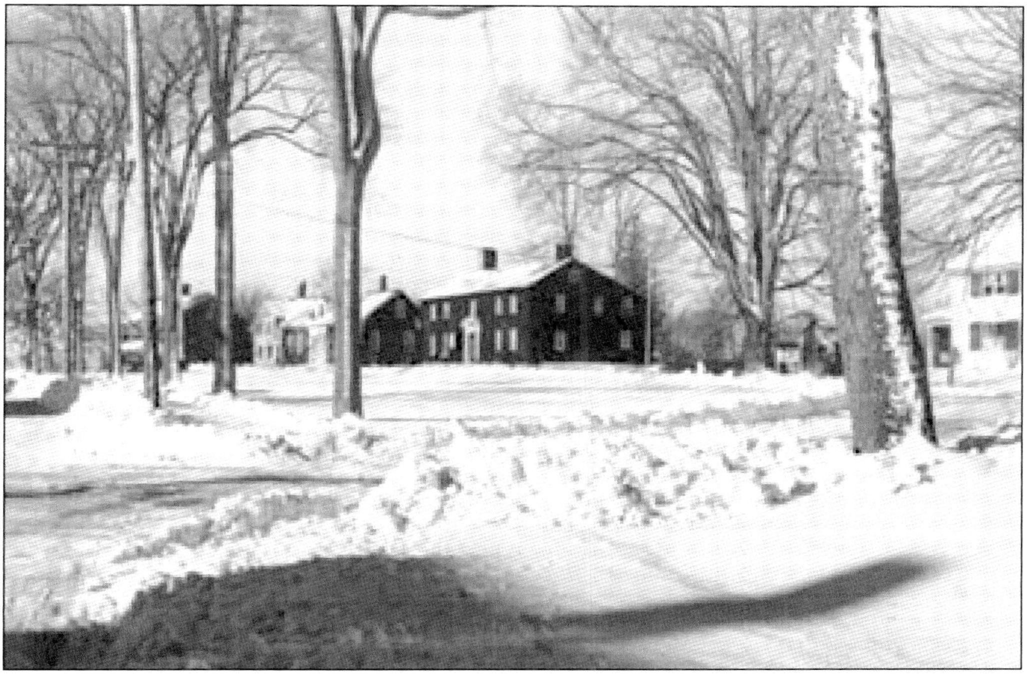

In 1731, Joshua Bailey gave the front of his farm to the town for a training field, and it was used during the Revolutionary War, the War of 1812, the Civil War, and even during World War II. Here were pillories, one of the town's first post offices, a covered bandstand, and two stores. The Farmers' Fair of the late 1800s was held here. (Courtesy of the GAR Memorial Library.)

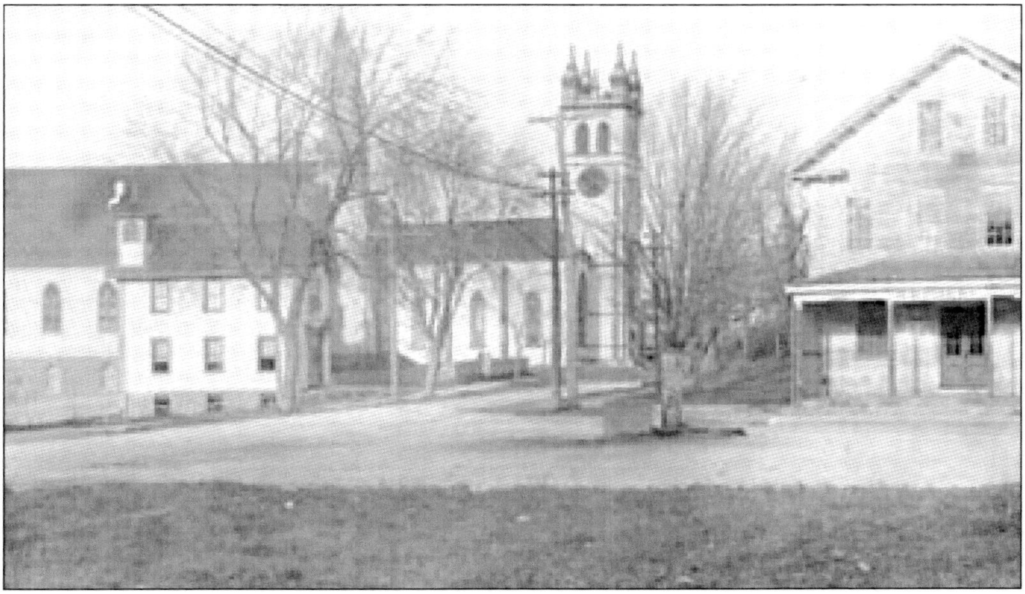

This view of the eastern side of Post Office Square shows, from the left, West Newbury's first fire station, built in 1884; St. Ann's Catholic Church, built in 1879; the Second Congregational Church, moved here in 1856 from Maple Street; the town pump; and George Whittier's Store, built about 1830. (Courtesy of the West Newbury Historical Society.)

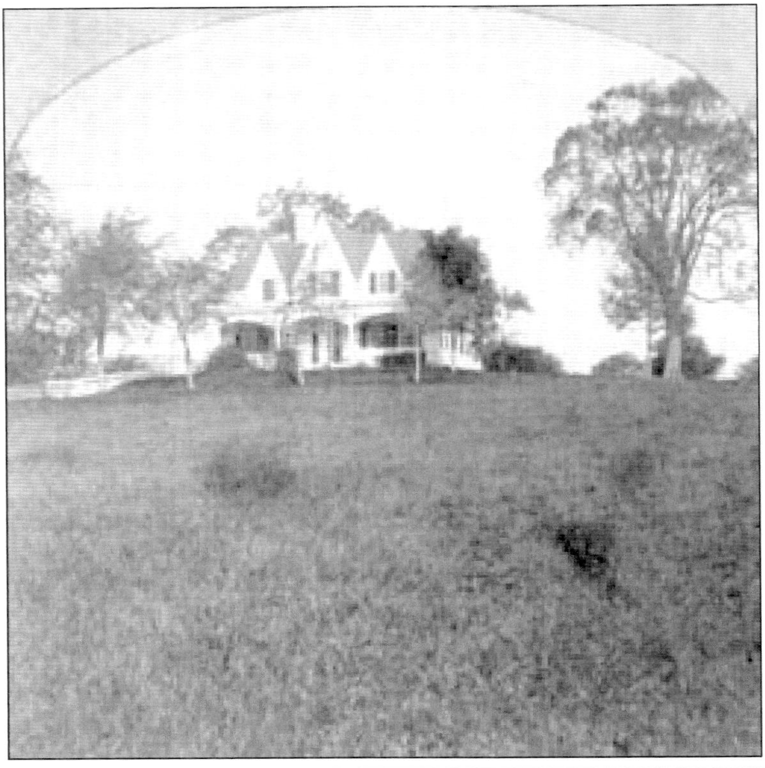

In 1842, Dr. Dean Robinson purchased this house on the top of Pipestave Hill and lived there until his death. After Tristram Dalton's house was taken down, this house was probably built sometime around 1835–1840 and was at the approximate location of the Dr. John C. Page School. (Courtesy of the West Newbury Historical Society.)

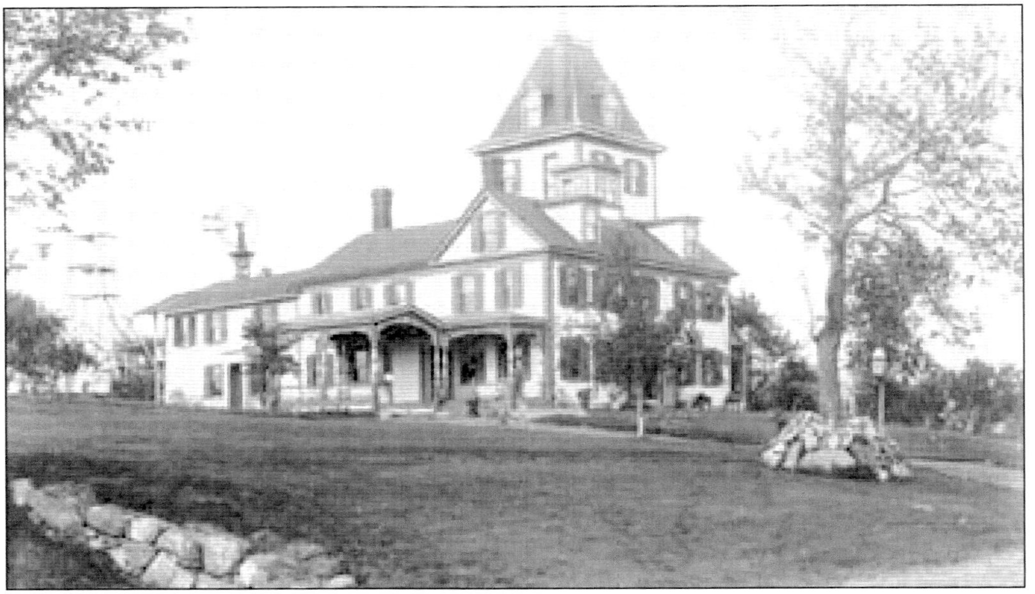

This mansion on Pipestave Hill was the home of E. Moody Boynton, a well-known inventor. It was said that on a clear day one could see Mount Washington from the tower. After Moody moved away, the house fell into disrepair and was totally destroyed by fire in September 1930. Visible to the left of the house is an observation tower. (Photograph by E.E. Bartlett; courtesy of Donald Laing.)

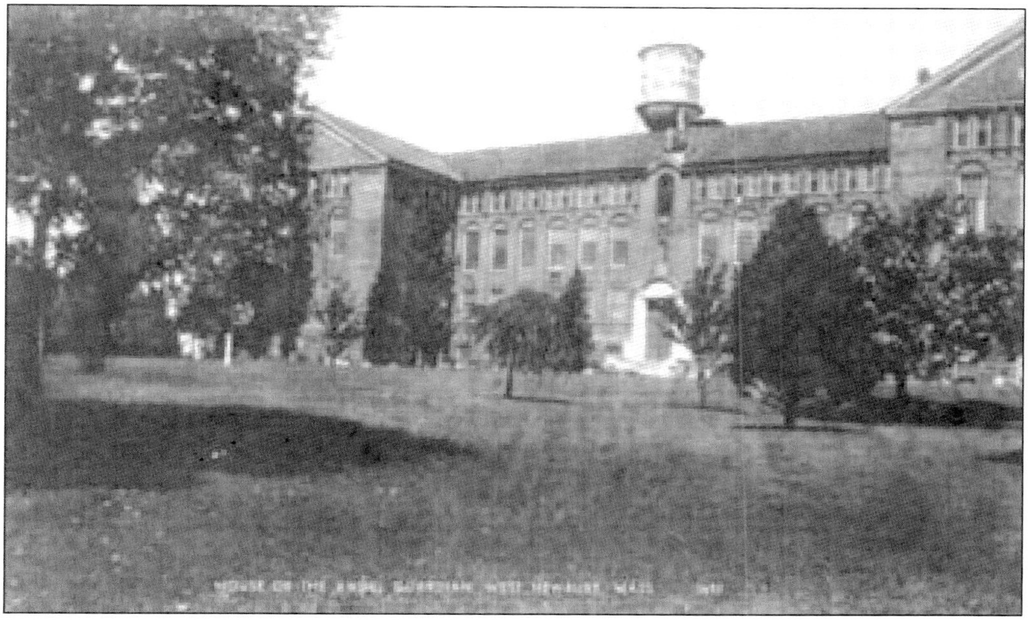

In 1928, the Brothers of Charity built an orphanage, the House of the Angel Guardian, on top of Pipestave Hill. The name was changed in 1951 to Boyhaven and, in 1963, to Cardinal Cushing Academy, a private boys' high school. The town purchased the 300-acre property in 1972, and the main building became the town's elementary school. (Postcard by American Art Postcard Company, Boston, Massachusetts; courtesy of Joyce Burnham Dixon.)

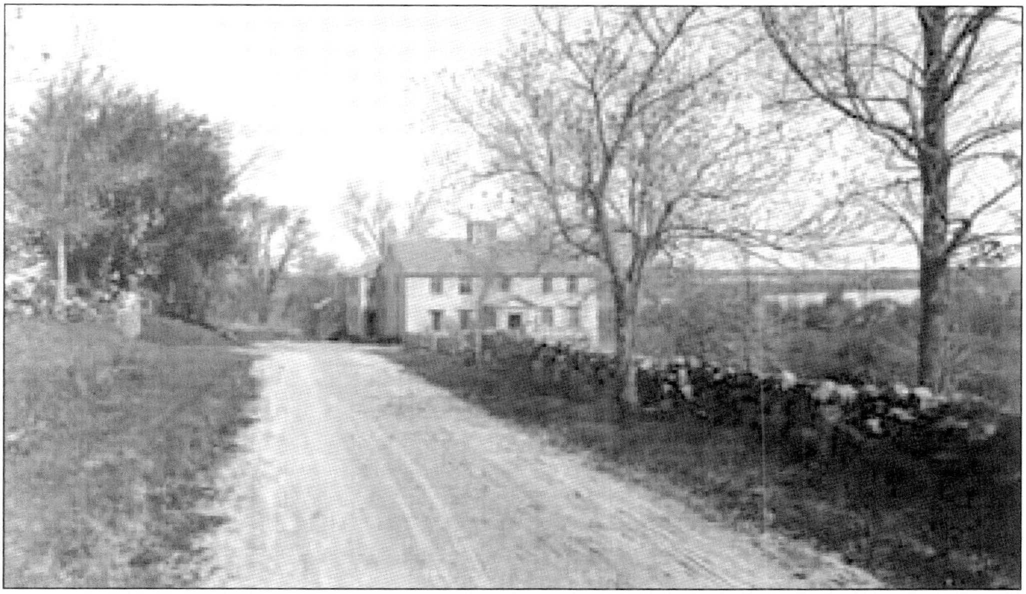

The Emerys first settled in this area in 1635. Their descendants Rev. Samuel Moody Emery and his wife, Mary Emery Emery, retired to their family homestead at 21 Emery Lane with their six unmarried children, and when the last child, Georgianna, died in 1952, the house was willed to the Society of St. John the Evangelist, an Episcopal religious order for men. (Courtesy of the West Newbury Historical Society.)

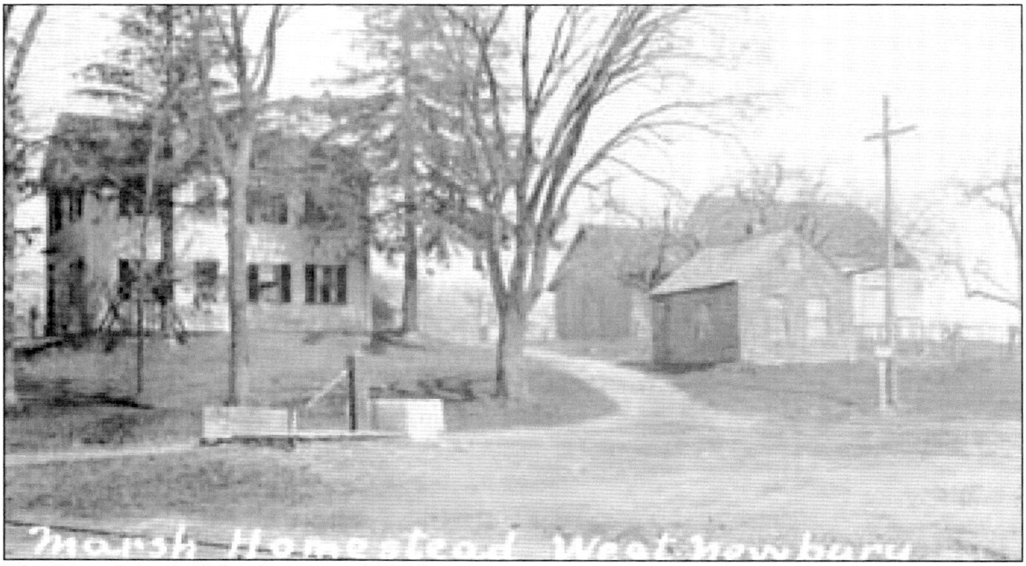

The Huse-Marsh-Kelso house at 875 Main Street, now renumbered 2 Garden Street, was built before 1729. In the late 1700s, it was known as Sawyer's Tavern; John Quincy Adams in his diary mentioned dancing there. A town pump and watering trough were located at this intersection for many years. (Courtesy of Joyce Burnham Dixon.)

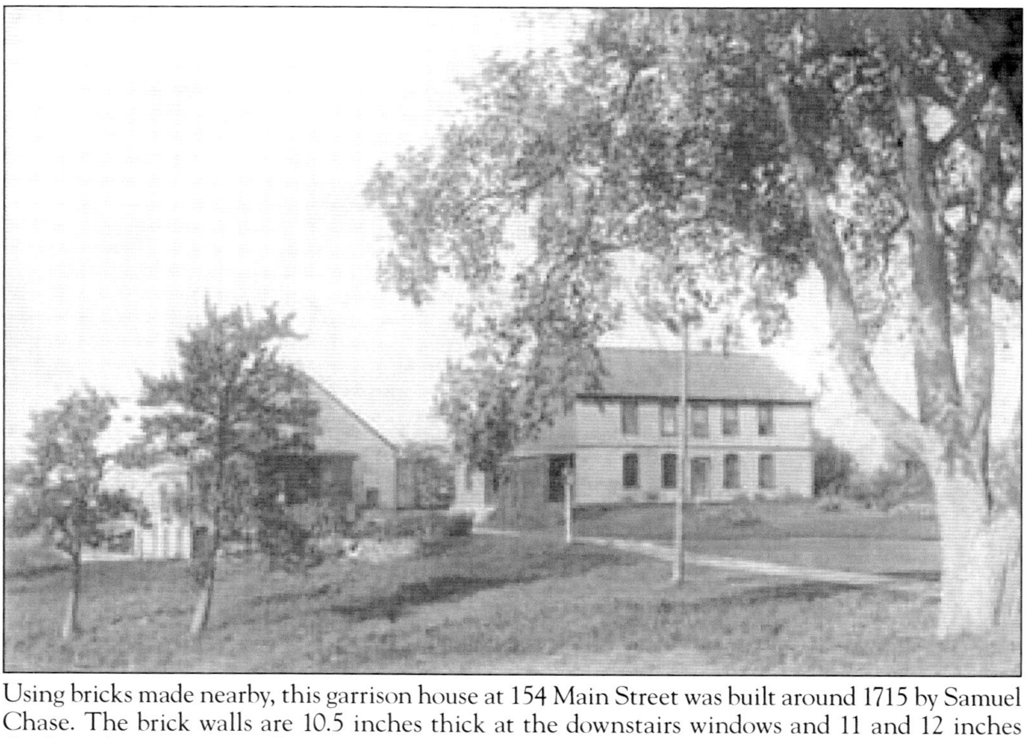

Using bricks made nearby, this garrison house at 154 Main Street was built around 1715 by Samuel Chase. The brick walls are 10.5 inches thick at the downstairs windows and 11 and 12 inches thick at the upstairs windows. There are tiny windows peering out from under each attic eave and under the second-story eaves from where settlers could watch for the approach of Indians. (Courtesy of Joyce Burnham Dixon.)

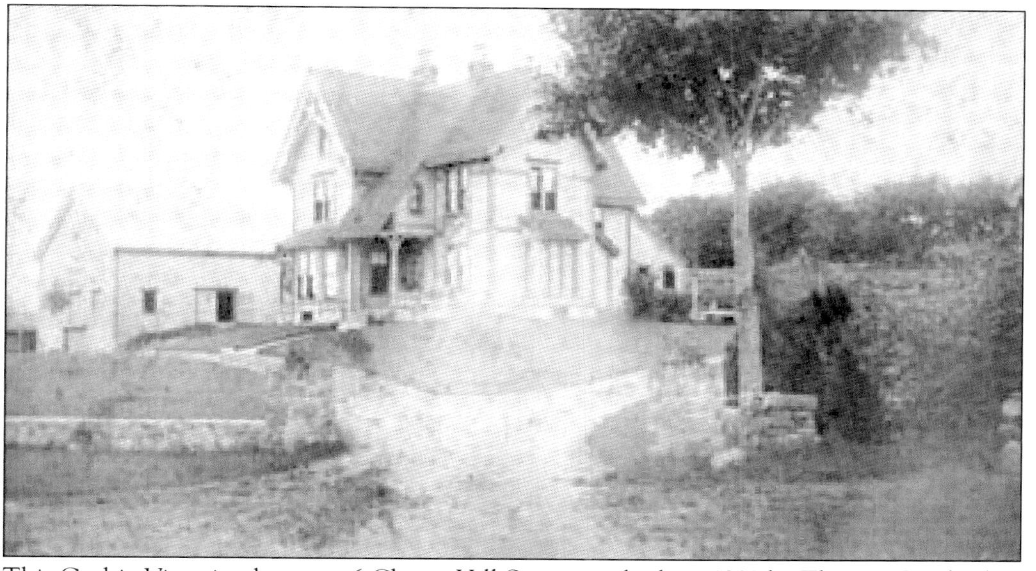

This Gothic Victorian house at 6 Cherry Hill Street was built in 1881 by Thomas C. Thurlow and remains in the Thurlow family to this day. Originally, a two-story garage and a three-story barn were also on the property, and unfortunately, the barn is no longer there, but the house and garage remain. (Courtesy of John Thurlow.)

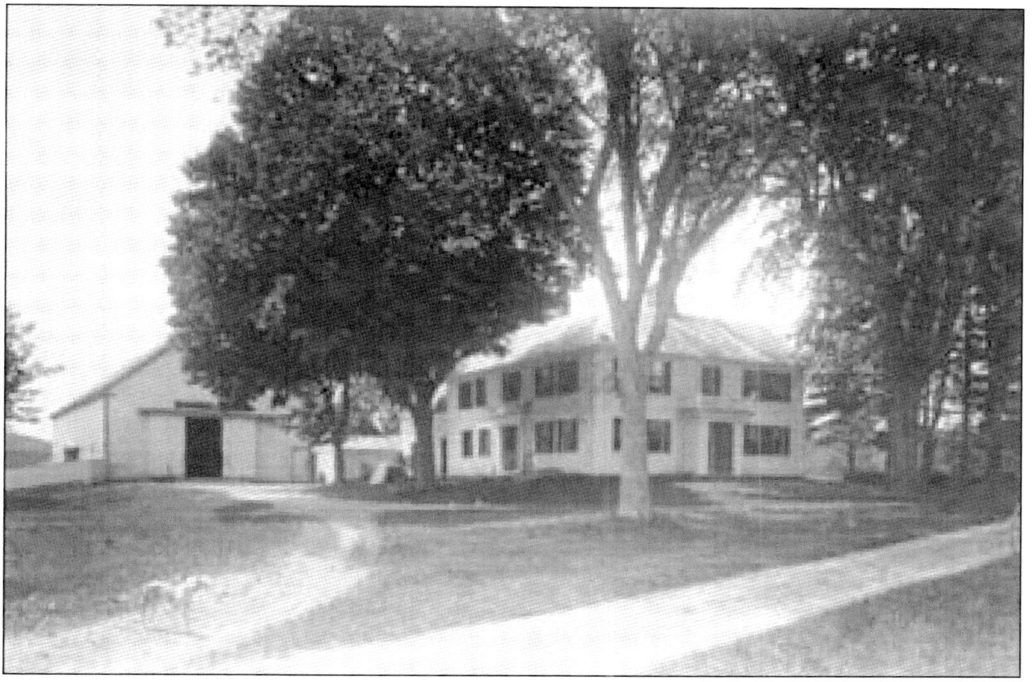

The Chase-Thurlow house at 5 Moulton Street was built in 1731 by Thomas Chase and has been owned by his descendants since that time. There was an earlier house on this site, which was destroyed prior to 1731, probably by fire. George Thurlow, the husband of Susan Chase, started the Cherry Hill Nurseries in 1832. (Courtesy of John Thurlow.)

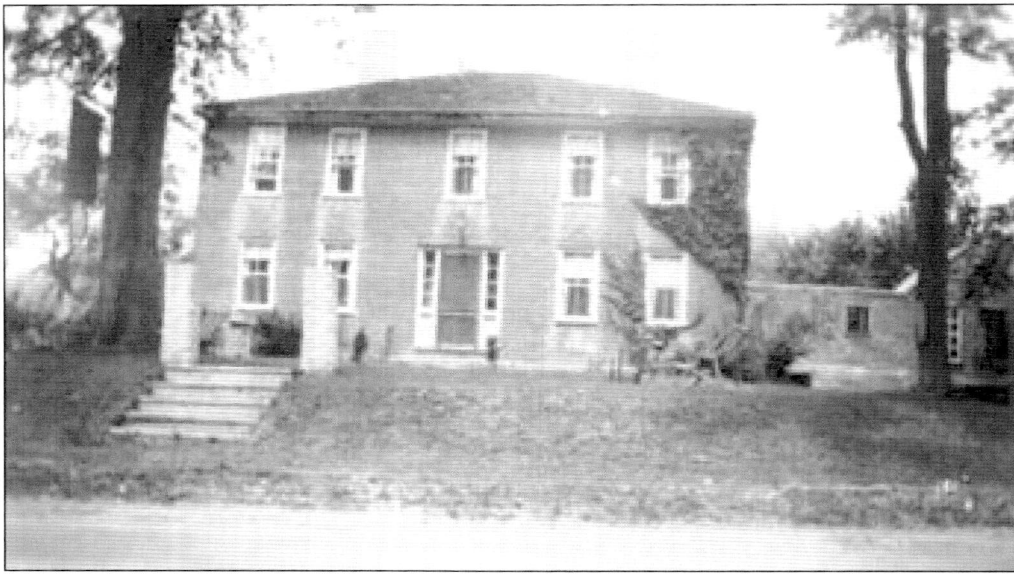

David Noyes, a comb manufacturer and inventor, built this house about 1790 at 74 Main Street, using bricks made in the Ordway and Newell brickyard, located where Pentucket Junior High School now stands. In the 1920s Marion and Margaret Dawson ran the Crane Neck Coffee House here and served dinners, teas, and lunches according to their advertisement in the 1926 *Automobile Green Book*. (Courtesy of the West Newbury Historical Society.)

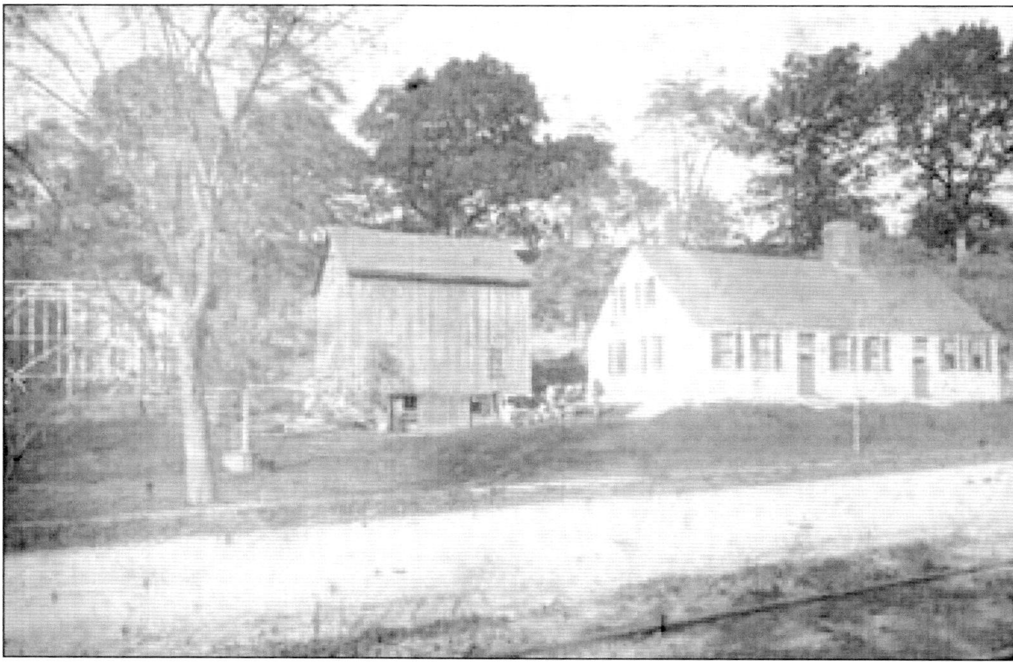

The right-hand portion of this unusual double-entrance Colonial cape at 102 Main Street was built before 1750, and legend states it had been moved to this location. The left-hand portion was built about 1830. The framed structure at the left is supposedly a dovecote built by Warren Sargent. (Courtesy of Peter Haack.)

The house at 209 Main Street was built about 1800. In this picture, Romulus Jacques, Ellen Follansbee Chase Jaques, and their cat are standing at the intersection of Merrill Street. The house was sold out of the family in the 1930s or 1940s. (Courtesy of the West Newbury Historical Commission.)

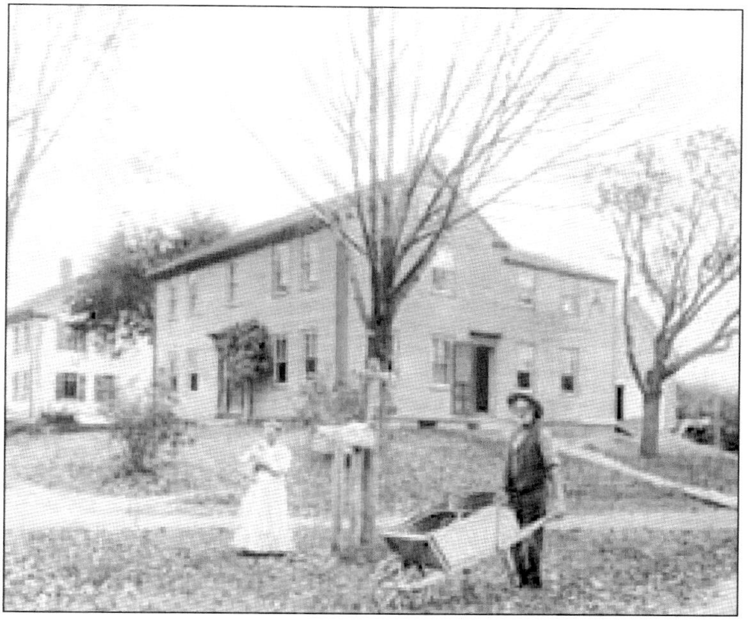

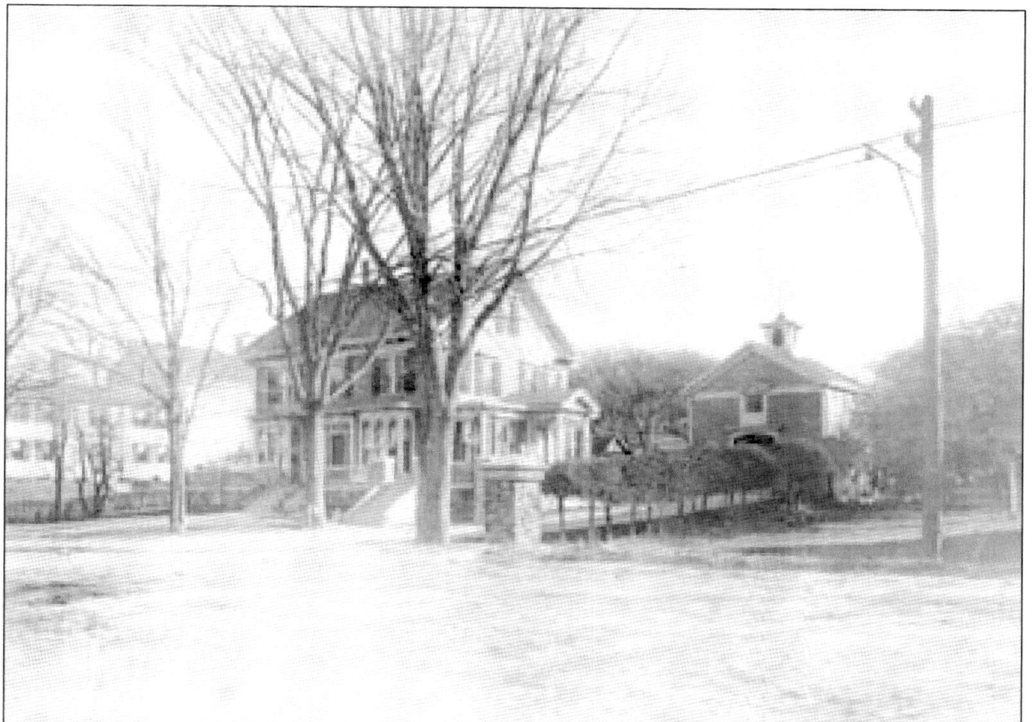

This Italianate house at 323 Main Street was built about 1862 by Somerby Newton Noyes and has been called the "Comb Factory Mansion." After Somerby's death, his son Horace Noyes, a prominent musician, hired famous musicians to give concerts there. Dr. John C. Page—a teacher, principal, and superintendent in West Newbury schools, for whom the local elementary school is named—lived here later. (Courtesy of the West Newbury Historical Society.)

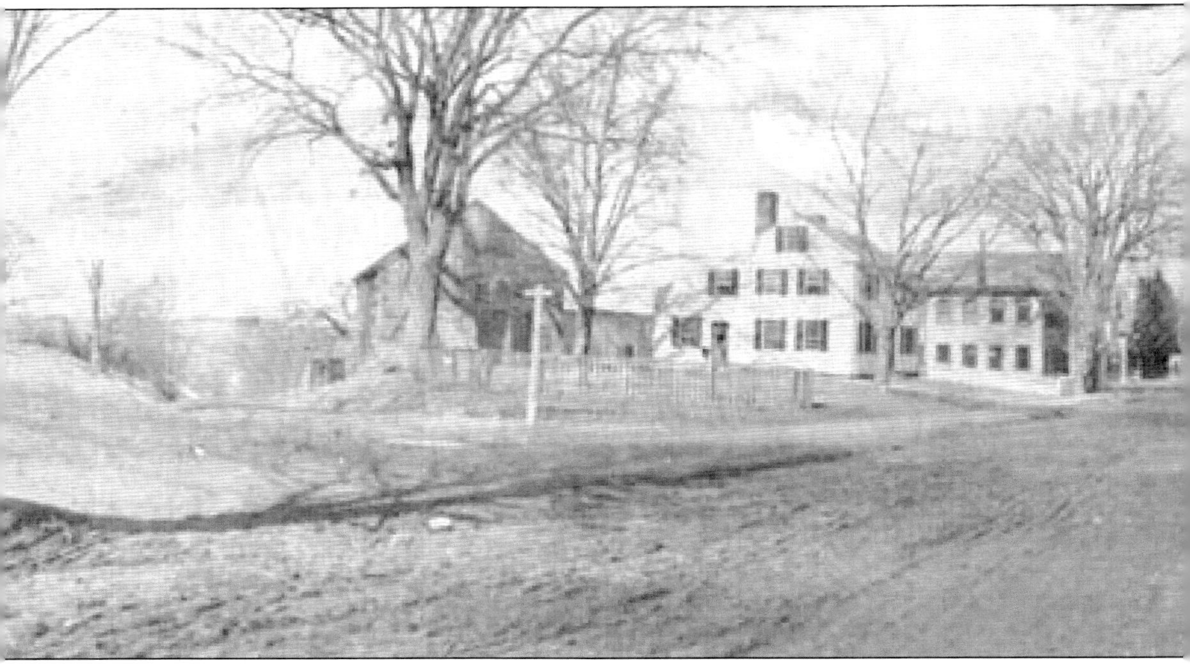

This panoramic view of the center of West Newbury was taken in the late 1800s or early 1900s. Whetstone Street is at the far left. Continuing from left to right, the Isaac Lane barn and house are at what is now 278 Main Street. The James Durgin and Sons Shoe Shop is beside it at 282 Main Street. Although there are buildings in between, the next visible building is the Second Congregational Church, which was moved to 308 Main Street in 1856. The parsonage is also

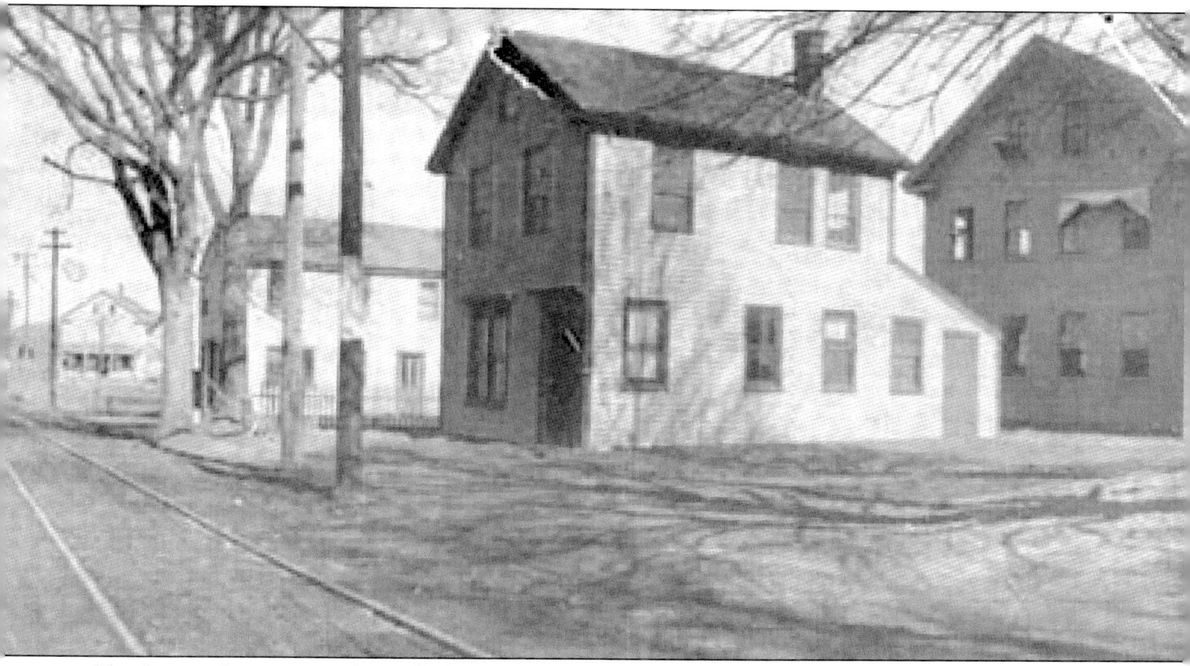

visible. Car tracks running through the center of the picture were laid in 1886. George Whittier's store is at the corner of Maple Street, followed by Isaac Lane's comb shop, which has since been torn down. The two buildings on the right comprise Haydn Brown's machine shop at 275 Main Street. (Courtesy of the West Newbury Historical Society.)

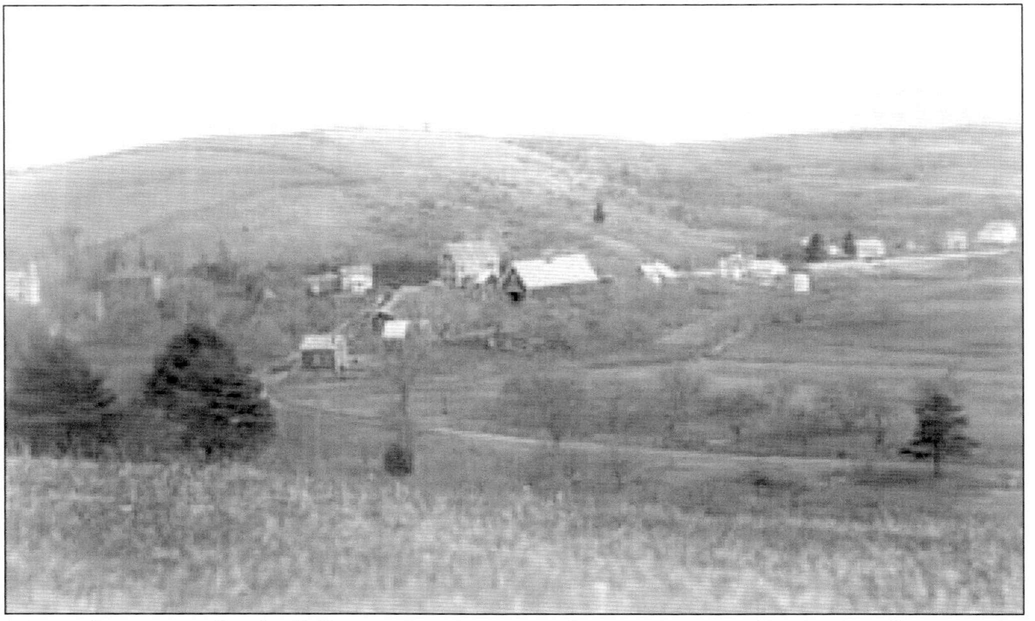

This early picture of Brake Hill was taken from near the top of Farm Hill. The large house in the center of the picture is at 66 Main Street; the barn behind it was used as a slaughterhouse. The road in the center of the picture went to the Dole farm on Dole Place. (Courtesy of the West Newbury Historical Commission.)

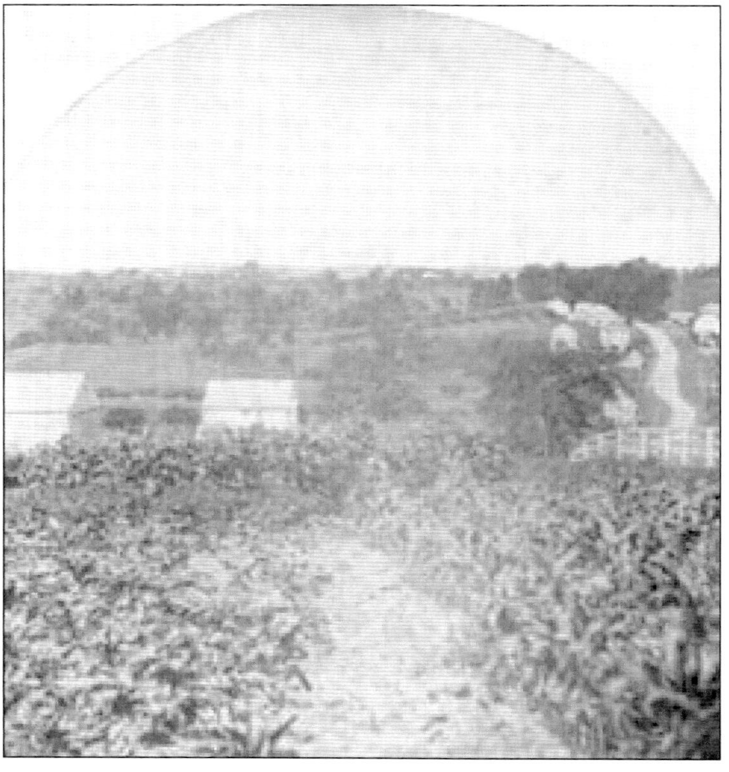

This stereopticon view is labeled "West Newbury from Pipestave Hill." Pipestave Hill was named for the dense forests of oak and birch. The trees were used for making pipe (barrel) staves, which were assembled into barrels for molasses, apples, and the like. Photographer Philip Coombs, who was active between 1860 and 1865, took this picture. (Courtesy of the Historical Society of Old Newbury.)

Four

Residents
Famous and Not-So-Famous

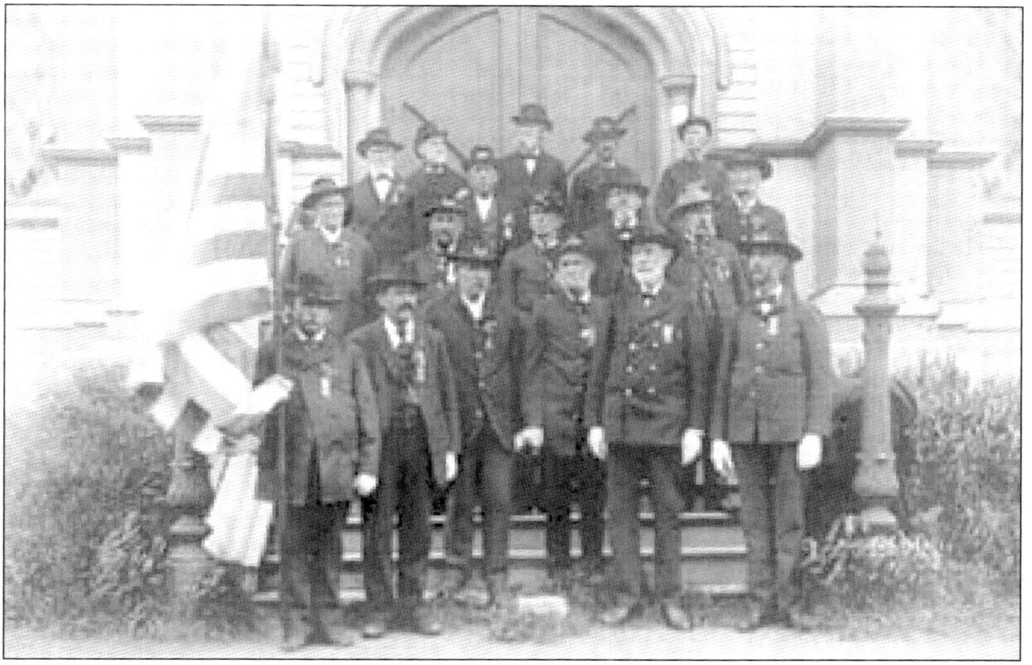

Civil War veterans gathered here about 1900 on the steps of the Second Congregational Church are, from left to right, (first row) Charles Bradley, John Bradley, Charles Gowen, Henry D. Lay, Col. Eben Stanwood, and Lawrence H. Bailey; (second row) James Porter, Randall B. Curtis, James Short, George Kennett, Charles Appleton, and John B. Clancy; (third row, in no particular order) Richard Lynch, David E.N. Carleton, Rufus Chase, Jeremiah Adams, William Kennett, and James Willard. (Courtesy of the GAR Memorial Library.)

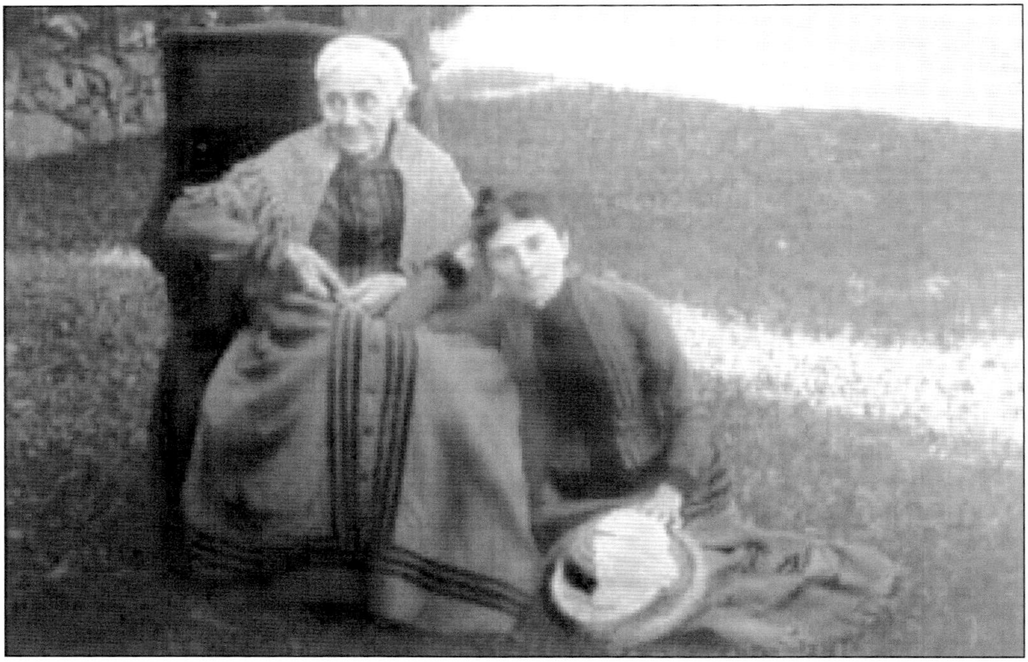

Susan Chase Thurlow and her granddaughter Alice Poore share a quiet moment. Alice lived with her grandmother at the Thurlow house at 5 Moulton Street from her infancy, her mother having died. Alice married Frederick Stultz from Nova Scotia as his first wife. This picture was taken in the early 1880s. (Courtesy of John Thurlow.)

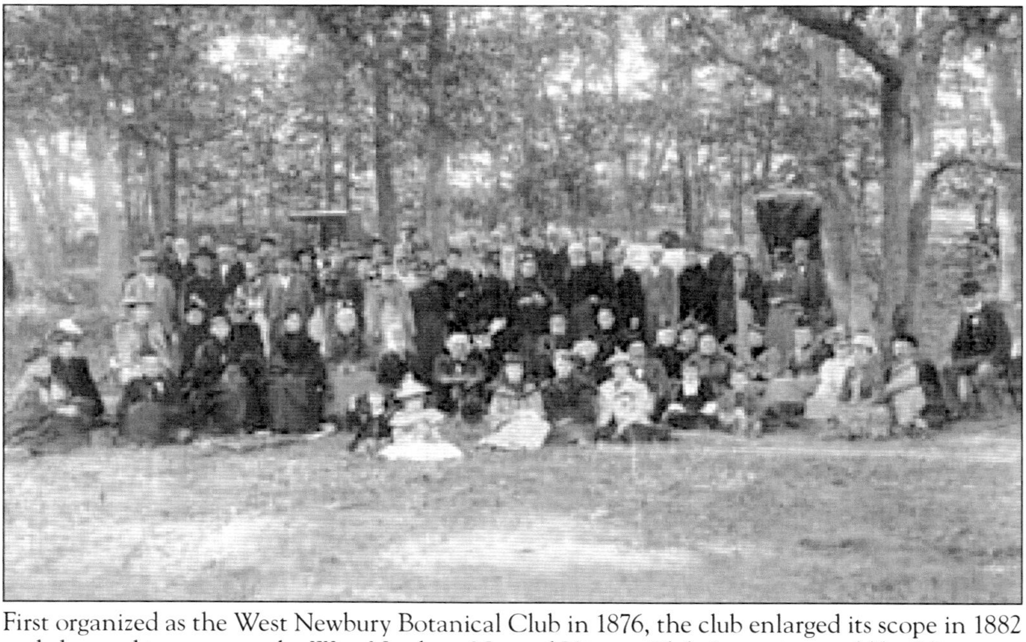

First organized as the West Newbury Botanical Club in 1876, the club enlarged its scope in 1882 and changed its name to the West Newbury Natural History Club. It met in an old building near the legion hall. In 1897, members were granted use of the top floor of the legion hall for their library room. (Courtesy of the West Newbury Historical Society.)

Out of the 77 who served, Charles L. Carr was the only West Newbury man killed in action in World War I. He died on October 15, 1918, in Cornay, France, during the Meuse-Argonne Offensive at the age of 30. Carr was a native of the town and left a wife, father, and brother. The American Legion Post now bears his name. (Courtesy of Elinor Spofford.)

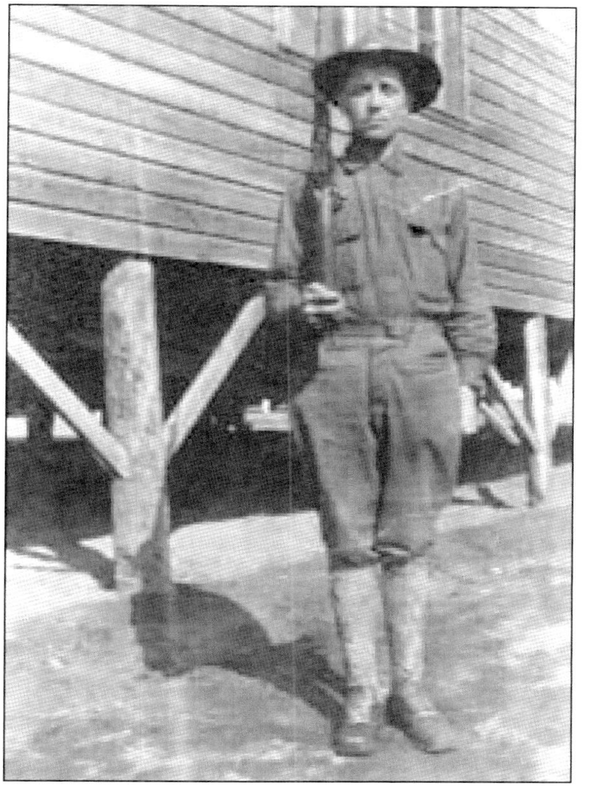

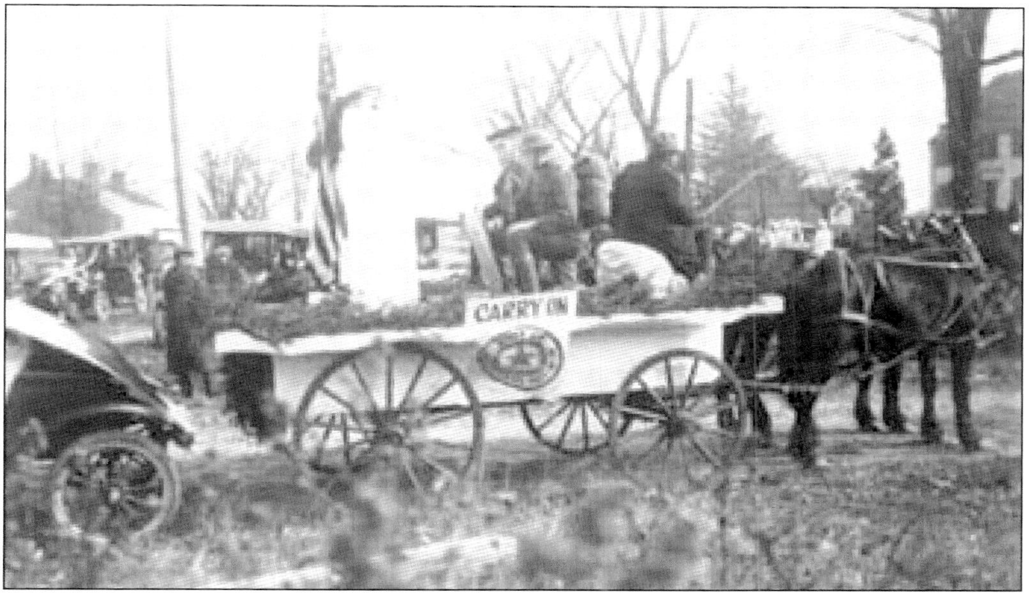

A large parade in 1919 celebrated the town's centennial and the return of its men from the First World War. Several cars follow the horse-drawn float of the Charles L. Carr Post, American Legion, that carried returning servicemen. The parade circled the Training Field. (Courtesy of Joyce Burnham Dixon.)

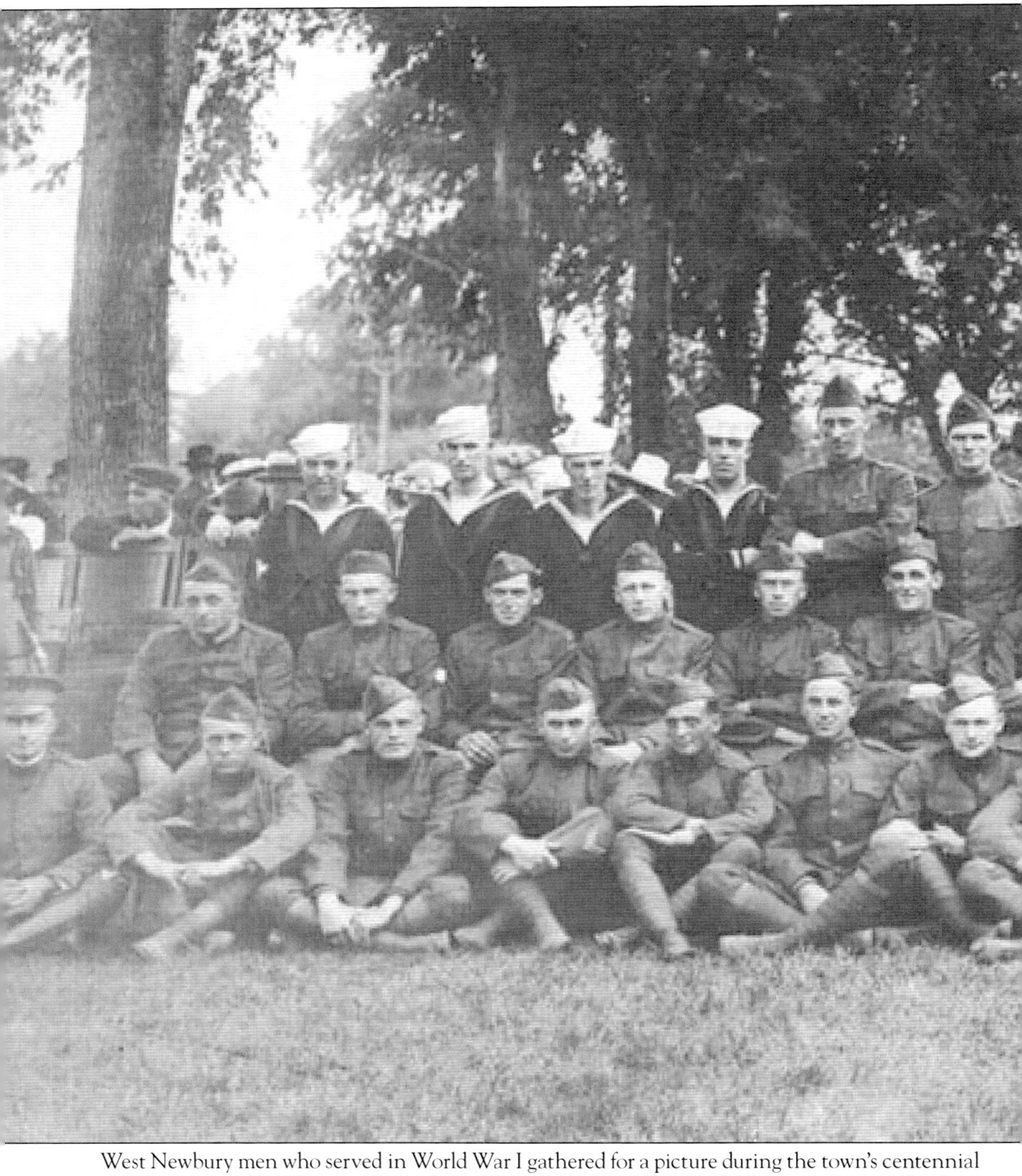

West Newbury men who served in World War I gathered for a picture during the town's centennial celebration in 1919. Pictured here, from left to right, are (first row) Thomas Hogan, Harrison Chase, Lincoln Peirce, Stanley Sawyer, Lester Kirkpatrick, Elmer Burnham, Russell Noyes, Leroy McDonald, Elmer Coskery, Vincent Sullivan, Frank Norris, Clarence Durland, and Harry Chase; (second row) Edgar Chase, Everett Watson, Walter Willis, Chester Colcord, Marshall Bacheller, John Kirkpatrick, William Thompson, William Melville, Spencer Poore, Winthrop Thurlow,

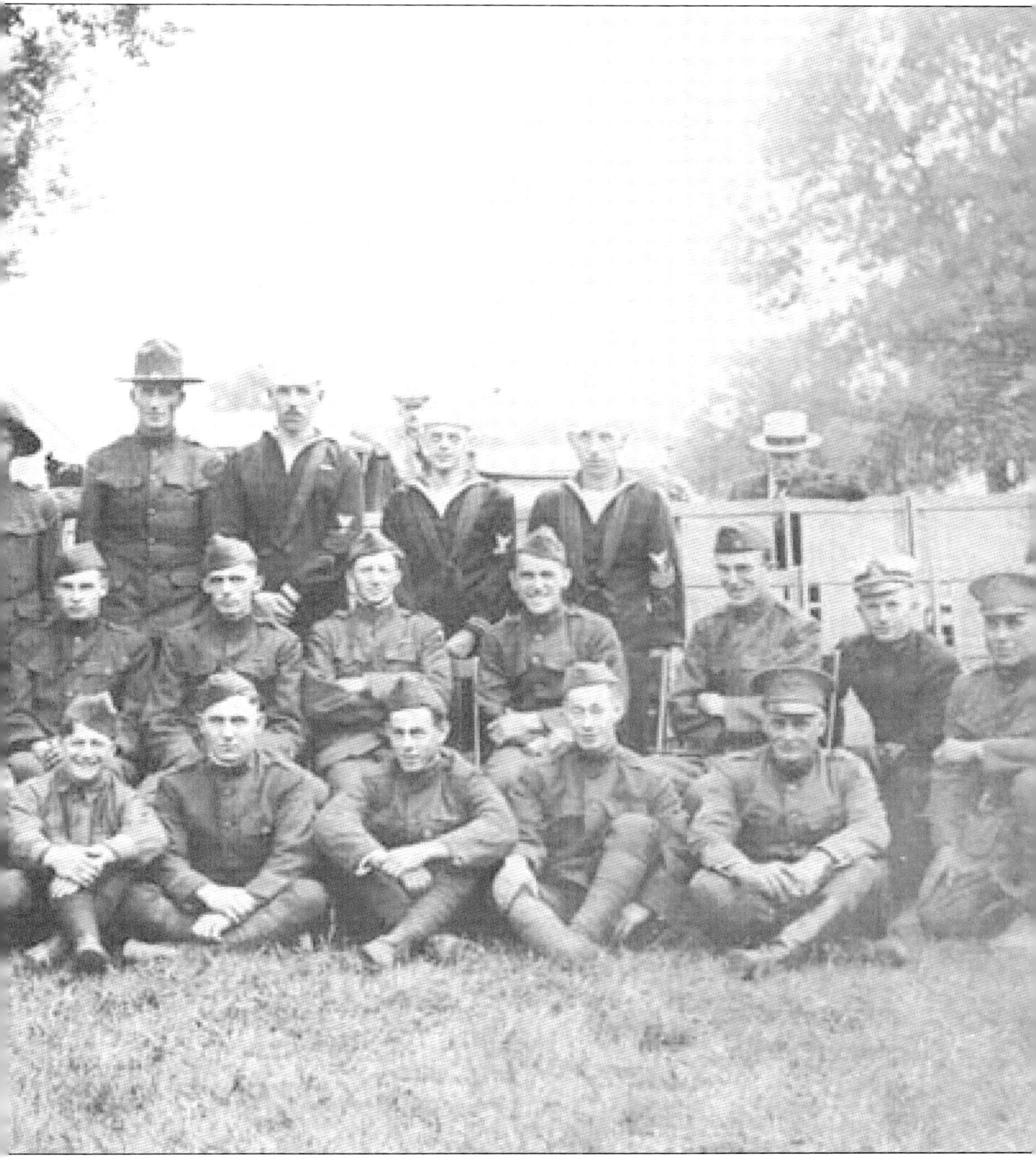

Stanwood Gordon, Harold Winchester, and Walter Swap; (third row) Caleb Allen, Chester Hall, Joseph Ryan, Rexford Bailey, Percy Tarleton-Shute, Charles Rogers, Patrick Hogan, Henry Bailey, Russell Peirce, and Edward Sullivan. Three West Newbury servicemen died during the war: Charles Carr was killed in action, Charles Knapp was killed by accident, and Herman Sonier died of disease. (Courtesy of John Thurlow.)

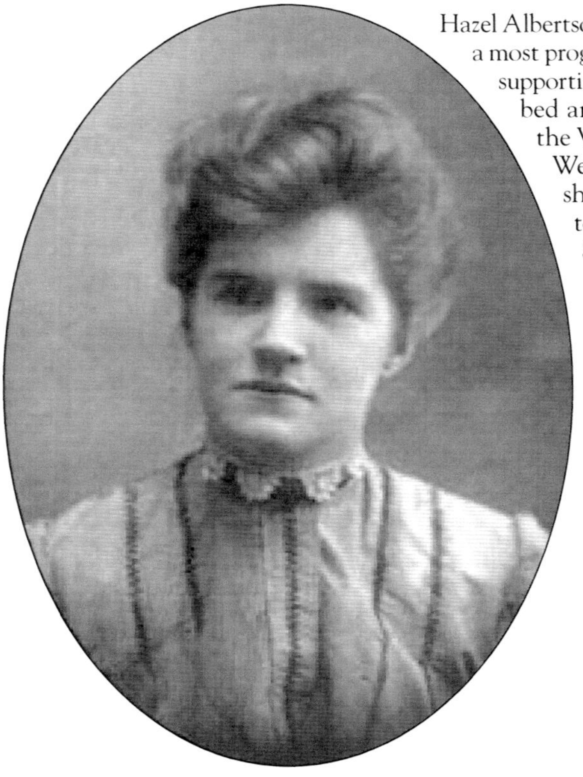

Hazel Albertson, matriarch of the Berkenbush family, was a most progressive woman for her time. In addition to supporting Chestnut Hill Farm with an avant-garde bed and breakfast for many years, she founded the West Newbury Woman's Club and the first West Newbury Girl Scout troop in 1914, and she wrote and directed the pageant for the town's centennial celebration. (Courtesy of Sandra Berkenbush.)

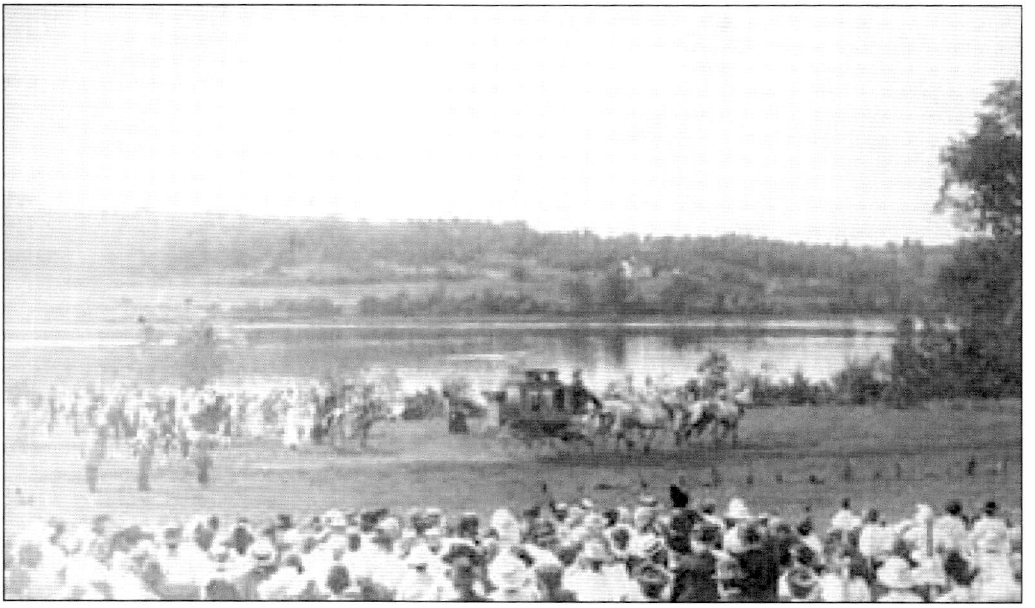

West Newbury's centennial pageant in 1919 was an amazing feat for a small town. Written by Hazel Albertson, the cast included more than 300 people. The pageant, "The Spirit of the Merrimack," told the history of the river from prehistoric times to the present. It was held at the Dole farm at the end of Dole Place on the banks of the Merrimack River. (Courtesy of Donald Laing.)

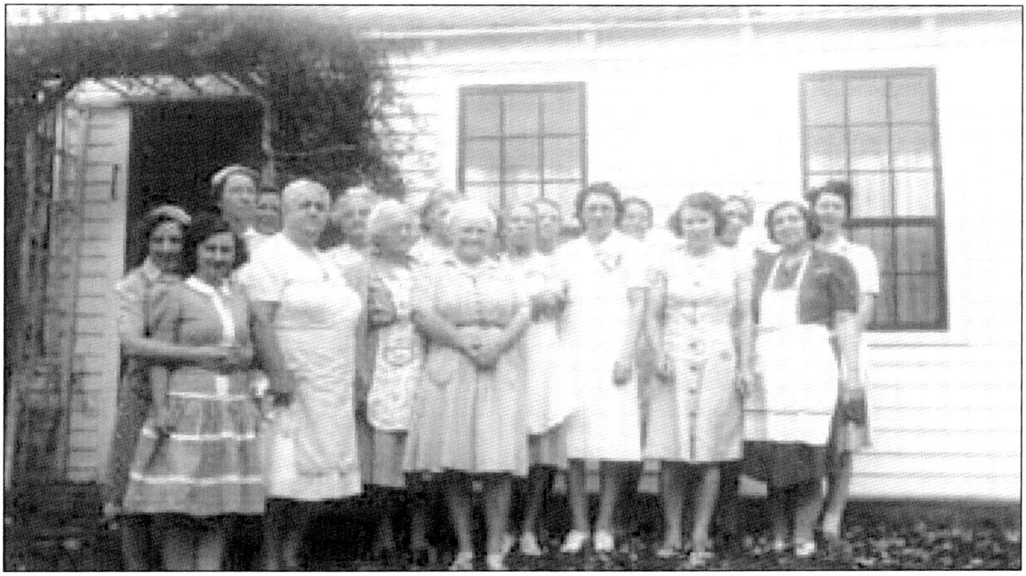

These women were perhaps typical of those in West Newbury during the Depression years. The group met regularly in this house at 200 Main Street to discuss ways to economize during hard times, such as cooking with chicken fat, and to enjoy the company of other women. Pictured, from left to right, are four unidentified, Eva Flook, unidentified, Etta Hale, unidentified, Madeline Collister, and eight unidentified. (Courtesy of Elinor Spofford.)

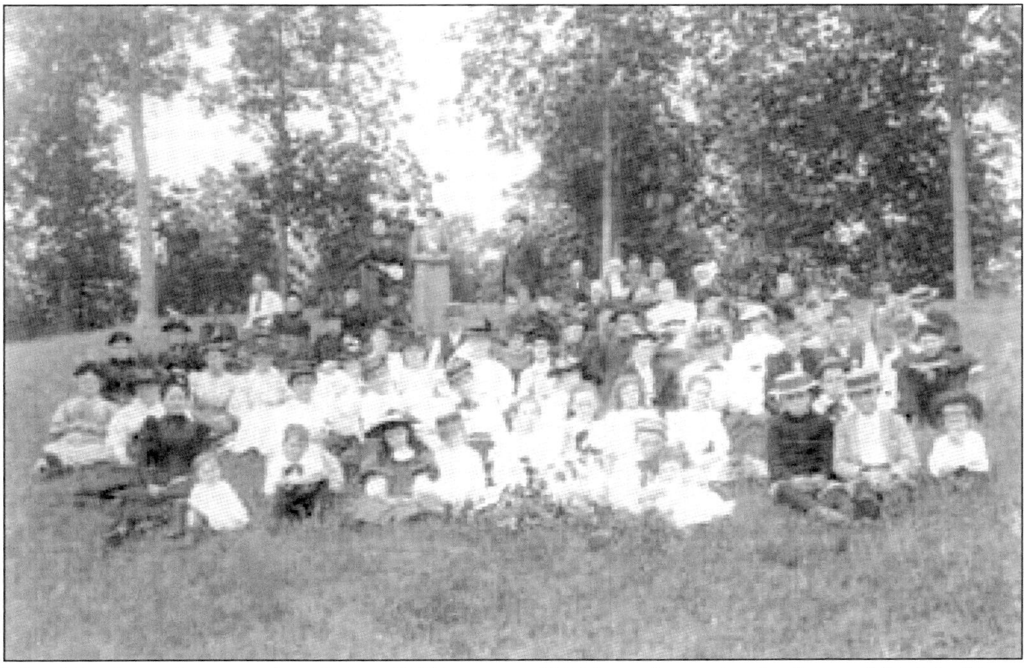

West Newbury Grange, founded in 1887, met at 320 Main Street in the Second Parish. Here, members are shown at a picnic at the Romulus Jaques farm, now called Chestnut Hill Farm. Laurel Grange, organized in 1888 in the First Parish, is still in existence and is an active grange today. (Courtesy of the West Newbury Historical Society.)

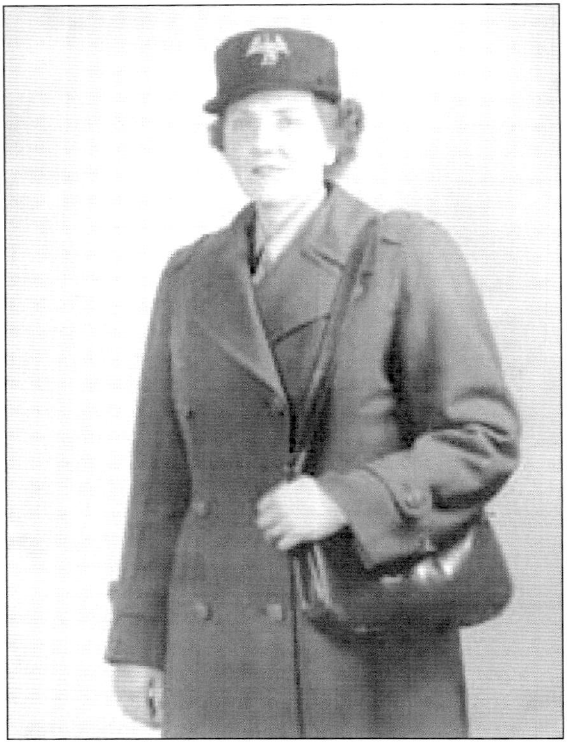

Capt. Frances Keegan Marquis, a West Newbury native, was commander of the first overseas detachment of the Women's Army Auxiliary Corps in 1943, as well as a member of General Eisenhower's staff. National Guardsmen, below, pose in front of town hall during World War II. Those pictured are, from left to right, (first row) Warren Simmons, unidentified, Edward Germain, Norman Bilodeau, Henry Coffey, Francis Bartlett, unidentified, and Russell Noyes; (second row) Ralph Woodworth, Ronald Gibbons, Leslie Plumley, Howard Willis, J. Stanley Sawyer, Chester Fowler, two unidentified, Bernard Sargent, unidentified, and Marshall Bacheller; (third row) Harrison Chase, Leonard Burrill, Hugh Hardinger, unidentified, Ross Gadd, unidentified, and Bacrad Kassabian. (Both, courtesy of the West Newbury Historical Society.)

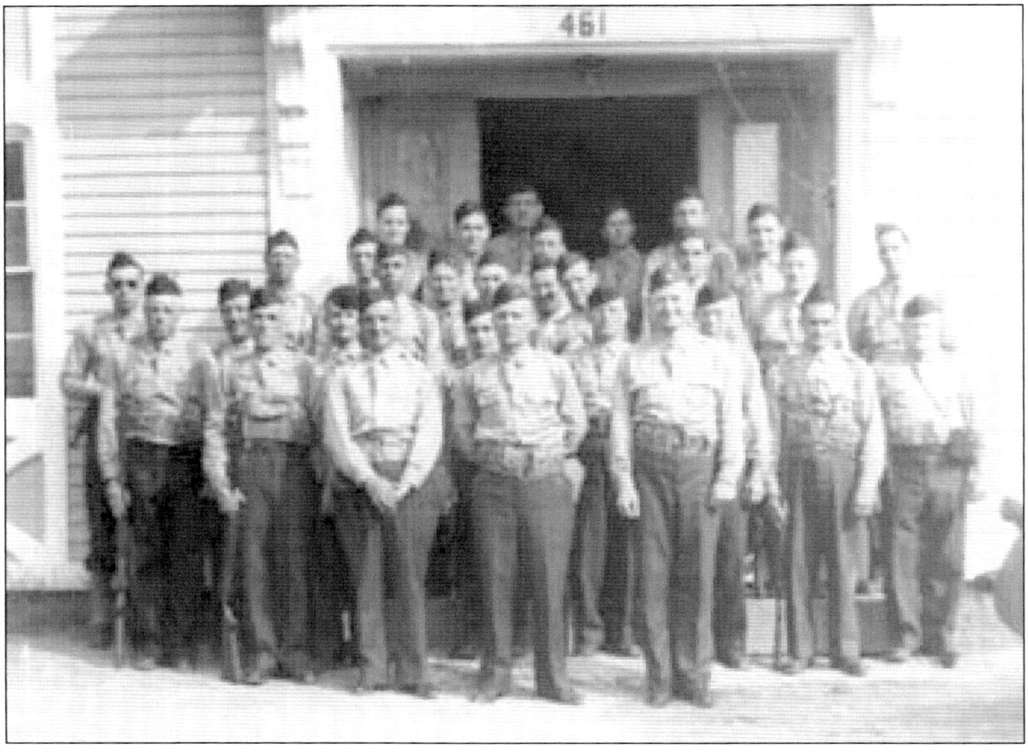

J. Appleton Brown was a West Newbury native and a nationally known landscape artist. His wife, Agnes Bartlett Brown, was an artist in her own right. He studied in Boston and in Paris and was elected to the National Academy in 1896. He and his wife were part of a group of artists living in the First Parish area near the Artichoke River. (Courtesy of the West Newbury Historical Society.)

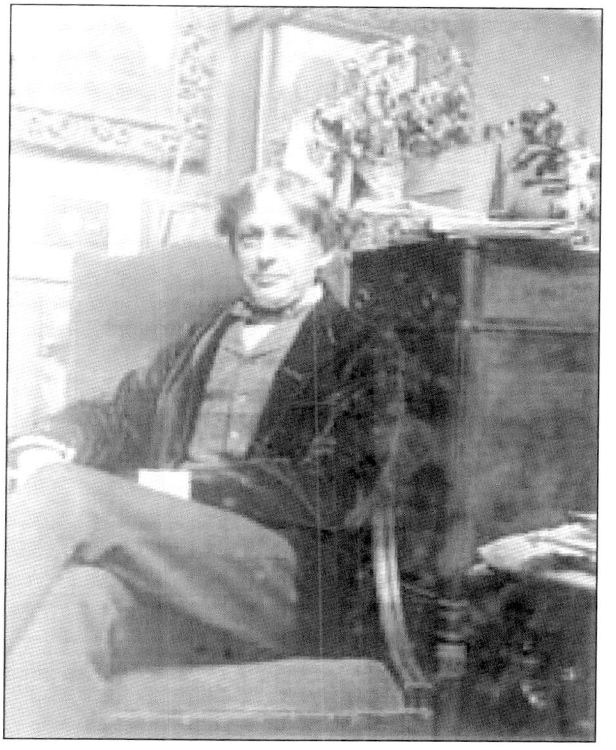

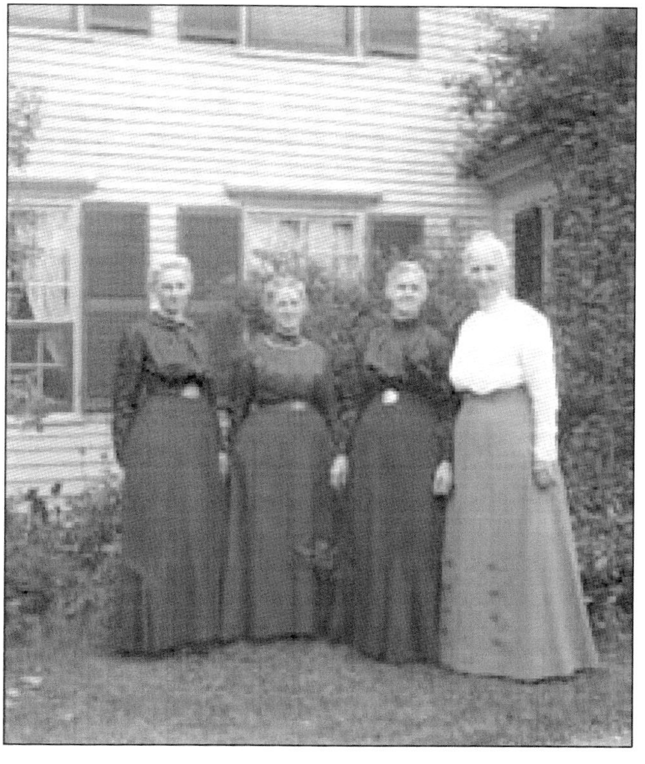

The five unmarried Emery sisters lived simply and frugally with their brother in their farmhouse on Emery Lane. In 1899, a distant cousin died, and the women found themselves millionaires. They used their money mostly to further God's kingdom and improve the quality of life in West Newbury. This picture, taken before 1927, shows the four youngest sisters from left to right: Louisa, Frances, Mary Elizabeth, and Georgianna. (Courtesy of the West Newbury Historical Society.)

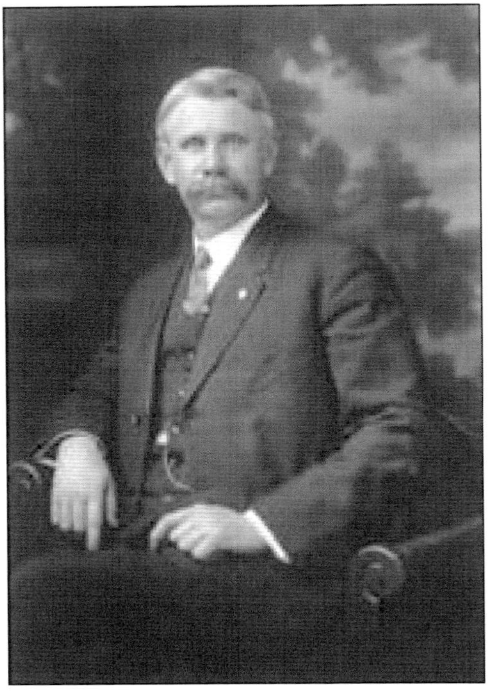

Parker Nason, a West Newbury native and the son of Ezekiel and Mary Salley Nason, was town clerk for 22 years. He also served as moderator for 21 years; selectman, assessor, and overseer of the poor for 12 years; school committeeman for six years; and library trustee for 15 years. He also served a term in the Massachusetts General Court. (Courtesy of the West Newbury Historical Society.)

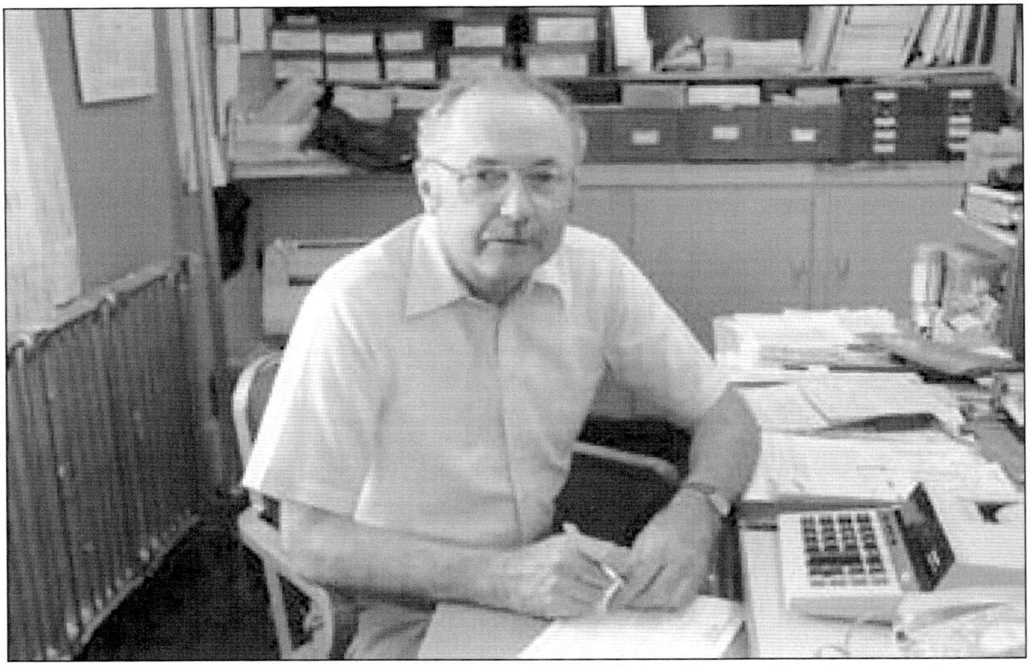

Norman Hobson, a West Newbury native, was town clerk for 38 years. He also served as town treasurer for 32 years, assessor for three years, and fire department dispatcher for many years. Hobson, with his father, Frank, organized four Little League baseball teams in 1953, beginning boys' league baseball in West Newbury. (Photograph by Bill Lane; courtesy of the Newburyport Archival Center at the Newburyport Public Library.)

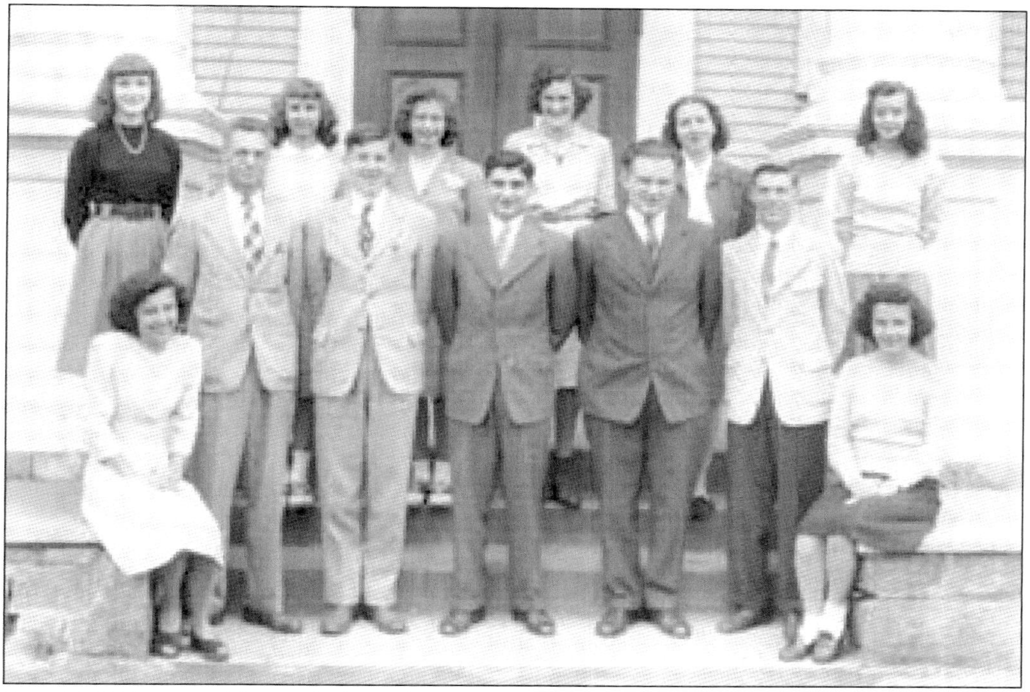

Ronald Gibbons and his wife, Dorothy, were well known in West Newbury for their years of teaching and for their homemade chocolates. Pictured here with students in 1947 are, from left to right, (first row) Janice Ellis, teacher Ronald Gibbons, Stanley Jackson, Kerkor Kassabian, George Bailey, John Gibbons, and Ann Leary; (second row) Marianna Possante, Ann Thurlow, Miriam Dennis, Idona Spencer, Susan Williams, and Phyllis Davis. (Courtesy of Doris Bailey-Jones.)

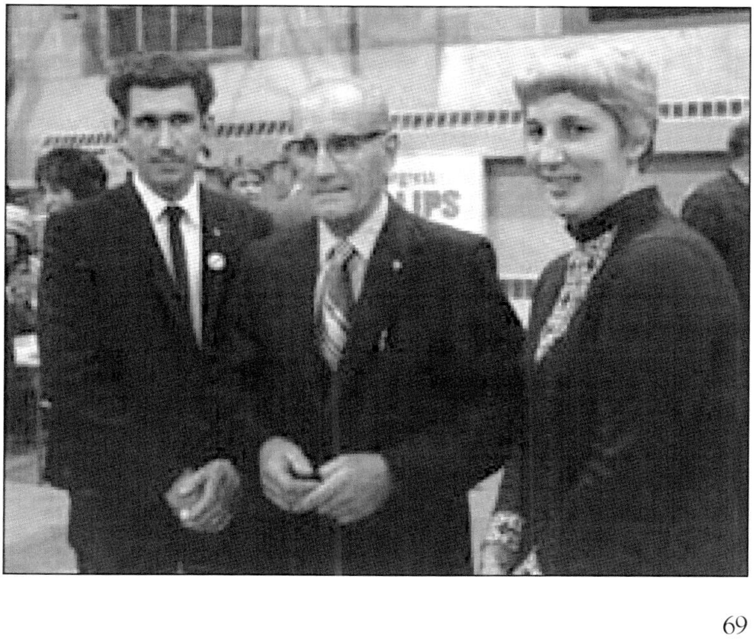

Albert Elwell moved to West Newbury in 1917 and was active in public service from then until his death in 1992. In 1928, he was the youngest selectman in the state. He served as selectman for 42 years, as state representative for four years, and as a school bus driver for 20 years. Albert is pictured between his two children, Richard Elwell and Nancy Elwell Lewis. (Courtesy of Nancy Elwell Lewis.)

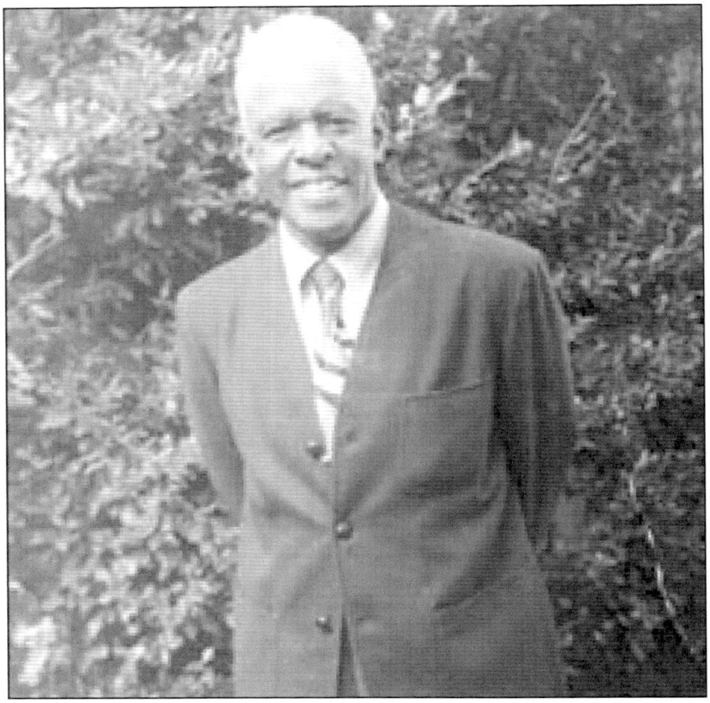

Roland Hayes, an internationally known concert tenor and son of a former slave, had a summer home in West Newbury. He sang before royalty at Buckingham Palace and at the Royal Palace in Madrid. In 1949, he gave a concert at town hall, accompanied by Reginald Boardman on Barbara Gove's concert grand piano, benefitting water main extension costs from Maple Street to Crane Neck Hill. (Courtesy of the GAR Memorial Library.)

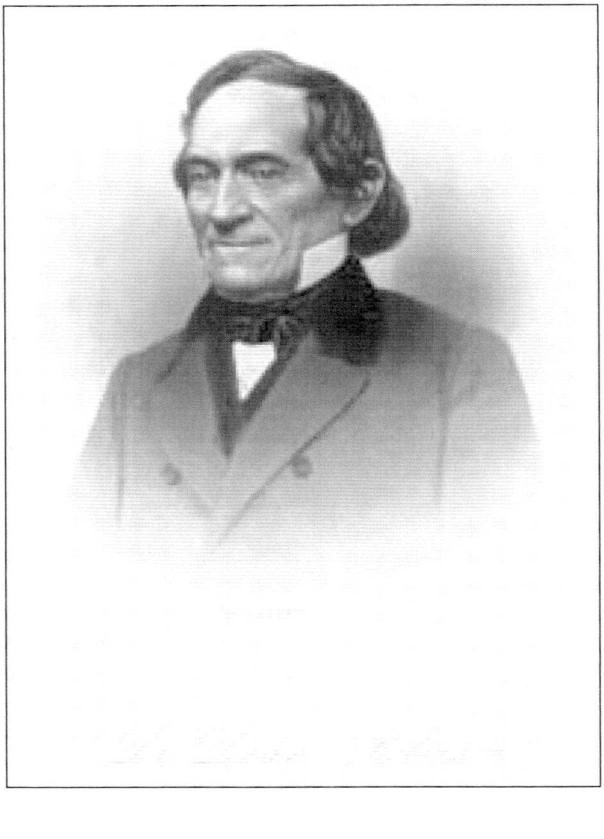

Dr. Dean Robinson was a physician in West Newbury from 1811 until his death in 1863. According to an article by Leonard Woodman Smith, Doctor Robinson was so loved and trusted that he wrote many of his patients' wills and administered their estates. He was the town moderator for many years and was one of the founders of the Essex County Agricultural Society. (Courtesy of Jane Wallace Wild.)

Dr. Orin Warren practiced medicine in West Newbury for 57 years, succeeding Doctor Robinson. He was a surgeon in the Civil War and was captured with the wounded he was tending at Camden but was unconditionally released by Gen. John T. Hughes, a Confederate. Warren was a member of the legislature in 1879 and was also on the school board. (Courtesy of Jane Wallace Wild.)

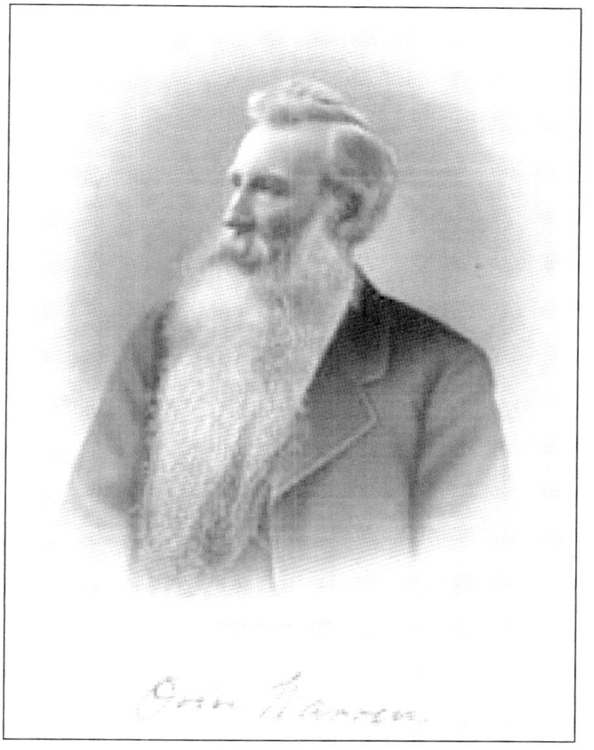

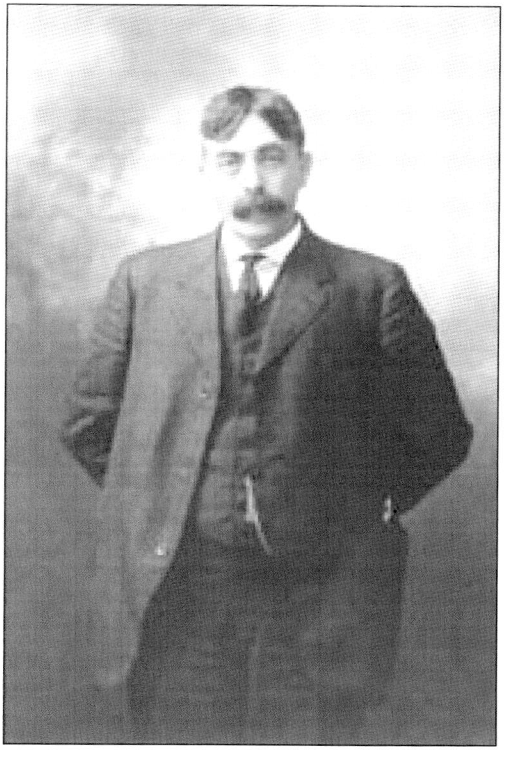

Dr. Amos Peirce was the leading doctor in West Newbury for 30 years until his sudden death in 1916 at age 54. He was a member of the school committee and a library trustee, as well as a member of many fraternal groups and the director of a savings bank in Merrimac. (Photograph by M.C. Oak, Merrimac, Massachusetts; courtesy of the West Newbury Historical Society.)

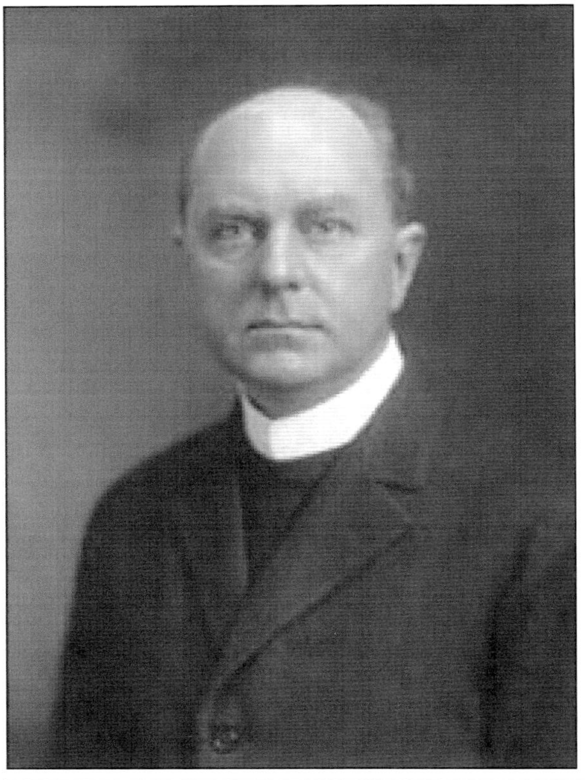

The Reverend Glenn Tilley Morse, founder and first minister of All Saints Church, served from 1910 to 1938. Deeply interested in his community, antiquities, and music, he served as a library trustee and a member of the school committee. He was chairman of the West Newbury Red Cross during the First World War. (Photograph by Notman Studios; courtesy of the West Newbury Historical Society.)

Alonzo P. Jaques, the oldest man in West Newbury when he died in 1921 at age 101, lived his entire life in the house in which he was born. He was at one time a comb maker, shoemaker, and farmer, and he was also an ardent abolitionist and steadfast advocate of the enfranchisement of women. He is shown here with his wife, Mary Bartlett Jaques. (Photograph by Jessie Jaques; courtesy of Sandra Berkenbush.)

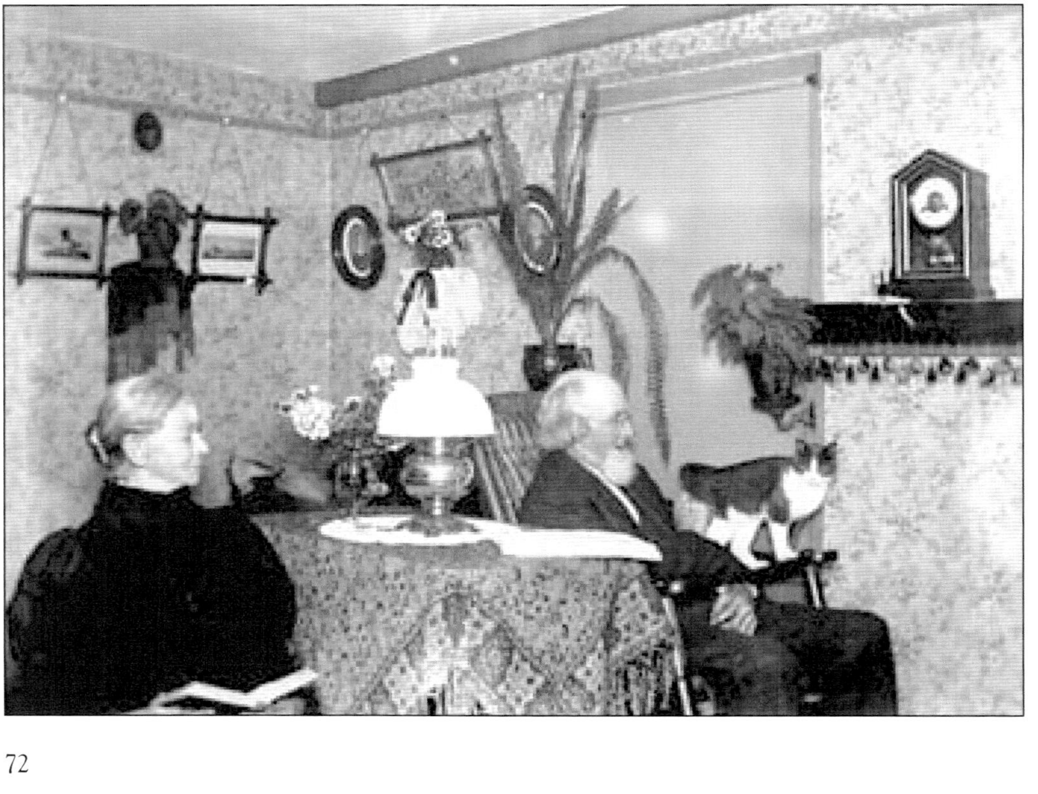

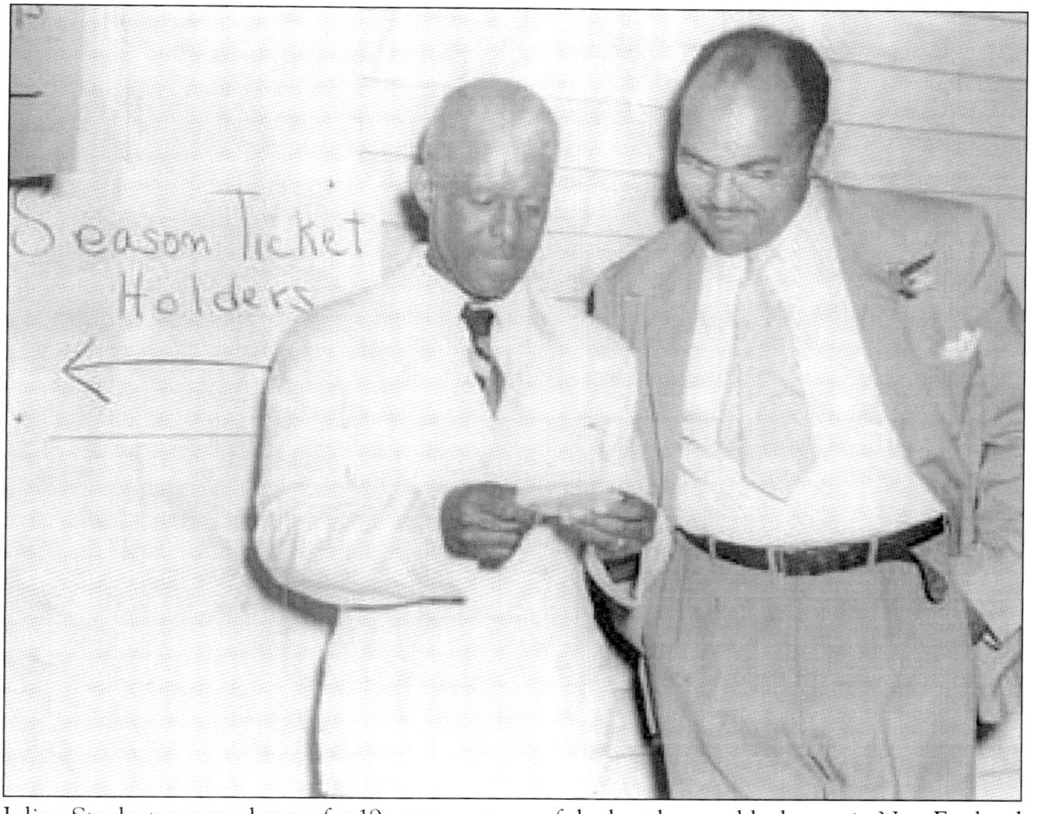

Julian Steele, town moderator for 19 years, was one of the best-known black men in New England and had achieved a national reputation as an expert in urban renewal on the federal, state, and local levels. He was commissioner of the Massachusetts Department of Community Affairs and deputy commissioner of the State Department of Commerce and Development. Pictured here are Roland Hayes (left) and Steele. (Courtesy of Emilie Steele.)

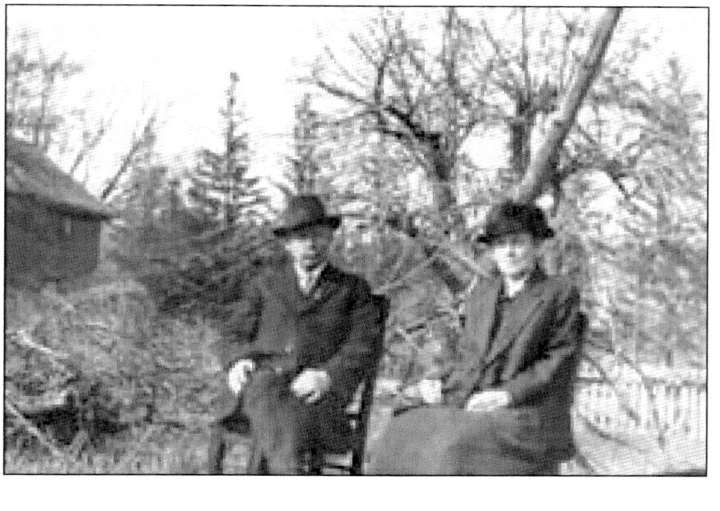

Herbert Brown and his wife, Ella Augusta Kimball Brown, were both West Newbury natives and lifelong residents. Ella bequeathed money to the town that was used to enlarge the stage at town hall and to add a heating plant, dressing rooms, and indoor rest rooms. There is a plaque commemorating her gift on the wall at town hall. (Courtesy of Charles Fowler.)

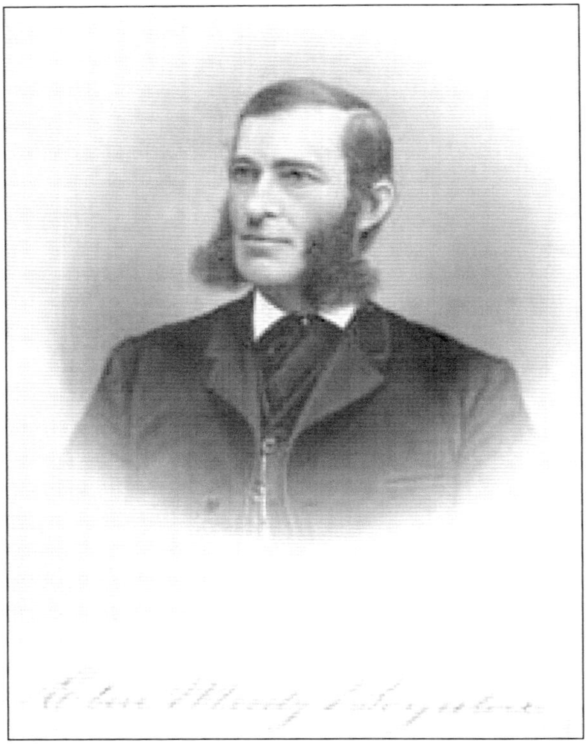

E. Moody Boynton invented the monorail "bicycle railway" and "lightning" M-toothed saw, which was such an improvement on saws of the time that he collected an estimated $500,000 in royalties. He proposed the construction of jetties at the mouth of the Merrimack River, and the US War Department appropriated $600,000 for their construction. Boynton lived in a mansion on top of Pipestave Hill. (Courtesy of Jane Wallace Wild.)

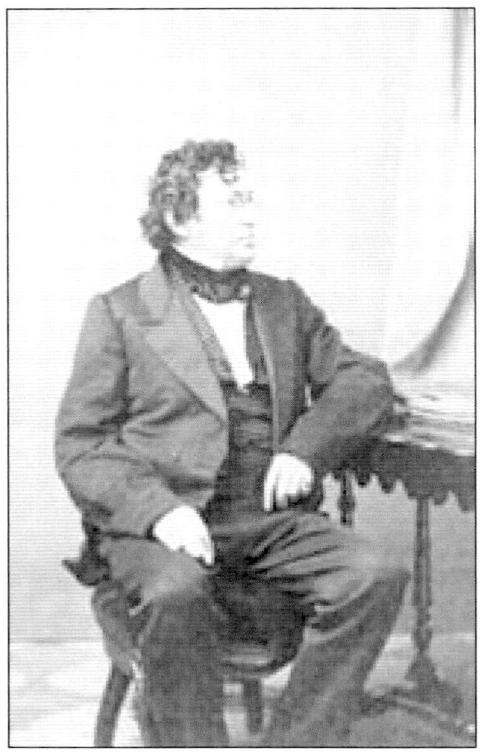

Cornelius Conway Felton was president of Harvard College from 1860 until his death in 1862. He was born in West Newbury in 1807; a historical sign noting his birthplace is located on Main Street a little to the east of and nearly opposite Garden Street. (Photograph by Warren of Lowell; courtesy of Peter Haack.)

Margaret Coit Elwell, a longtime West Newbury resident, won the Pulitzer Prize for biographies for her first book, *John C. Calhoun: American Portrait*, in 1951. She wrote seven other books, including a biography of Bernard Baruch. She was a professor of English, history, and political science at Fairleigh Dickinson University and a newspaper reporter for several area newspapers. (Photograph by E. Austin Benner; courtesy of Kim Sharpe.)

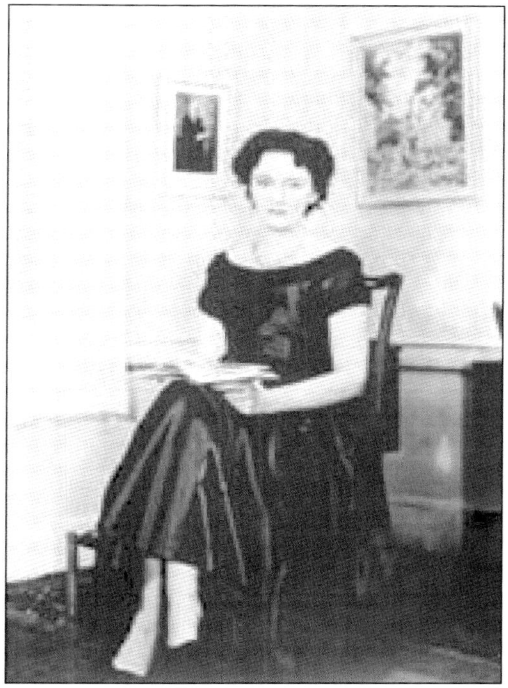

The West Newbury Insurance Company was formed in 1828 to provide insurance protection for the property and goods of town residents. Members of the company are, from left to right, Bailey Sargent, Capt. Richard Newell, Myron Goodwin, Charles William Ordway, George Emery Noyes, Ezekiel Nason, and Samuel Rogers. (Courtesy of the West Newbury Historical Society.)

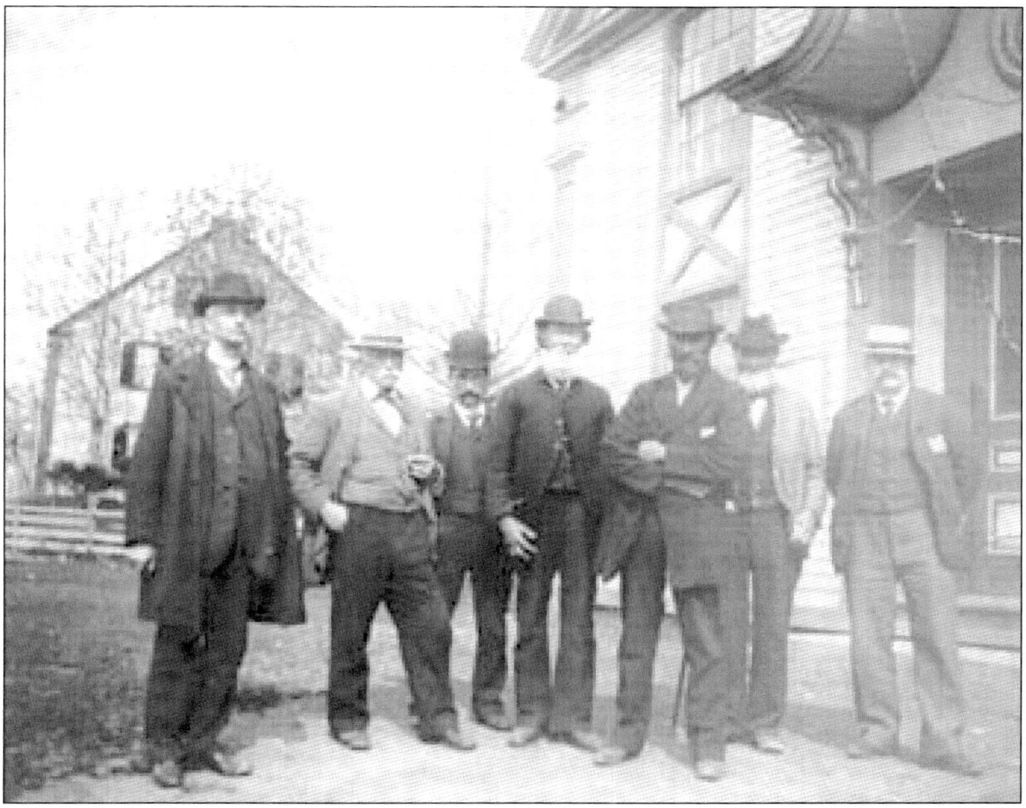

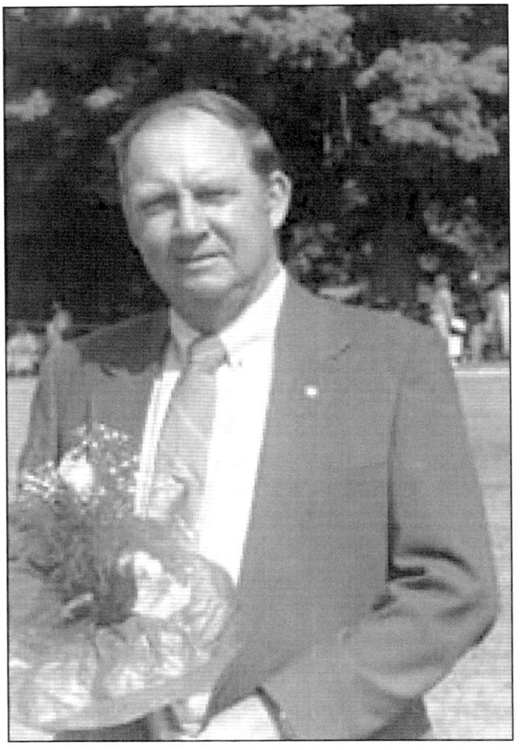

After serving several years as constable, Eugene M. "Shike" Willis was appointed chief of police in 1958 when he was 24, the youngest police chief in Massachusetts at the time. He served as police chief for 23 years, as a school bus driver for 34 years, and as organizer of the annual Memorial Day parade for more than 20 years. (Courtesy of Jacqueline Willis.)

Members of the West Newbury Police Department in 1948 or 1949 pose in front of the library. From left to right are special police officers Bernard Sargent, Howard Cox, Arthur Elwell, Vernon Burnham, Chief Buel Curry, special police officers Donald Adams, Roy Haynes, and Willie "Dar" Hudson. (Courtesy of Joyce Burnham Dixon.)

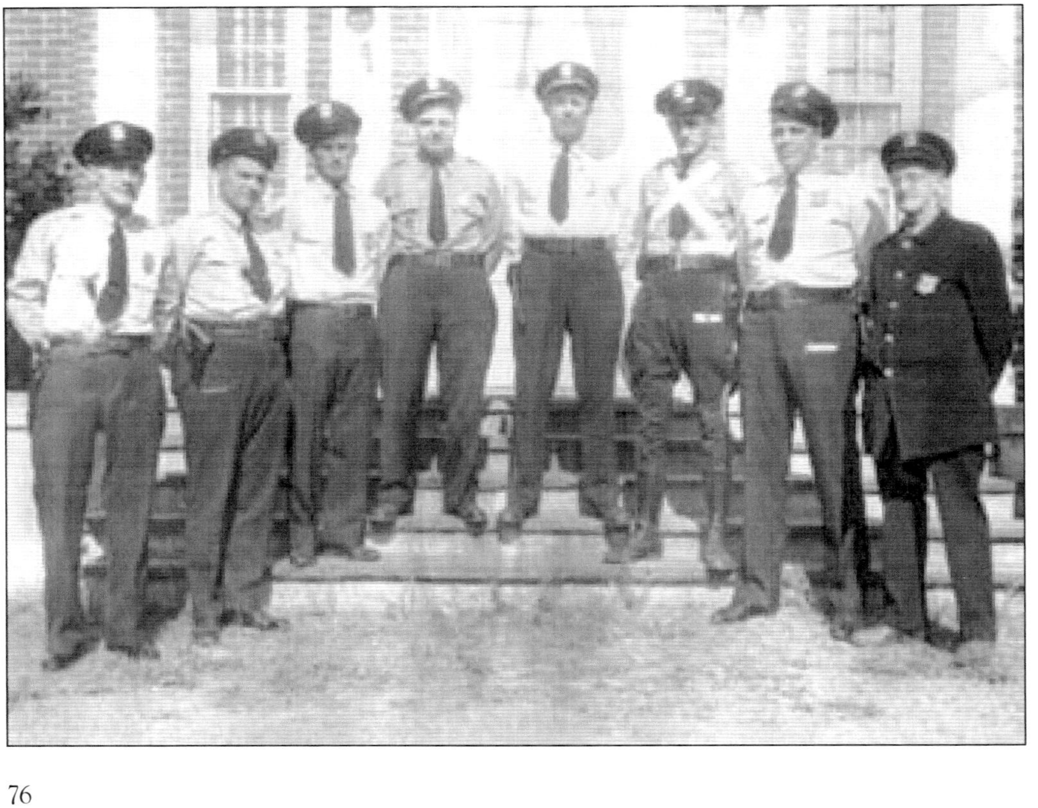

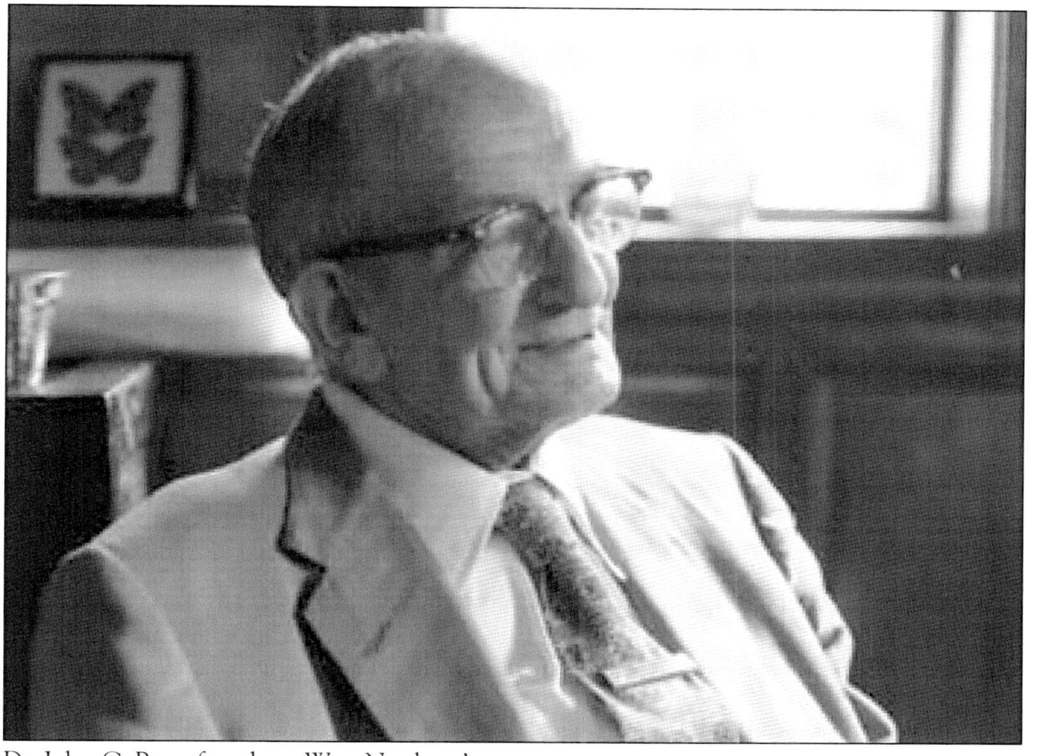

Dr. John C. Page, for whom West Newbury's elementary school is named, was principal and a teacher of mathematics and science at the former West Newbury High School for eight years beginning in 1914. He was superintendent of the school district composed of West Newbury, Merrimac, Salisbury, and Newbury from 1928 to 1955. (Photograph by Bill Lane; courtesy of the Newburyport Archival Center at the Newburyport Public Library.)

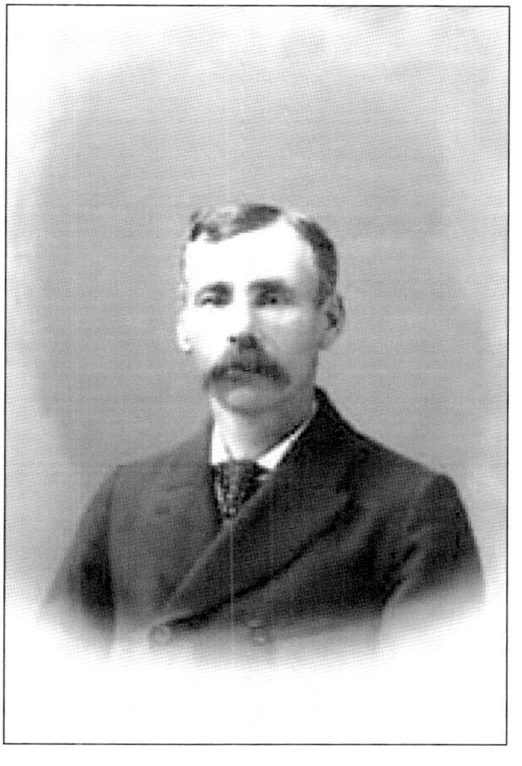

William E. Sharples was a lifelong resident of West Newbury, a shoe factory worker, a skilled photographer, and a taxidermist. From about 1900 until his death in 1926, he took many photographs of West Newbury scenes, several of Rocks Bridge, and of the construction of the Haverhill railroad station. (Photograph by William E. Sharples; courtesy of John McGrath.)

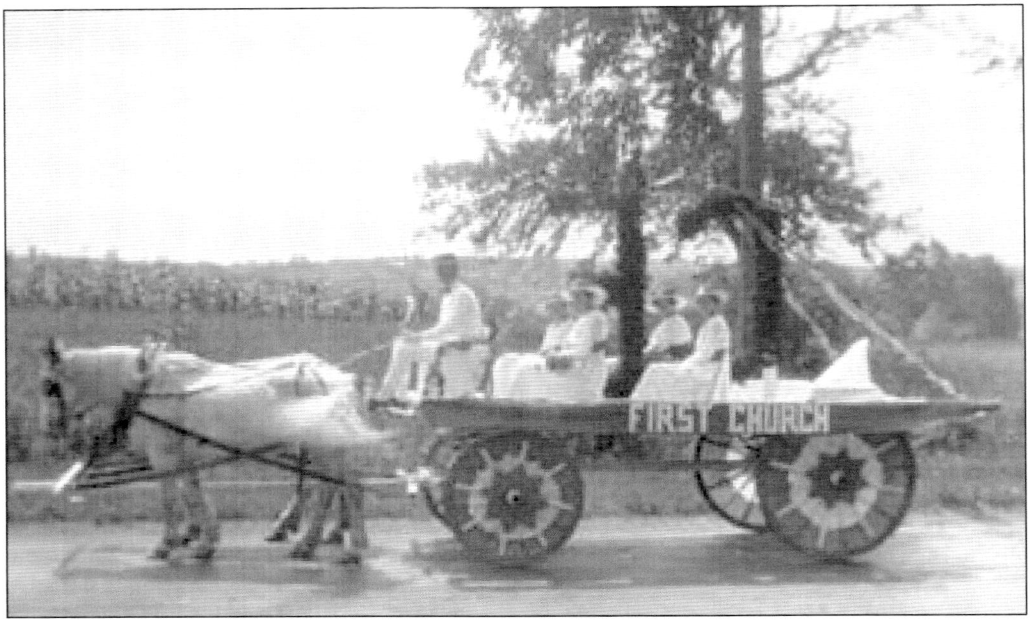

Decorated floats for the annual parade were an important part of West Newbury's celebration in the early 1900s. Here, women from the First Congregational Church sit in splendor on a decorated wagon behind matched white horses. Harold Evans is the driver; his wife, Pearl, and his sister Ethel are among the riders. (Courtesy of Elinor Spofford.)

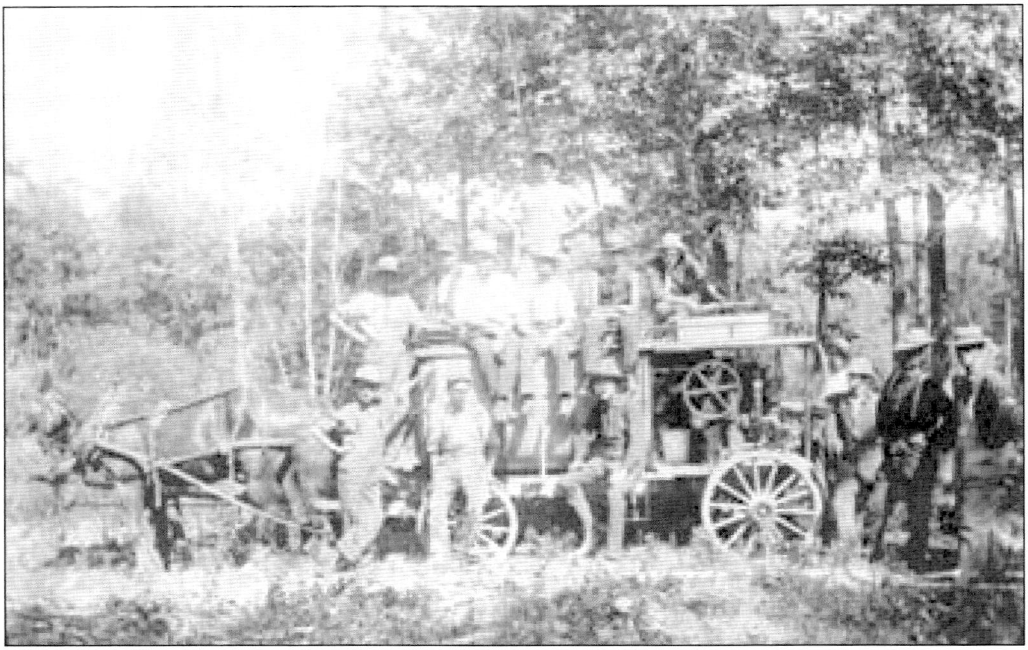

Gypsy moths were as much of a problem in 1908 as they are now. Members of West Newbury's moth gang, seen here with their machinery, include Wallace Ordway, Carroll Ordway, John Bartlett, William Preble, Richard Knight, Albert Noyes, Frank Bailey, and Fred Stevens. (Courtesy of the West Newbury Historical Society.)

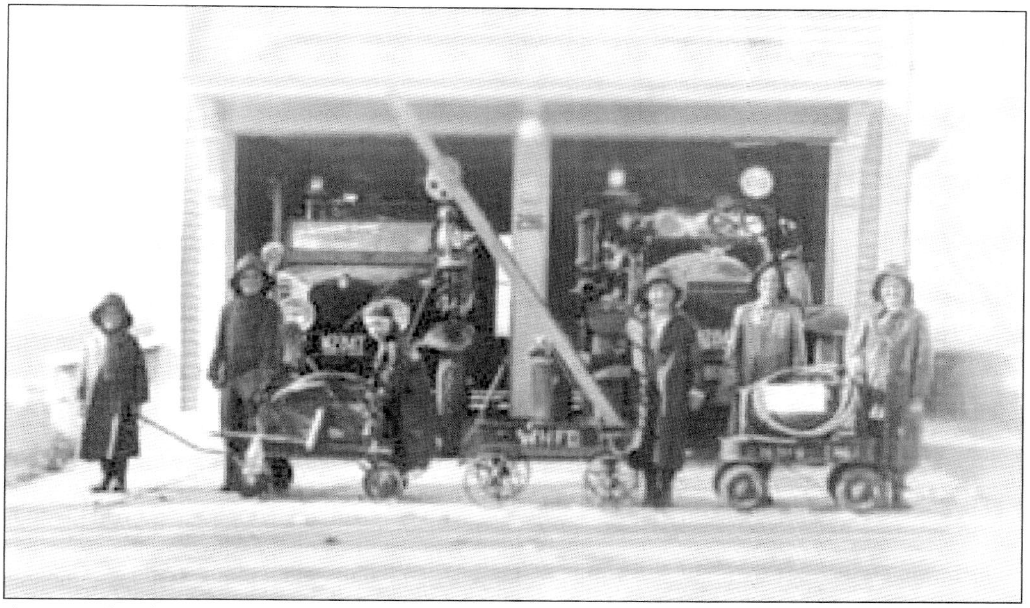

A junior fire department was trained by Russell Noyes in 1935. Pictured here in front of the original Central Fire Station at 296 Main Street are, from left to right, Clinton Whiting, Daniel Leary, John Leary, George Bailey, Chief Winfield Robin, and Richard Bacheller. (Courtesy of the West Newbury Historical Society.)

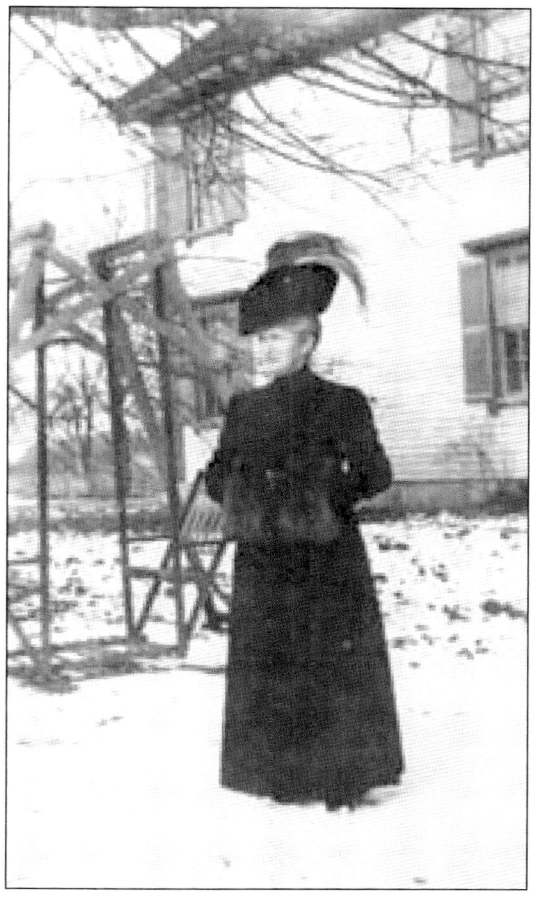

Mary Ann Sullivan was a native of West Newbury and one of nine children of Jeremiah and Margaret Sullivan, immigrants from Ireland. She was unmarried and worked as a stitcher in the shoe factories in Haverhill for many years. She is remembered as a loving and wonderful aunt. (Courtesy of John McGrath.)

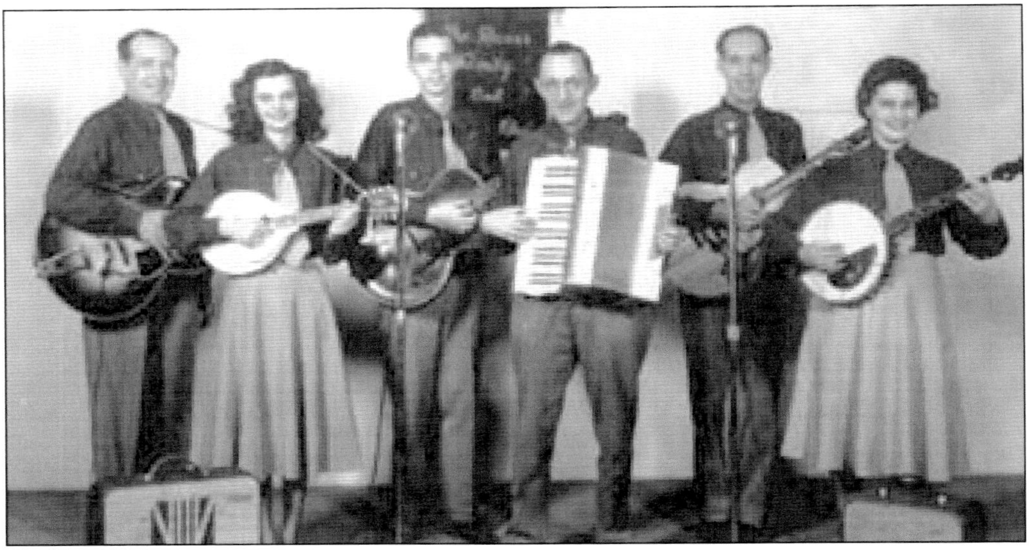

The Davis Family and Cousin Chet Band, pictured above, frequently entertained West Newbury and Georgetown at minstrel shows and other events in the 1940s. Other musicians occasionally joined them. From left to right are William Kelly, Phyllis Davis, Merle Davis, Percy Davis, Chet Colcord, and Gladys Davis. (Courtesy of Zella Haskell.)

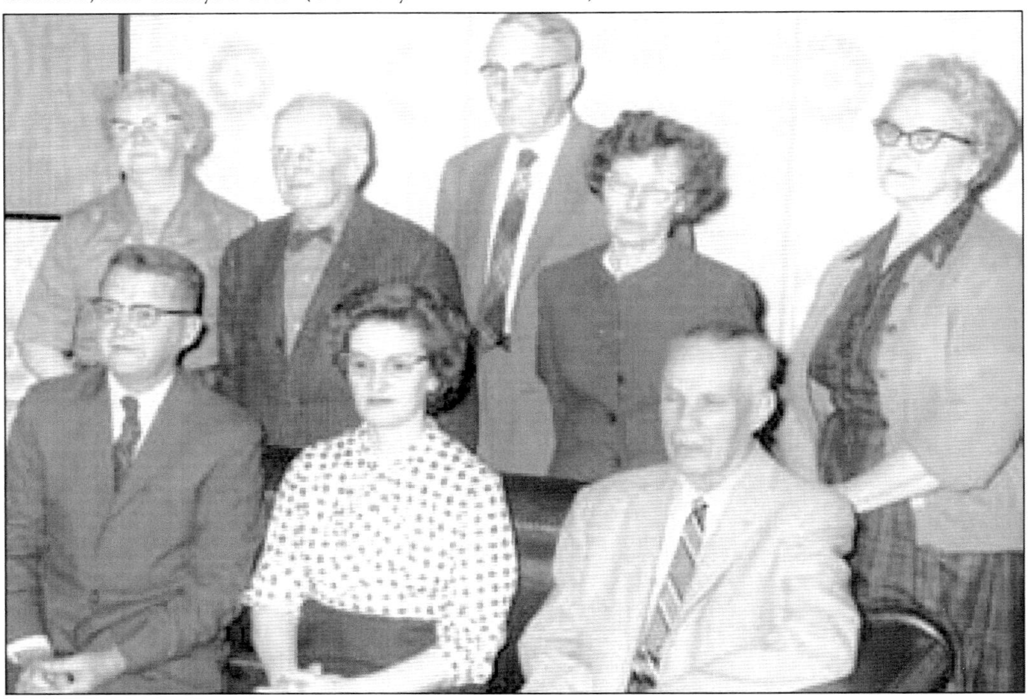

The West Newbury Historical Society was formed in 1957. Pictured in 1964 are the officers, from left to right, (first row) John Stevens, Dorothy Niles, and M. Paine Hoseason; (second row) Martha Gremore, Lawrence G. Dodge, Howard Poore, Miriam Thayer, and Elizabeth Thompson, who was considered West Newbury's historian throughout her life. (Photograph by Beckman; courtesy of the West Newbury Historical Society and the *Newburyport Daily News*.)

Five

Education
Then to Now

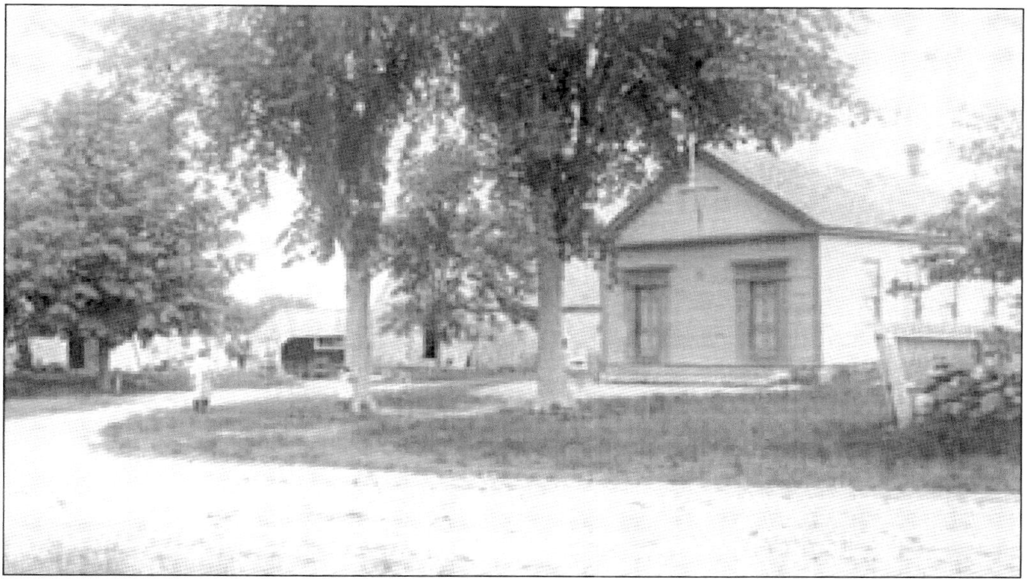

There were nine district schools scattered across West Newbury until 1910, when all of them, except No. 9, closed, and the students were transferred to the new Central School. Pictured here is District School No. 7, which was situated at the northeast corner of Crane Neck and Middle Streets. The building is no longer standing. (Courtesy of the West Newbury Historical Society.)

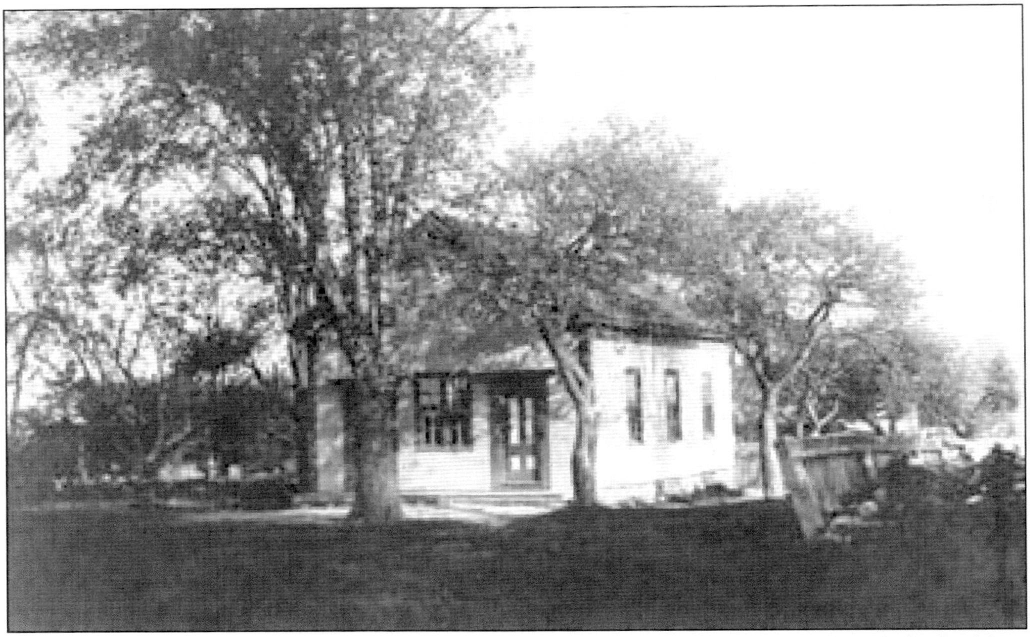

District School No. 1 was built in 1867 in the field at 835 Main Street. After it closed, the building was moved to 7 Garden Street and converted into a dwelling. The students and their teacher posing in front of No. 1 School in 1897 are, from left to right, (first row) Russell McIntosh, Herbert McIntosh, Chester Poore, Charles Titcomb, Sumner Tobey, LeBurton Marsh, Frank Congdon, and Fred Congdon; (second row) Idella Rowell, Alice Gambrell, Mabel Ridgway, Lizzie Tobey, Greta Bailey, Gladys Robinson, unidentified, and Annie Tobey; (third row) George Rogers, Wallace Ordway, Waldo Bailey, Russell Watson, Harold Robinson, Samuel Congdon, Harry Rogers, Wallace Watson, Richard Knight, Carroll Ordway, and teacher Grace Bailey. (Above, courtesy of Rachel Adams; below, courtesy of the West Newbury Historical Commission.)

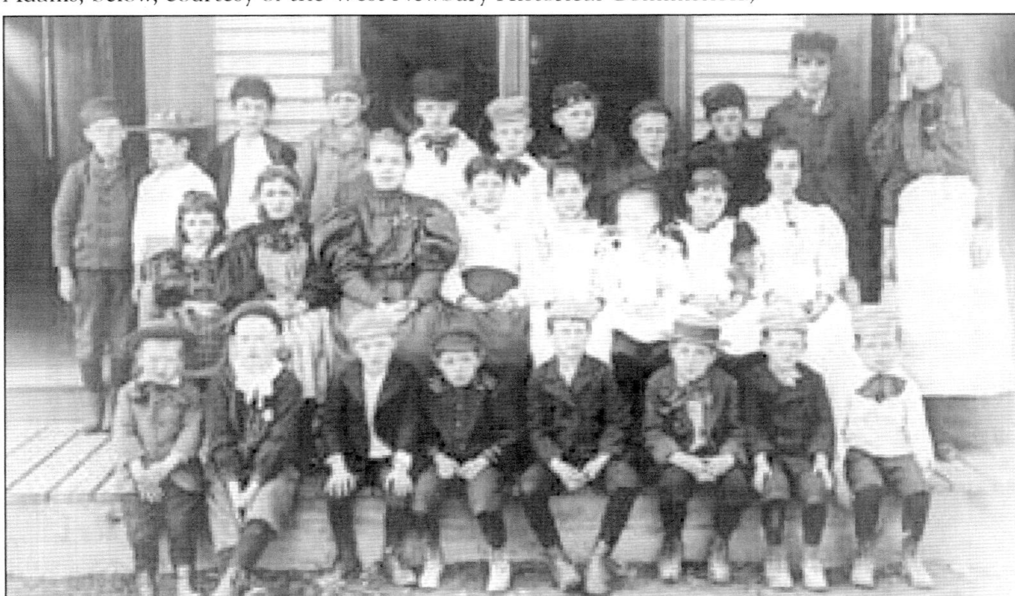

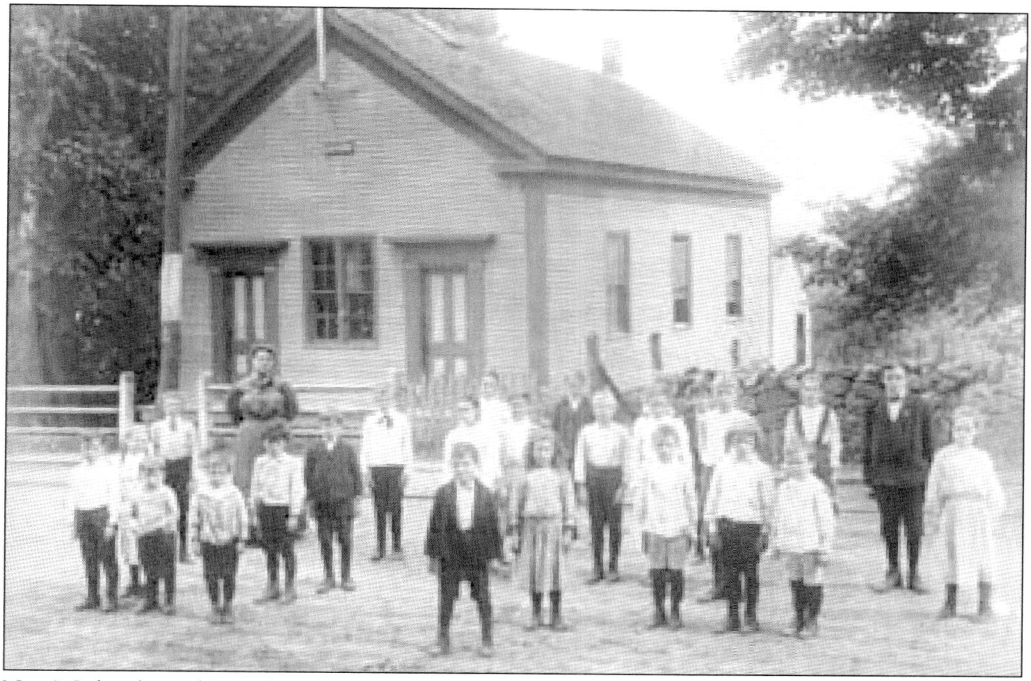

No. 2 School was located at 563 Main Street and has since been made into a dwelling. In 1864, it was reported that No. 2 School had 60 seats but 75 pupils for part of the year. No. 2 students, pictured here in 1909–1910, are, from left to right, (first row) Mildred Shute, Hazel MacDonald, unidentified, Helen Dunn, Mabel Hudson, unidentified, Raymond Shute, Joseph Goldberg, unidentified, Julius Goldberg, John MacDonald, and Aldworth Jackson; (second row) Edith Shute, Edith Batten, Rebecca Goldberg, William Hull, teacher Mary H. Poore, art teacher Miss Aiken, Carl Jackson, ? Smith, two unidentified, Verdo Jackson, and Nelson Gile. (Above, courtesy of the West Newbury Historical Society; below, courtesy of the GAR Memorial Library.)

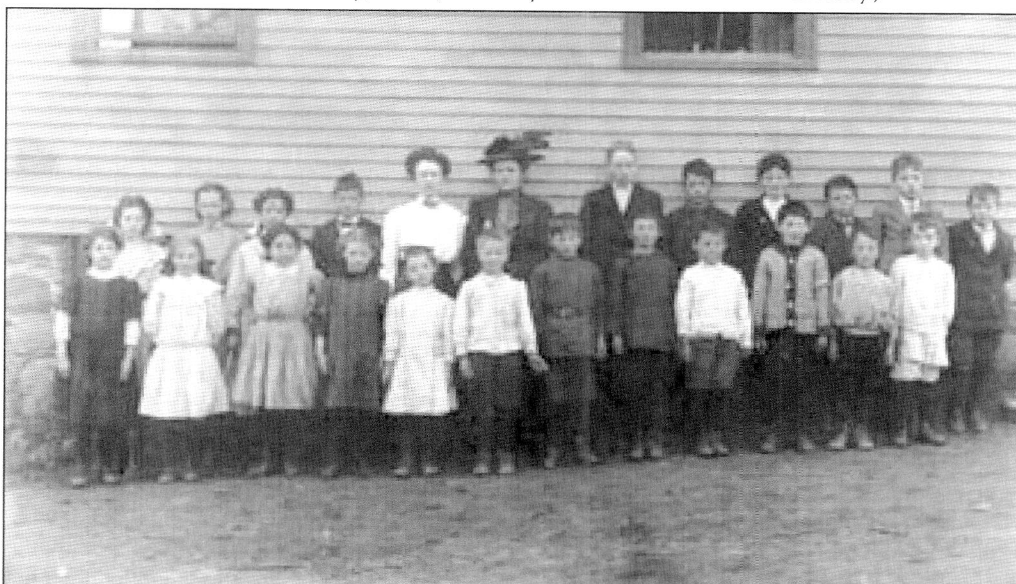

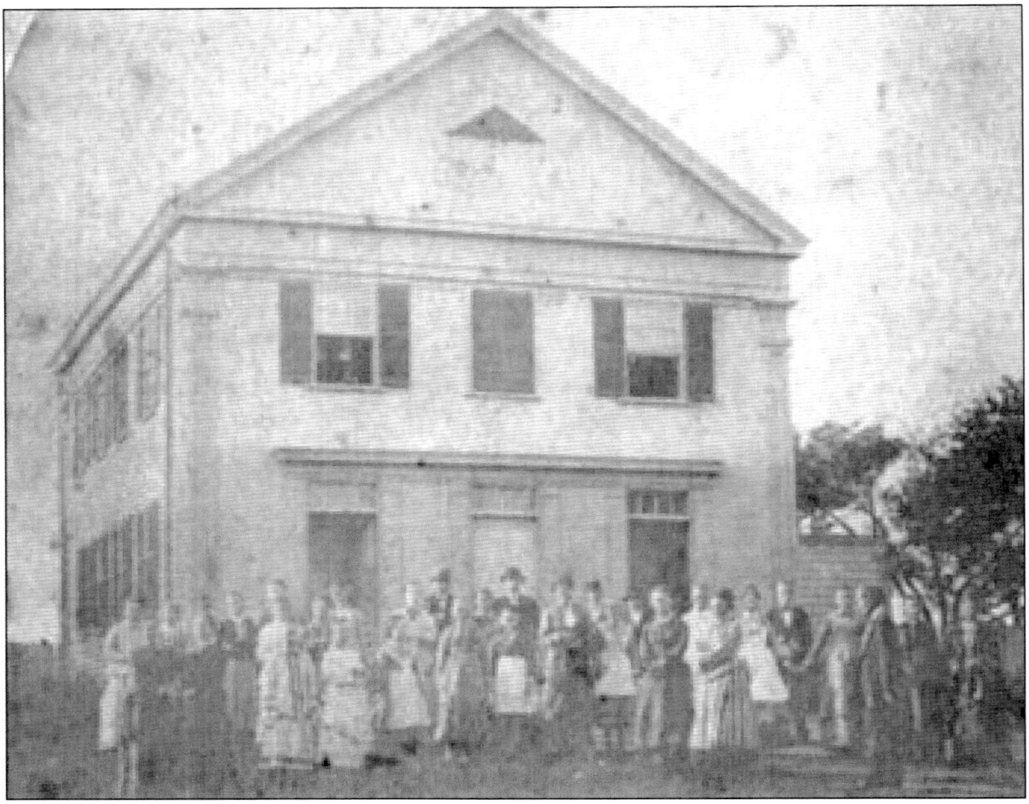

No. 3 School was built at 446 Main Street. The building was later moved across the street to Stewart Street and was torn down around 2001. The first high school was located here from 1875 to 1902. No. 3 students, pictured below in about 1911, are, from left to right, (first row) Gardner Carr, Chester Hall, Russell Peirce, Rodney Gadd, Arnold Gadd, unidentified, Gertrude Hardy, Helen Kennett, unidentified, Susan Thompson, Verna Hills, Charlotte Gile, unidentified, and Gladys McIntosh; (second row) unidentified, Leroy MacDonald, Viola Shute, Elsie Poore, Sadie Kennett, Ora Drake, Christabel Freeman, Clara Hibbs, Gladys Coskery, Greta Poore, ? Watson, unidentified, and Mary Sonier; (third row) Edwin Whittemore, unidentified, George Stevens, Rexford Bailey, unidentified, Caleb Allen, Beatrice McIntosh, Edith Willis, Erdine Bridges, and Mabel Smith. (Both, courtesy of the West Newbury Historical Society.)

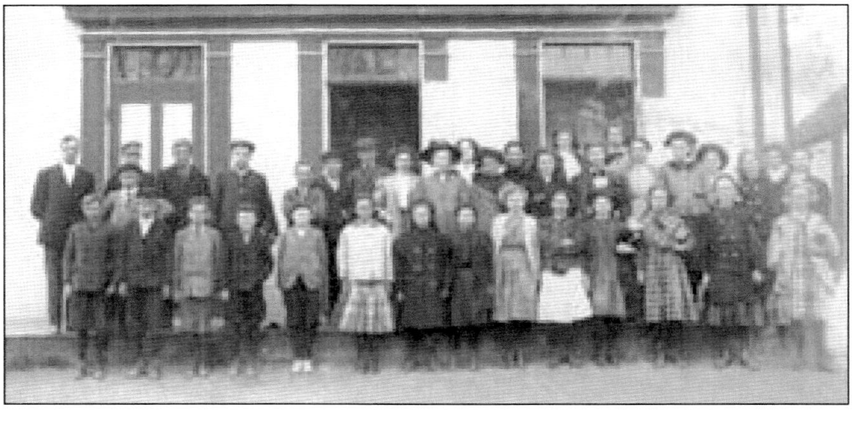

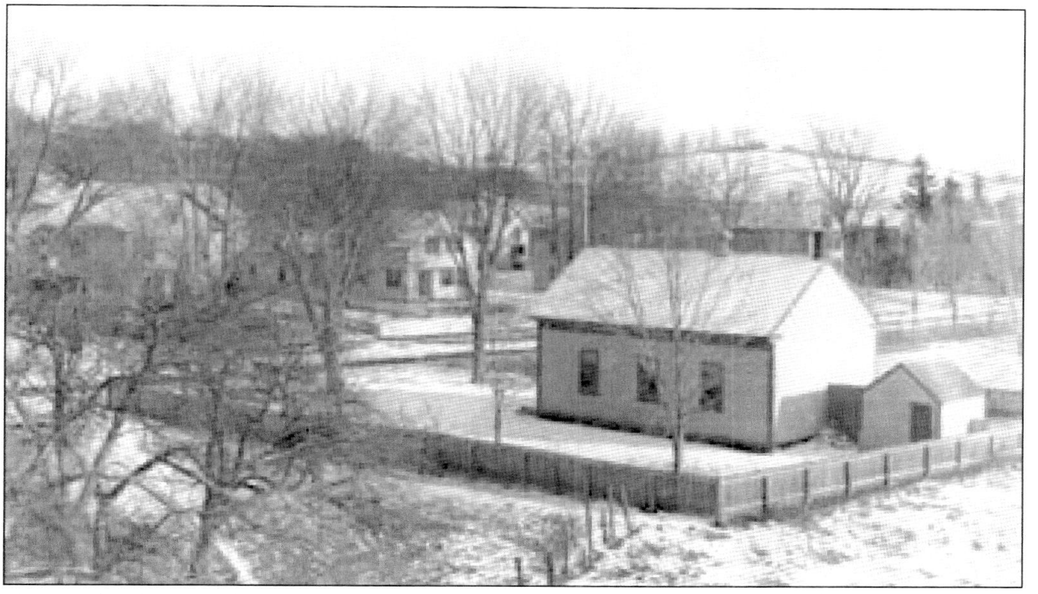

No. 4 School, located at 13 Maple Street, is now a private dwelling. The following 1850 school committee report states some of the problems of the district schools: "No. 4 has one blackboard 4 feet by 2 1/2 feet, which is nailed up over the woodpile, so that only one scholar can work at one time." (Courtesy of the West Newbury Historical Society.)

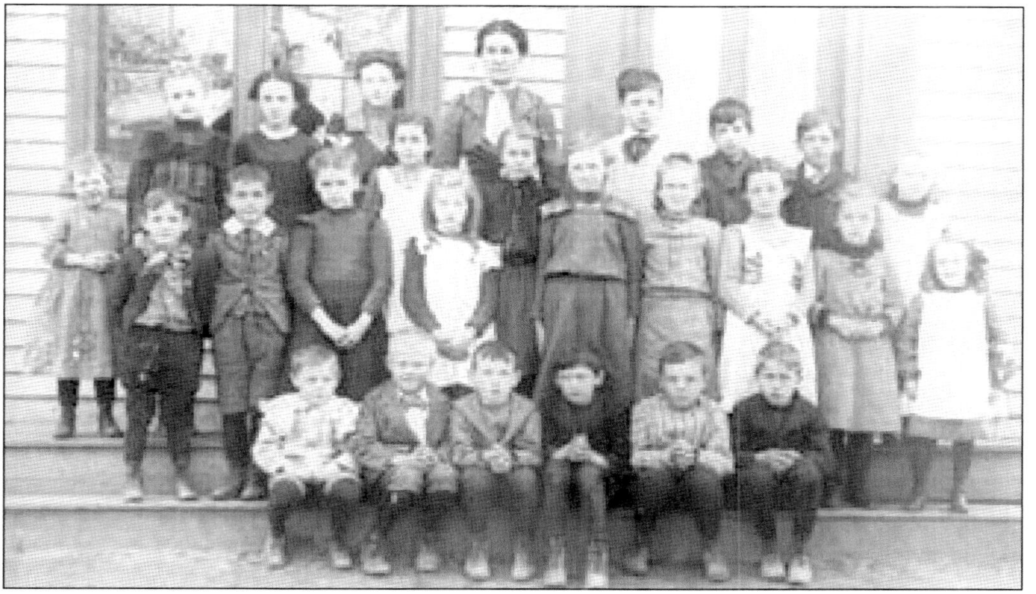

No. 4 students, pictured here about 1900, are, from left to right, (first row) Lincoln Peirce, Willie Knowles, Edward Sullivan, Walter Willis, John Peirce, and Merrill Swap; (second row) Richard Connell, Edward Connell, Marguerite Johnson, Frances Keegan, Mollie Silk, Edith Fowler, Mary Carroll, Mary Johnson, and Sadie Johnson; (third row) Helena Connell and Madeline Goodwin; (fourth row) unidentified, Edith Johnson, Nellie Hayes, Annie Willis, Edith Forsythe, Henry Bailey, Horace Brown, Robert Willis, and unidentified. (Courtesy of the West Newbury Historical Society.)

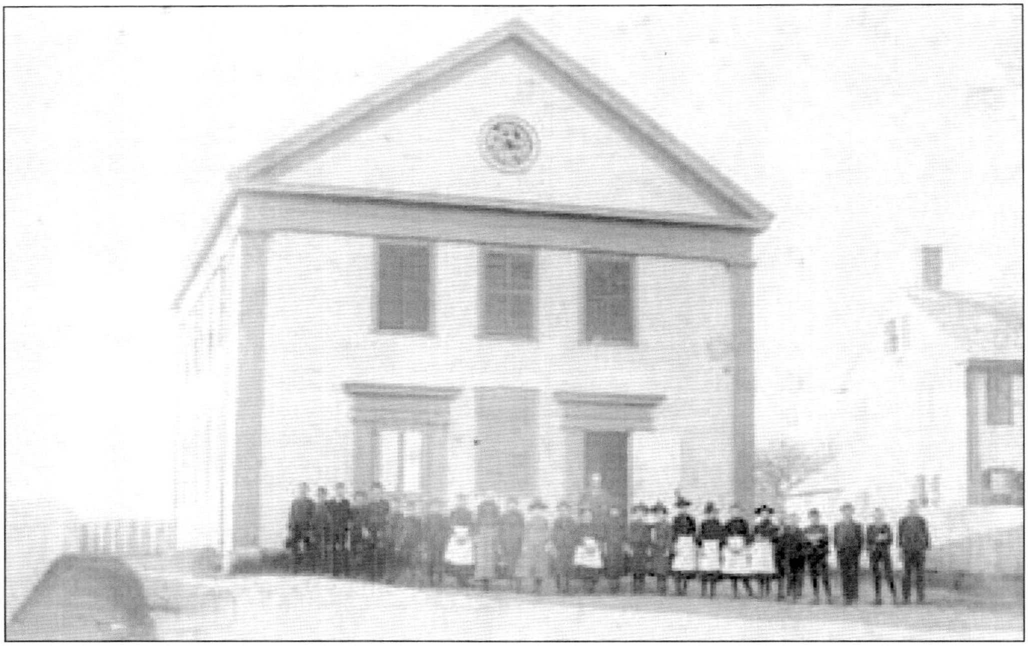

No. 5 School was located at 270 Main Street and was used as the high school from 1902 until 1930, when the building was condemned and torn down. No. 5 students, shown below in 1906, are, from left to right, (first row) Robert Willis, Fred Shute, Charles Adams, and Russell Noyes; (second row) Alice Cooney, Abbie Goodrich, Rachel Smith, Sadie McIntosh, Mary O'Loughlin, Irene Powers, Annie Kennedy, Mattie Bartlett, and Violet Kennedy; (third row) Ethel Evans, Gertrude Scanlon, Maude Mosley, Minnie Boody, Mary Griffen, Lucy Noyes, and Roland Evans; (fourth row) George Rogers, Helen Burnham, Georgeanna Clark, Harry Merritt, Lillian Weir, Mildred Drake, Blanche Cooney, and Patrick Hogan; (fifth row) Idella Rowell, Blanche Coffin, Leslie Marshall, William Baker, Wilbur Dunn, Annie Keegan, Mildred Burnham, Irene Keegan, and Mary Hogan. (Both, courtesy of the West Newbury Historical Society.)

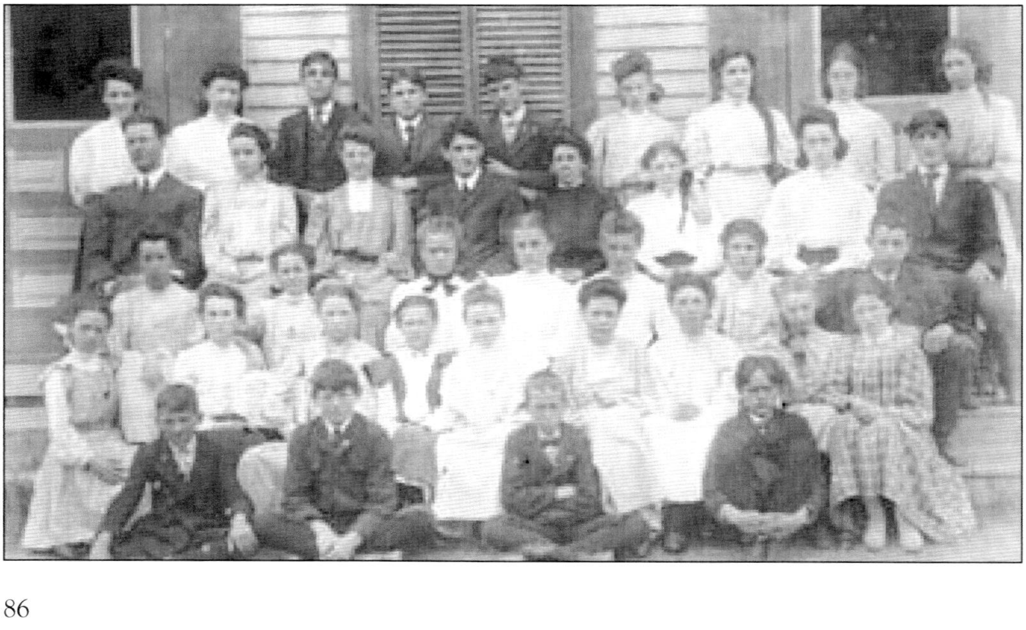

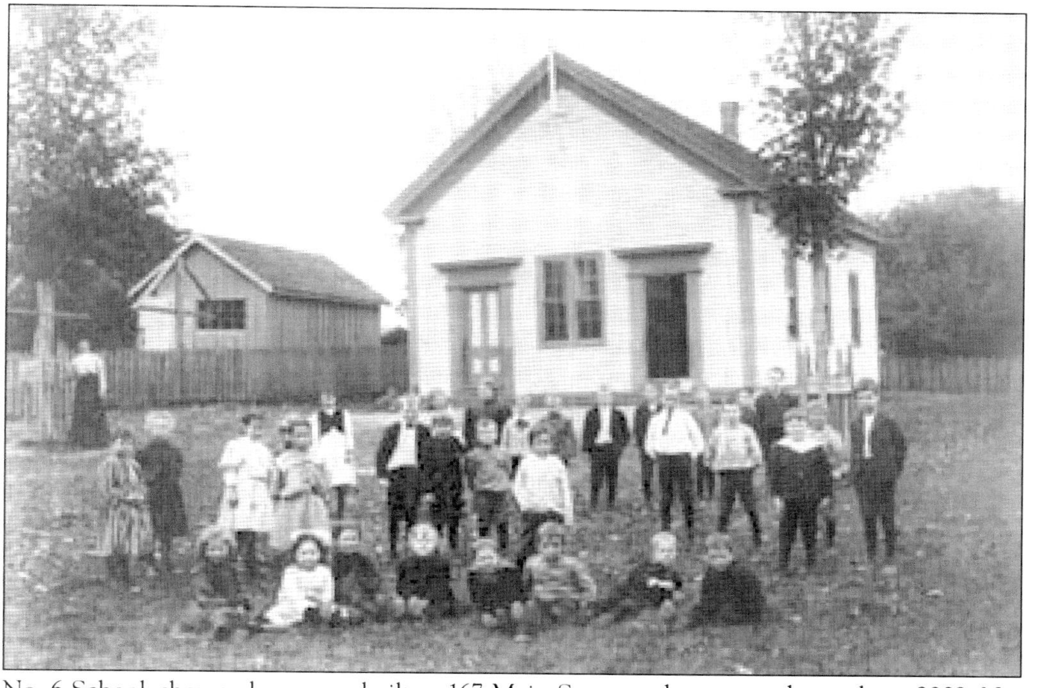

No. 6 School, shown above, was built at 167 Main Street and was torn down about 2002. No. 8 School (no picture) is now a private home at 157 Bachelor Street; it was originally across the street. If attendance at one school was too few, pupils attended another school. (Courtesy of the West Newbury Historical Society.)

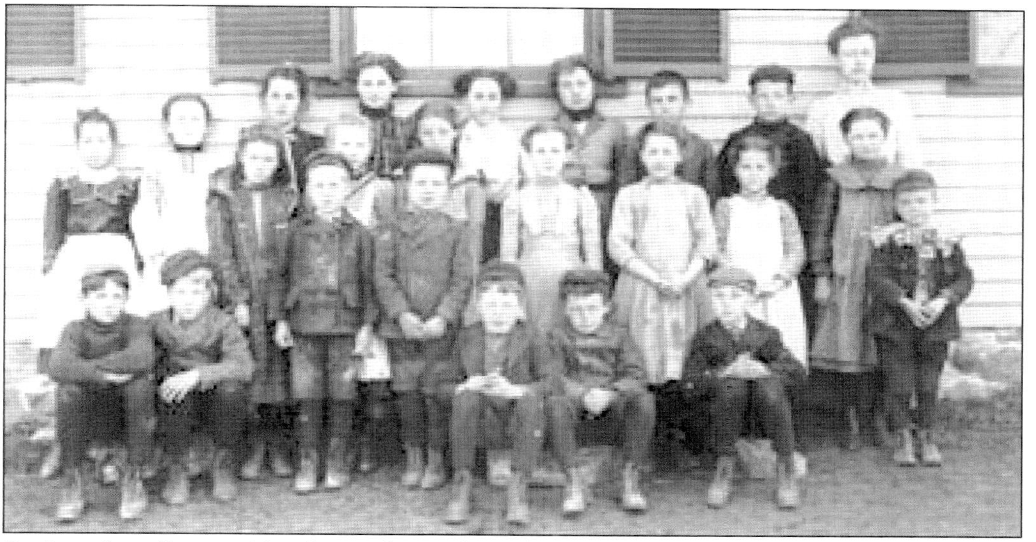

Students from Districts Nos. 7, 8, and 9 are shown here, from left to right, (first row) Albert Willis, Earl McDonald, Perley Jaques, Warren Jaques, and Earl Shute; (second row) Ernest McDonald, Frank Merritt, and Roy McDonald; (third row) Jennie Merritt, Mattie Bartlett, Mary Griffin, Abbie Goodrich, Emily Callahan, Olive Smith, and Rachel Smith; (fourth row) Ethel Evans, Dora Jaques, Kate Callahan, Mildred Goodrich, Mary Callahan, Gertrude Merritt, Thomas James, Harold Evans, and Alice Sargent. (Courtesy of the GAR Memorial Library.)

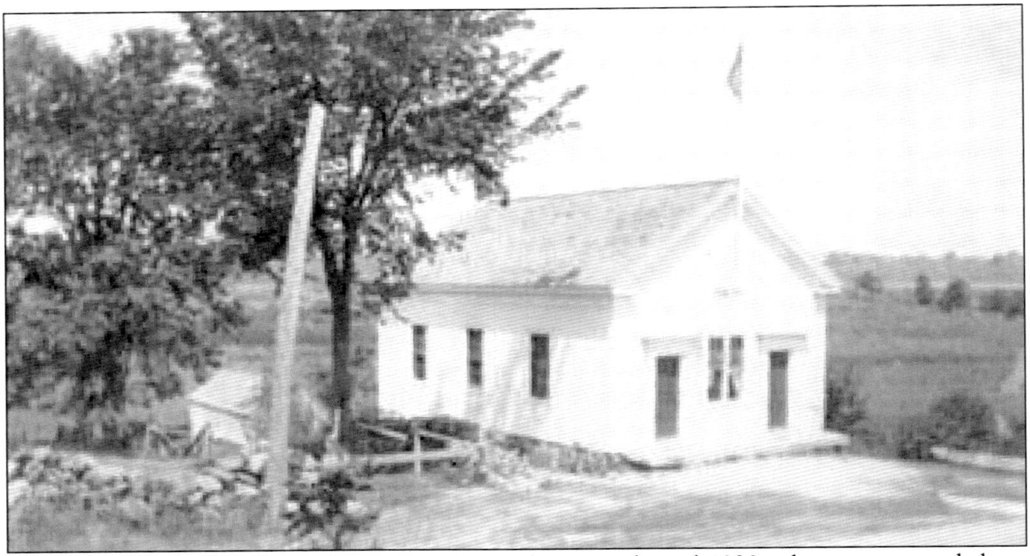

No. 9 School was built sometime after 1856 and was used until 1930, when it appeared there would only be three students the following year. It was used as a sort of community center for a time, but in 1941, the building was dismantled, and the lumber was used to build the Garden Street Fire Station. (Courtesy of Emily Poore.)

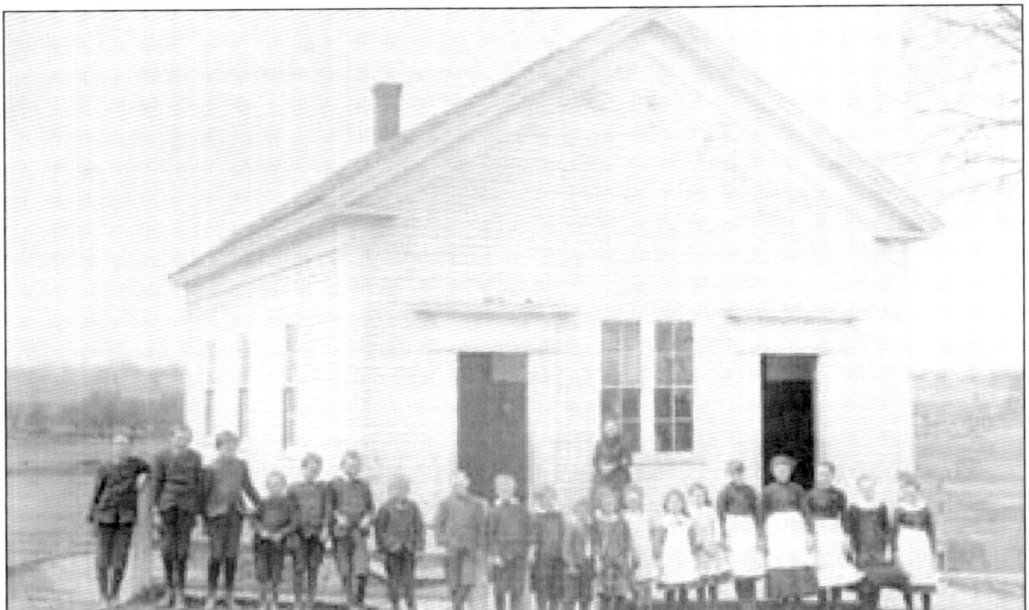

No. 9 students, shown here in 1887–1888, are, from left to right, Spencer Goodridge, Eugene Dow, Frank Rogers, Arthur Titcomb, Louis Rogers, Albert Rogers, Albert Swap, Eben S. Poore, Jay Knight, Elton Bradley, Marshall Bradley, Emma Woodwell, Lena Campbell, Dora Goodrich, Georgie Titcomb, May Poore, Cora Rogers, Mary Woodwell, Florence Goodrich, and Myrtis Woodman. Teacher Belle Rogers stands in the back. (Courtesy of the West Newbury Historical Society.)

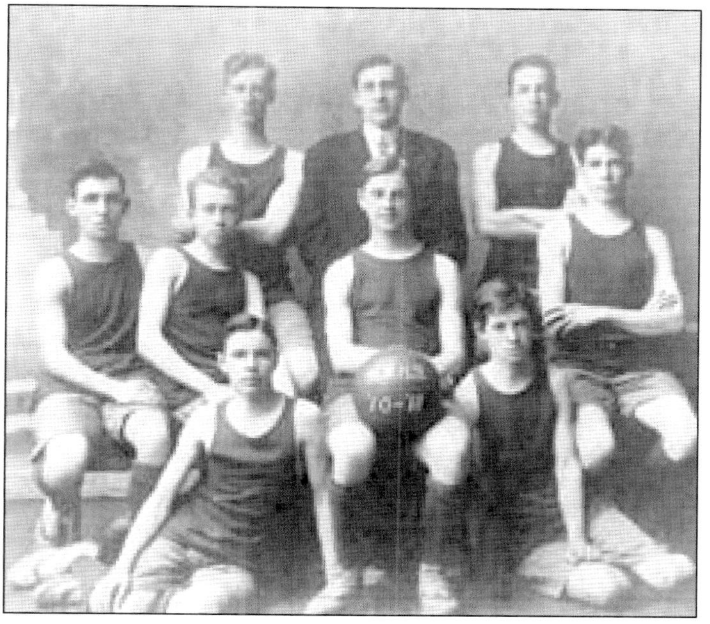

Members of West Newbury High School's basketball team, pictured in 1910–1911, are, from left to right, (first row) Ted Richards and Bernard Heath; (second row) Edward Sullivan, Marshall Bachellor, Elmer Burnham, and William Thompson; (third row) Perry Tarleton, principal E. Tucker, and Henry Bailey. Elmer Burnham has been called one of college football's most outstanding coaches. He was inducted into the Indiana Football Hall of Fame in 1975. (Courtesy of the West Newbury Historical Society.)

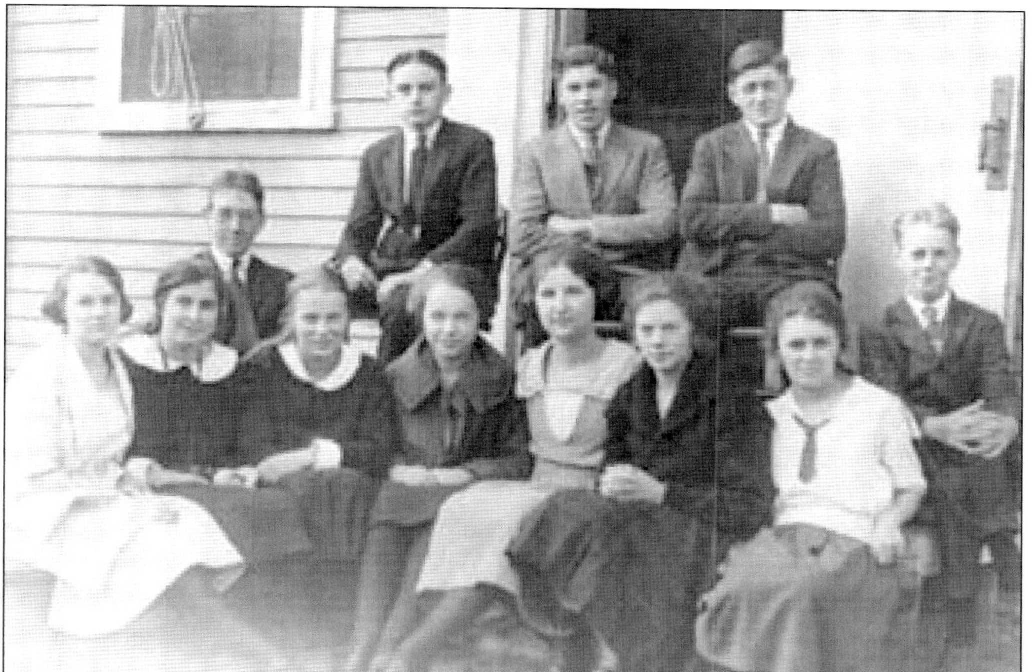

Pictured are members of the West Newbury High School class of 1923. From left to right are (first row) Olive Marshall, Mae Stranger, Mary Zink, Mary Gowen, Marguerite Ellis, Bessie Shupe, and Margaret Bickford; (second row) Howard Poore, Howard Sheys, Hugh McCarron, John McGrath, and Lloyd Ray. Missing from the picture is Norman Bilodeau. (Courtesy of the West Newbury Historical Society.)

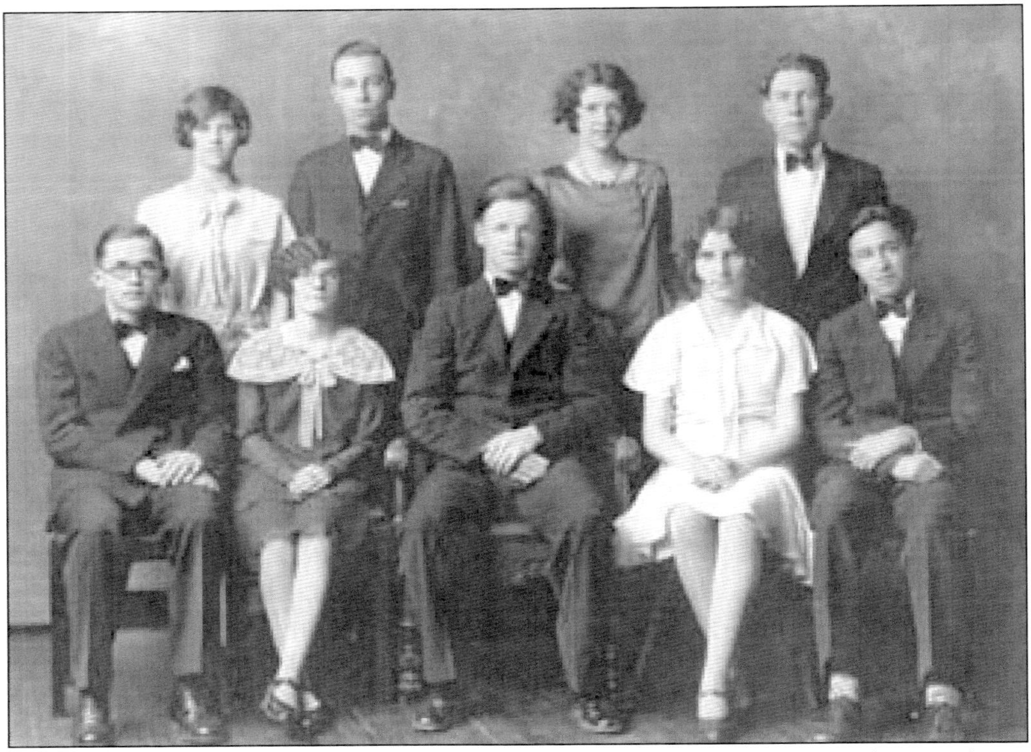

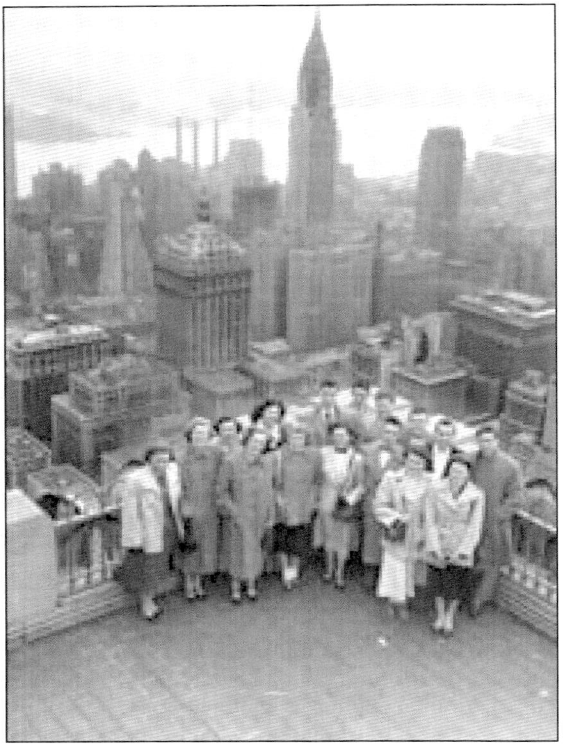

Students of the West Newbury High School class of 1930, the last class to graduate from the high school before it was moved to the Central School Building, are pictured. From left to right are (first row) Walter Briggs, Helen MacDonald, Mark Rogers, Christine Ellis, and C. Alan Merrill; (second row) Helen Evans, Russell Mingo, Margaret McGrath, and Chester Fowler. (Courtesy of Charles Fowler.)

Shown here on their class trip to New York City in 1951 are members of the last class to graduate from high school in West Newbury. Listed in no particular order are Irving Burrill, Merle Davis, Shirley Ford, Ernest Frye, Bernard Guilford, Marion Hall, Betty Hamilton, Beverly Thompson, Lois Thompson, Marilyn McCrillis, Frederick Emery, Leonard Greany, Richard Preble, Bryant Spencer, Thomas Thurlow, Connie Knight, and Eugene Willis. (Photograph by Rockefeller Center Roof Studio; courtesy of Richard Preble.)

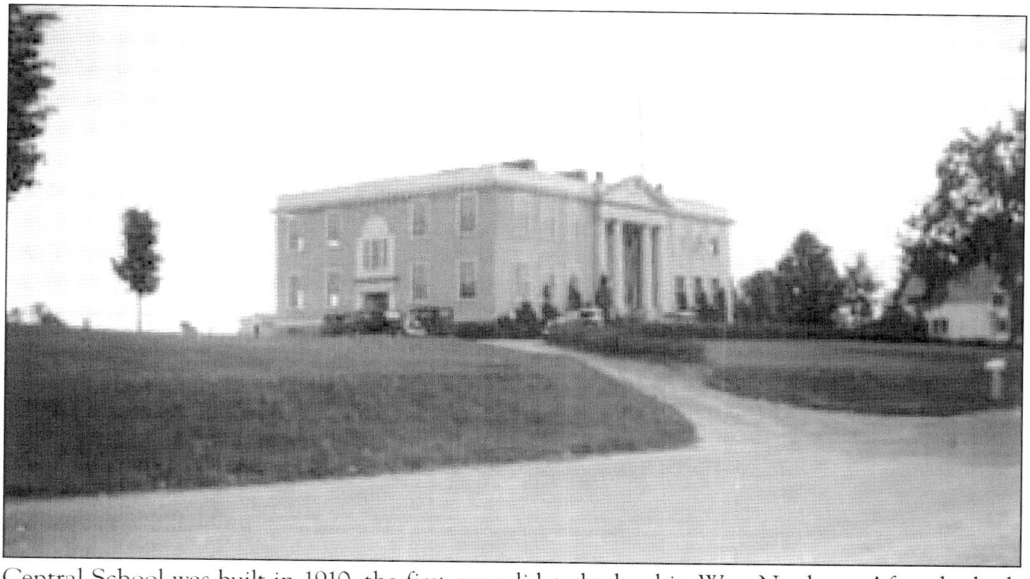

Central School was built in 1910, the first consolidated school in West Newbury. After the high school building was condemned in 1930, Central School served all grades, first through 12th, until 1951, when high school students were sent to Newburyport. On November 15, 1938, Central School was partially destroyed by fire. Classes were housed temporarily in the West Newbury Woman's Clubhouse, Second Congregational Church, Laurel Grange, and Newburyport High School. The school was reopened in May 1939. The town purchased the Cardinal Cushing Academy on Pipestave Hill in 1972 for its school, and the Central School Building then was used to house the town offices. (Above, courtesy of West Newbury Historical Society; below, courtesy of Rachel Adams.)

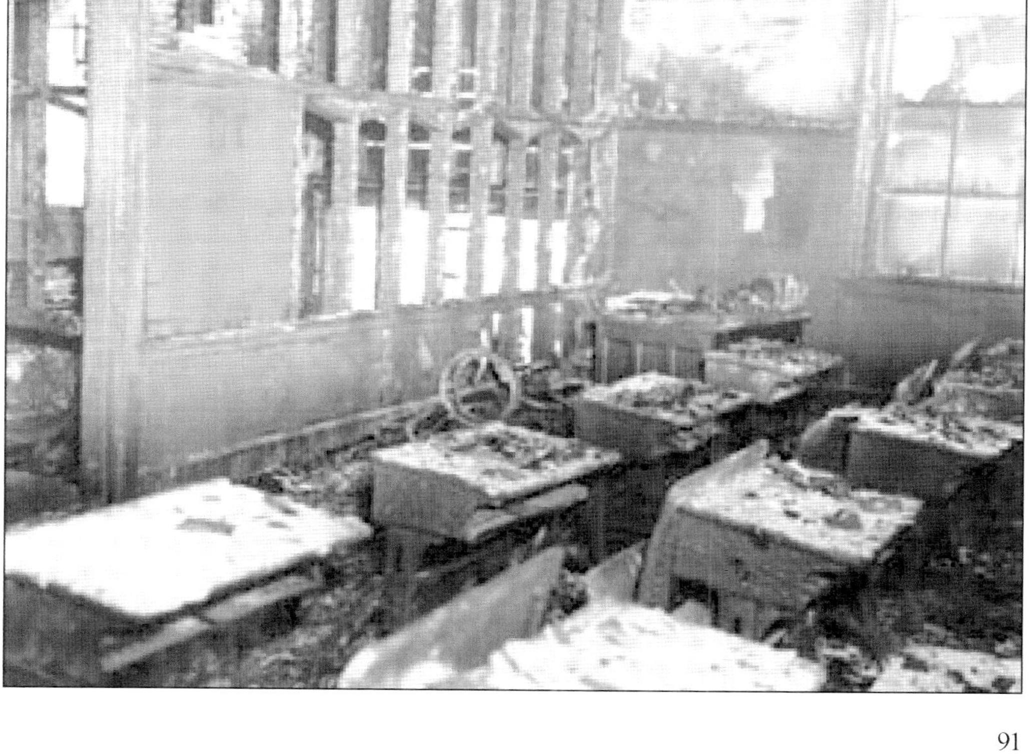

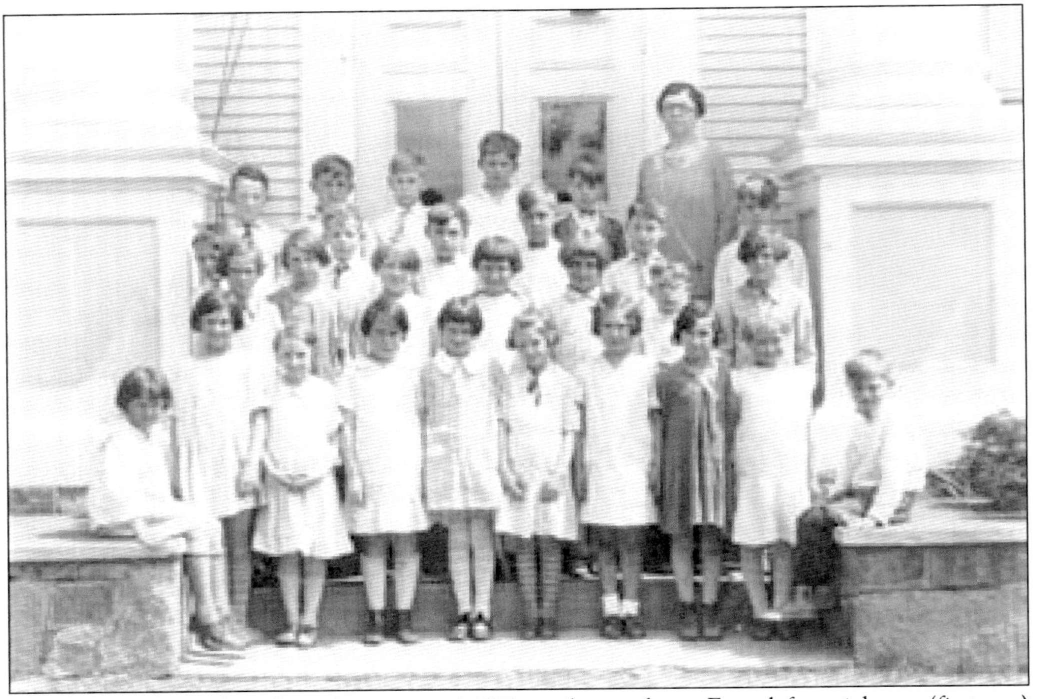

Central School third-grade students around 1929 are shown above. From left to right are (first row) Helen Girroir, Elinor Brown, Anita Spottiswood, Margery Thibideau, Eleanor Melville, Rachel Poore, Dorothy Cresswell, Grace Richer, Helen Coffey, and Walter Kamekowski; (second row) Vivian Spencer, Cynthia Hartford, Mary Ladd, Mary Clopek, Audrey Swap, John Morrill, and Vera Spencer; (third row) Bryant Page, Herbert Hale, Donald Dunn, Chester Colcord, Granville Jaques, and Charles Johnson; (fourth row) Robert Murphy, George Carr, Norman Theburg, Neil Gadd, Victor Ryan, and teacher Mary H. Poore. Pictured below is part of the cast of Central School's operetta in the late 1930s, *Six and Four are Ten*. Those pictured are, from left to right, (first row) unidentified, Priscilla Scarlett, and unidentified; (second row) Evelyn Dawkins, Phyllis Davis, unidentified, Delphine Kilgore, unidentified, and Alice Brewer. (Above, courtesy of Rachel Adams; below, photograph by Rudolph Currier; courtesy of the West Newbury Historical Society.)

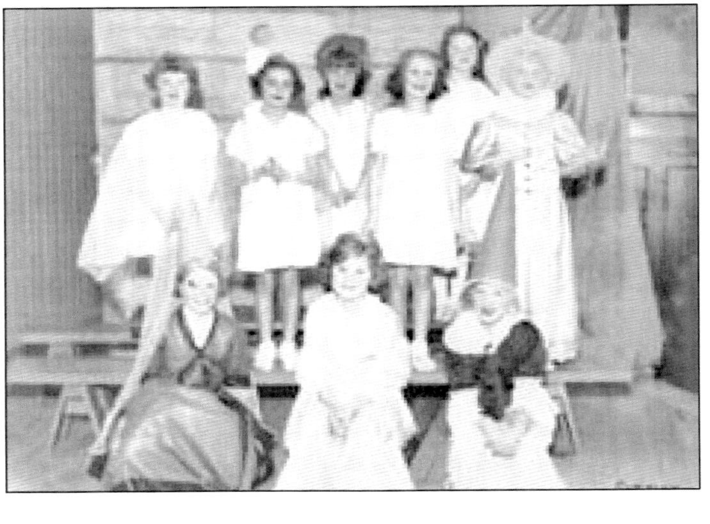

Six

Industries From Days Gone By

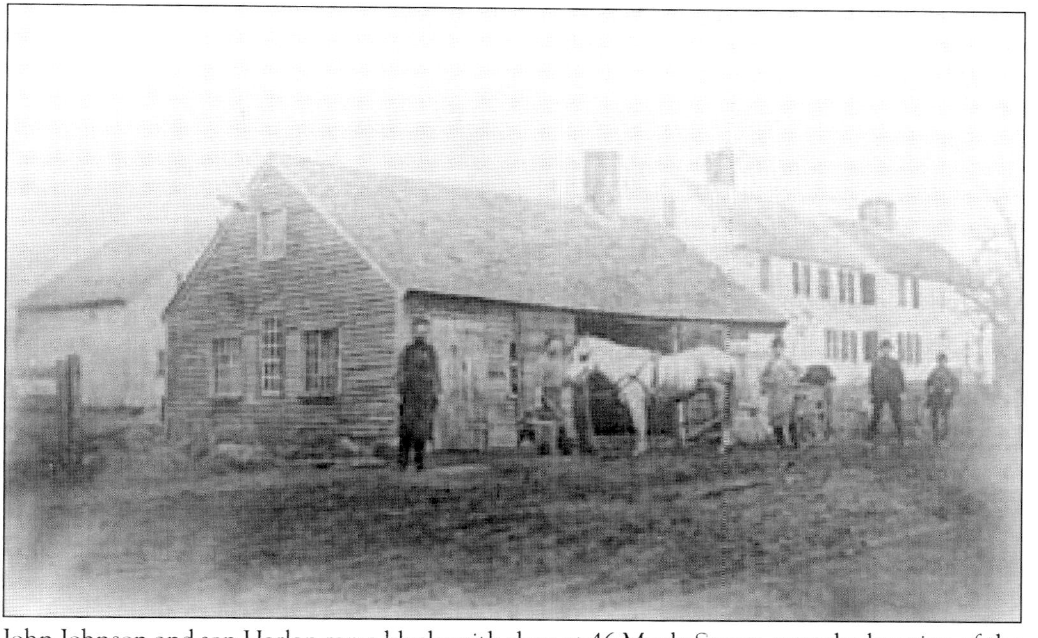

John Johnson and son Harlan ran a blacksmith shop at 46 Maple Street, near the location of the present St. Ann's Rectory. Blacksmithing saw a diminished use with the advent of the automobile until horses for pleasure became popular near the end of the 20th century. A handsome double house can be seen to the right of the shop. (Courtesy of Donald Laing.)

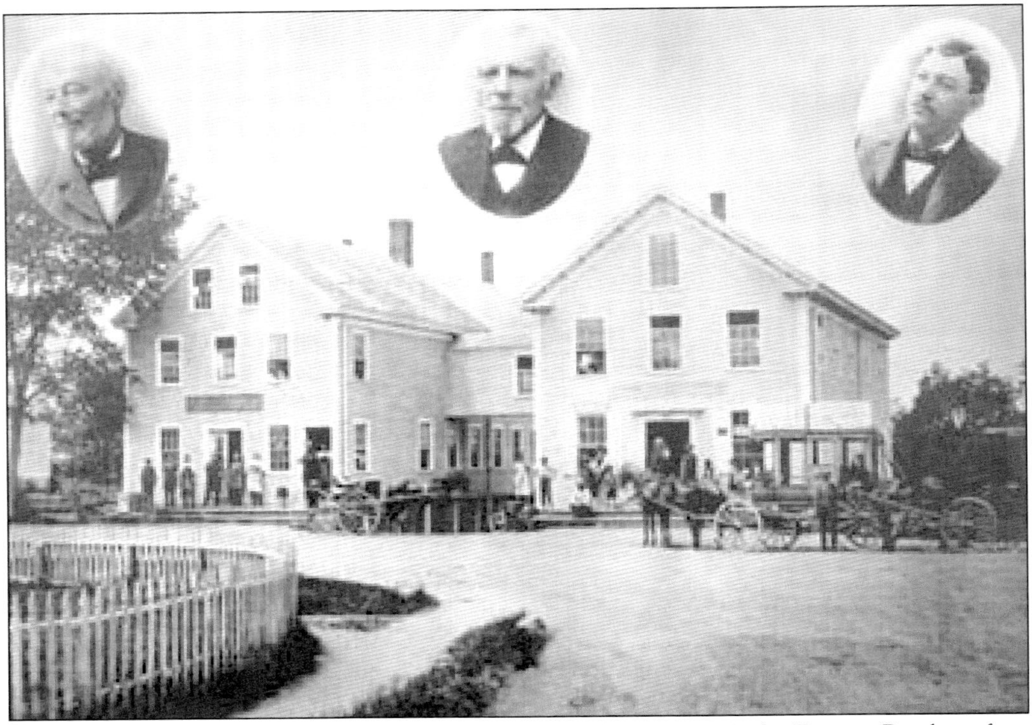

According to the *West Newbury Messenger* on November 16, 1889, the Durgin Brothers firm was formed in 1843, and for 46 years, its shoe shops were the centerpiece of Post Office Square. The two buildings were moved to this location, one from Maple Street and the other from the head of Mechanic Street. In 1889, the business relocated to Haverhill, and the buildings were used for a general store and a post office. The stagecoach on the right ran between Newburyport and Haverhill until the horsecars were introduced in 1886. Below, workers pose outside the shop. Deacon Durgin is the man in the dark suit in the second row. (Both, courtesy of the West Newbury Historical Society.)

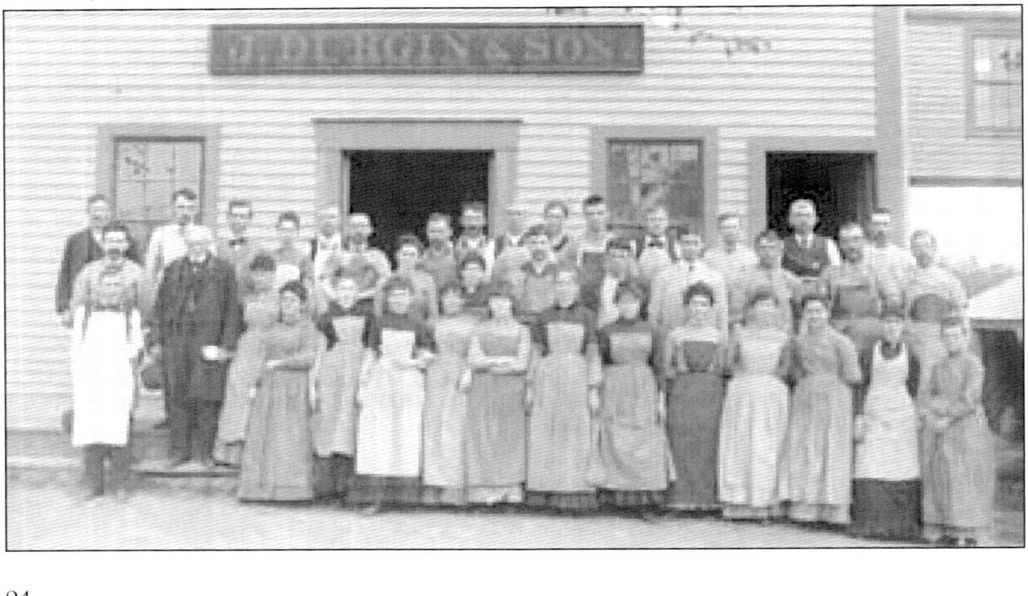

At one time, the Ruddock Shoe Factory employed 250 hands, of which 59 were female. Located at about 324 Main Street, it was destroyed in the big fire of 1884, along with the house next door. As soon as the fire was discovered, an alarm was given by ringing the church bell. The Protector Engine Company in Rocks Village quickly responded, but it was too late to save the buildings. As a result of this disastrous fire, the town voted to organize and maintain a fire department, and a firehouse was situated next to St. Ann's Church in Post Office Square. Pictured below are shoe workers plying their trade. (Both, courtesy of the West Newbury Historical Society.)

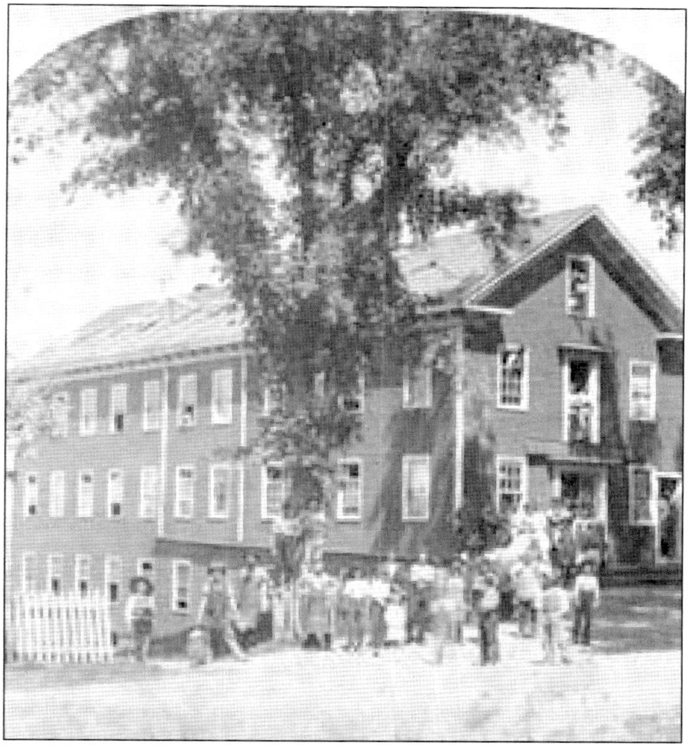

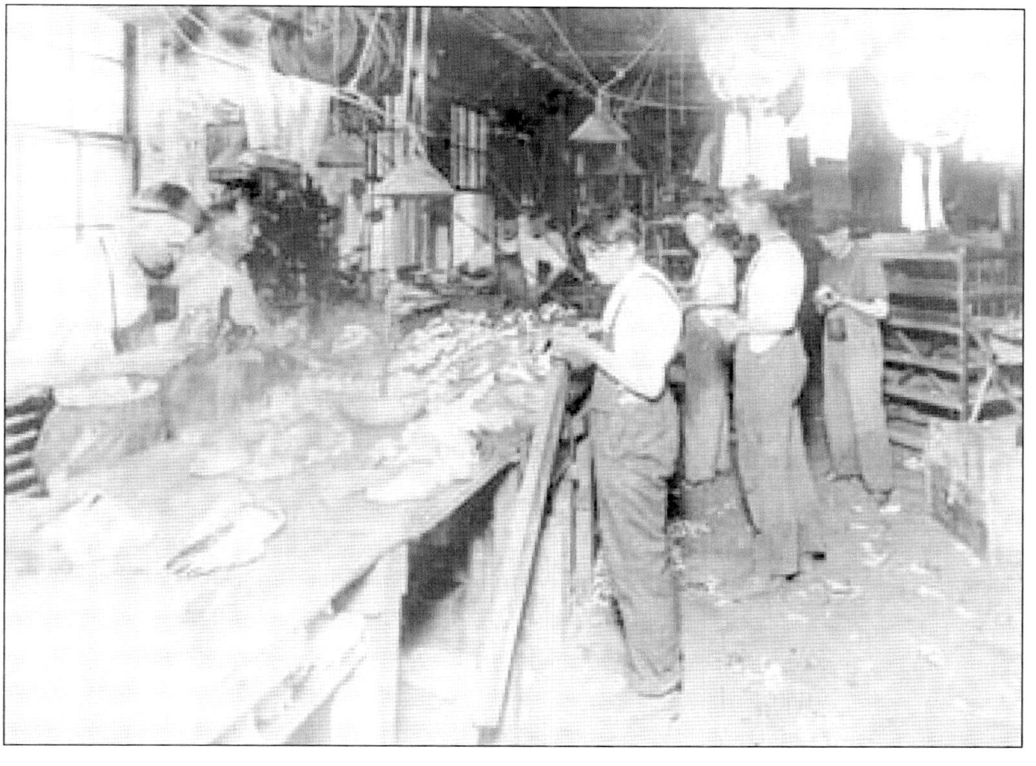

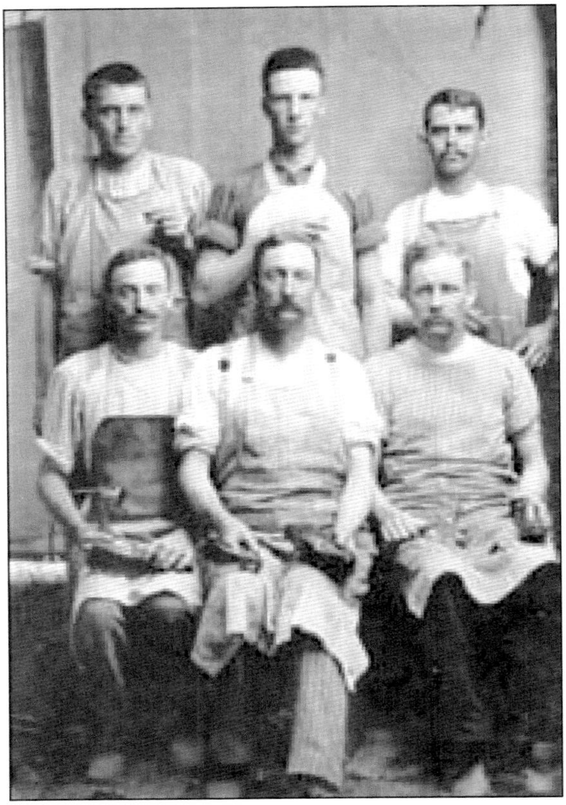

Some of the prize-winning shoes exhibited at the Chicago World's Fair in 1893 were made by West Newbury men and are now exhibited at the Haverhill Historical Society. Pictured from left to right are (first row) Arthur Hills, Jim Pattinson, and Joseph Fitzsimmons; (second row) William Hills, Daniel Pattinson, and Irving Brown. (Courtesy of the West Newbury Historical Society.)

After the Durgin Shoe Shops moved to Haverhill in 1889, this building on the left became Henry T. Bailey's store, later owned by William Harriman, followed by Earl Lewis, and more recently, the West Newbury Pizza Factory. The building on the right at the edge of the picture was torn down in 1964 to make way for the post office. (Courtesy of the GAR Memorial Library.)

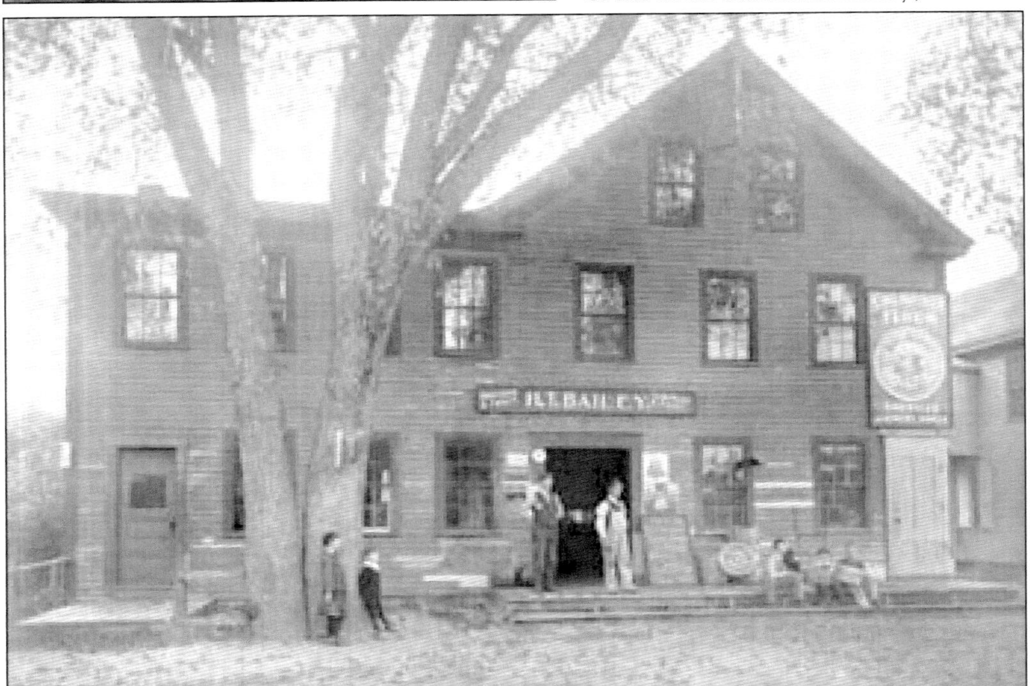

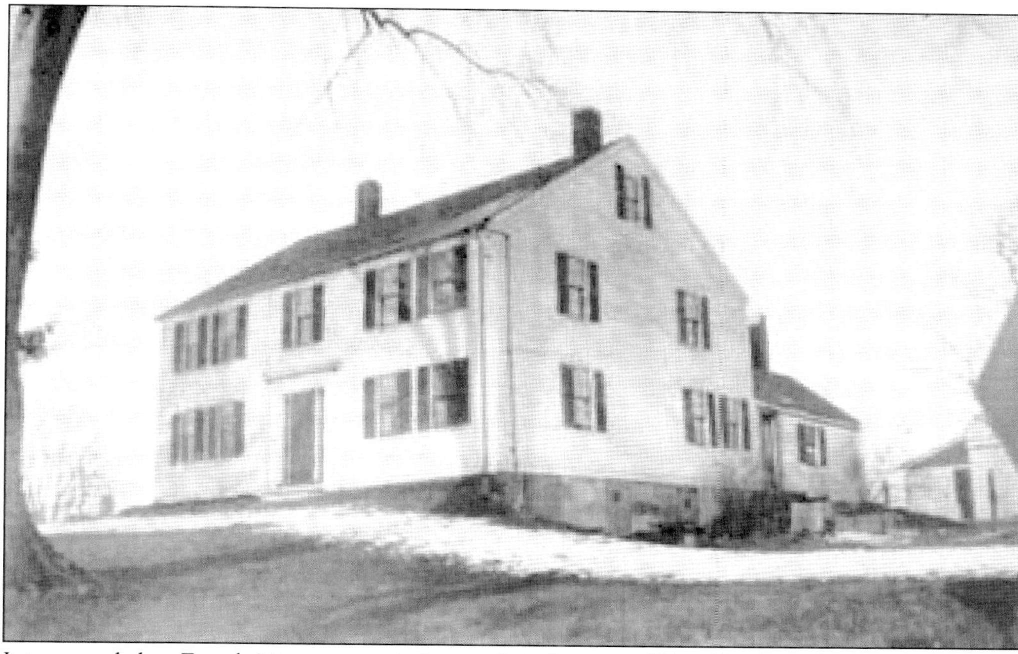

It is agreed that Enoch Noyes started the comb industry in West Newbury; however, there has been controversy over exactly where his comb shop was located. This house, built around 1825 on the foundation of an earlier house, is either on or near that site. Noyes began making combs with a jackknife around 1759. In 1777, or thereabouts, he joined in a partnership with William Cleland, a comb maker looking to ply his trade. Cleland was one of the Hessian soldiers captured at the Battle of Saratoga and housed at Turkey Hill farm. Shown below, the comb factory on Harrison Avenue was owned by Thomas Meady Chase and Harrison Gray Otis Chase, whose home is shown to the right of the factory. (Above, courtesy of the West Newbury Historical Commission; below, courtesy of the West Newbury Historical Society.)

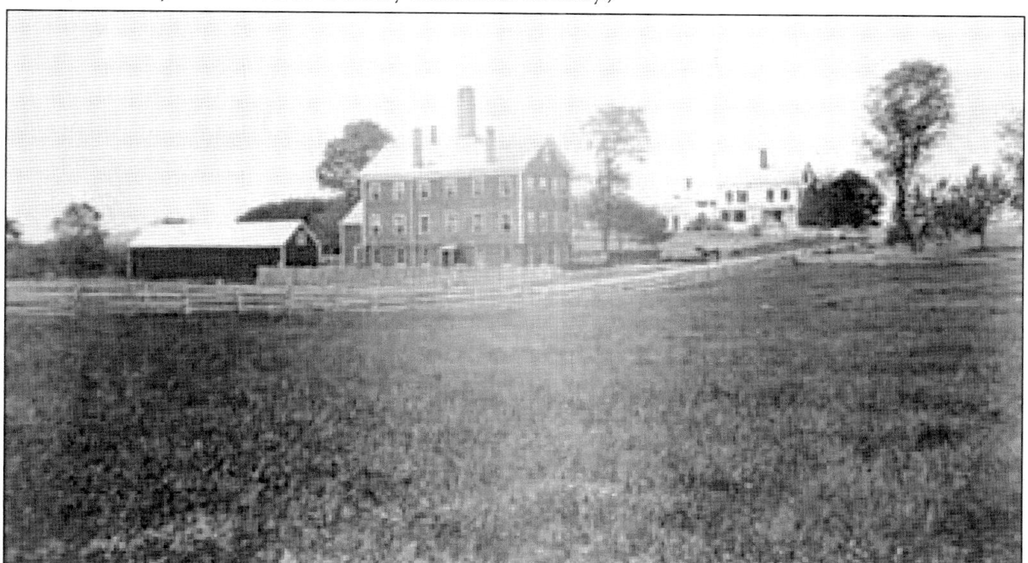

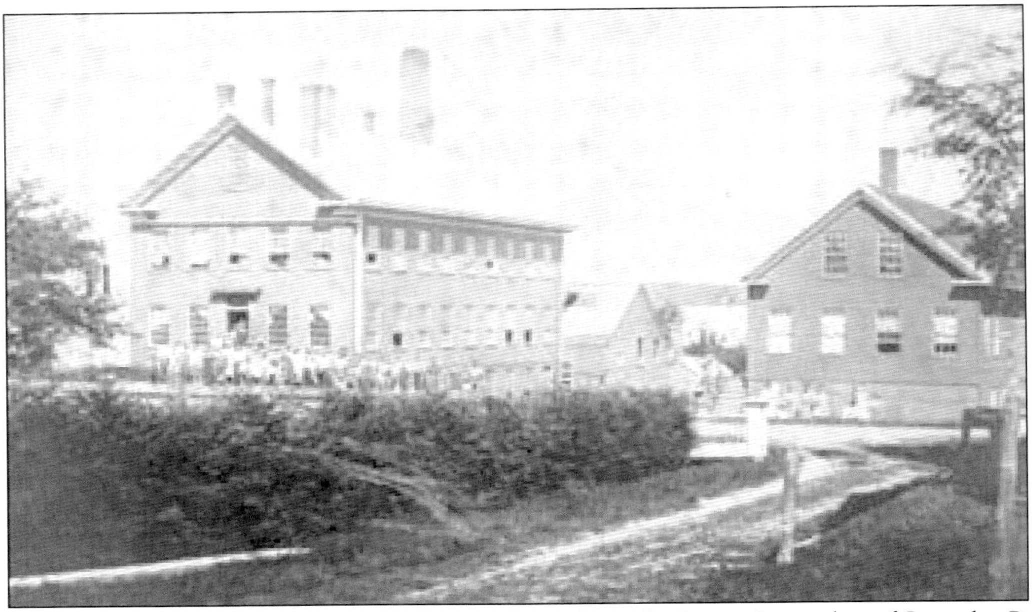

At one time, there were 30 comb shops in West Newbury, the largest being that of Somerby C. Noyes, pictured above and located at about 320 Main Street. Combs were made from tortoise shell and horn, with the work being done by hand. After machinery began to take the place of handwork, the power for running the machines was furnished by horses on a treadmill and later by steam. On October 15, 1904, at 12:00 p.m., the whistle at the factory of S.C. Noyes and Company was blown for the last time, ending the comb industry in West Newbury. Shown below are comb factory employees taking a break. (Above, courtesy of the Historical Society of Old Newbury; below, courtesy of the West Newbury Historical Society.)

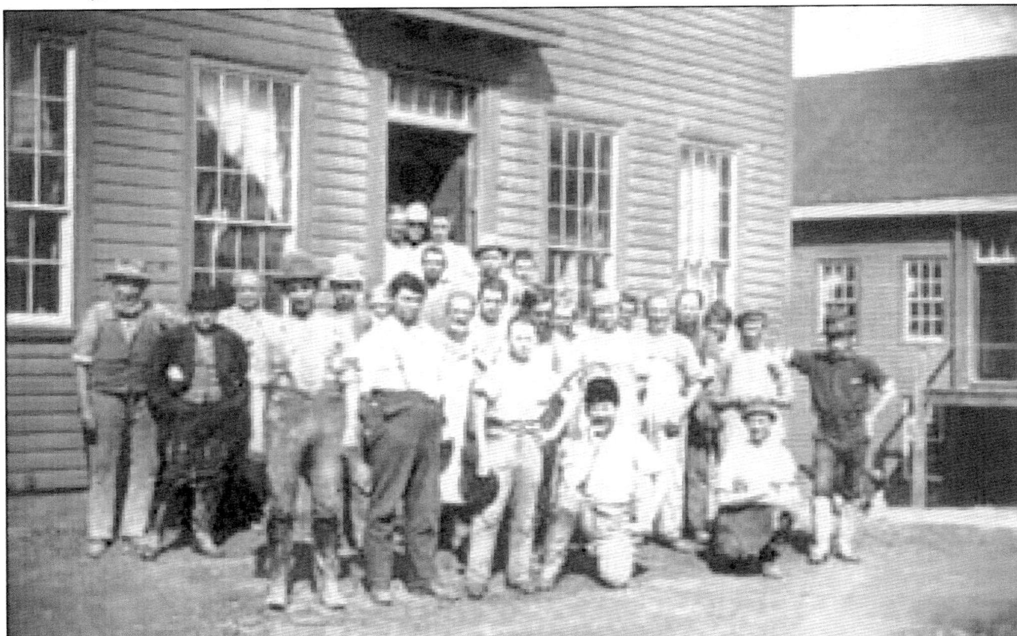

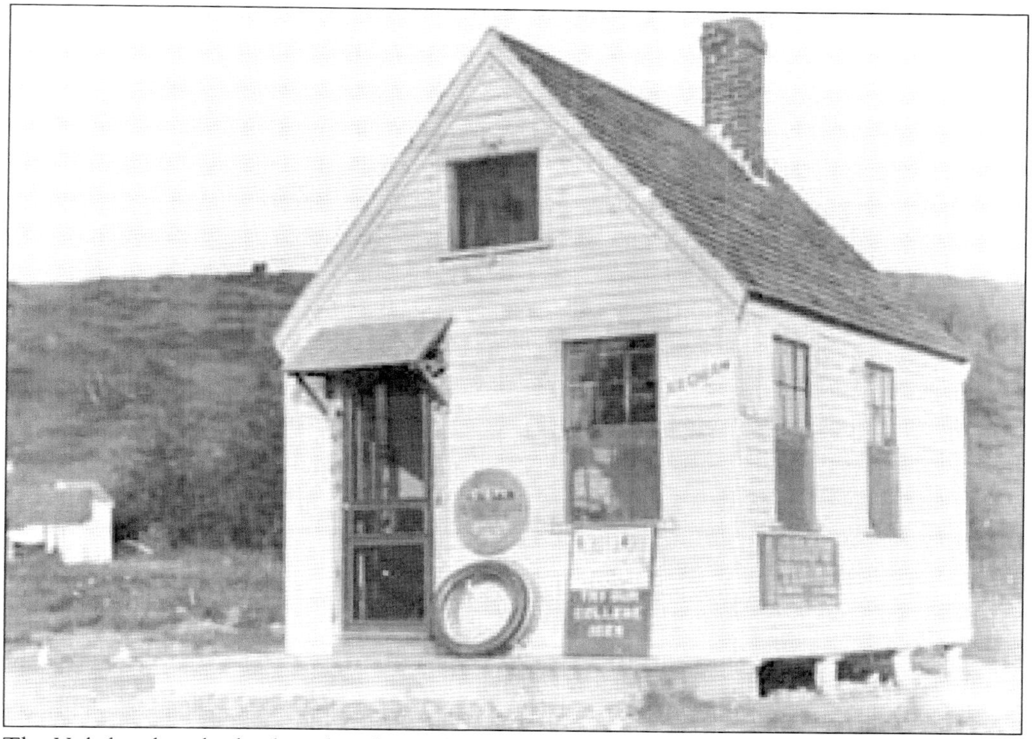

The Hale brothers had a shoe shop located at approximately 33 Main Street sometime previous to 1925. The building was then used to sell ice cream and tires, as pictured here. Later, it was enlarged to become Hales's Hot Dog Stand, famous locally for its steamed hot dogs, curlicue french fries, and homemade root beer. (Courtesy of the West Newbury Historical Commission.)

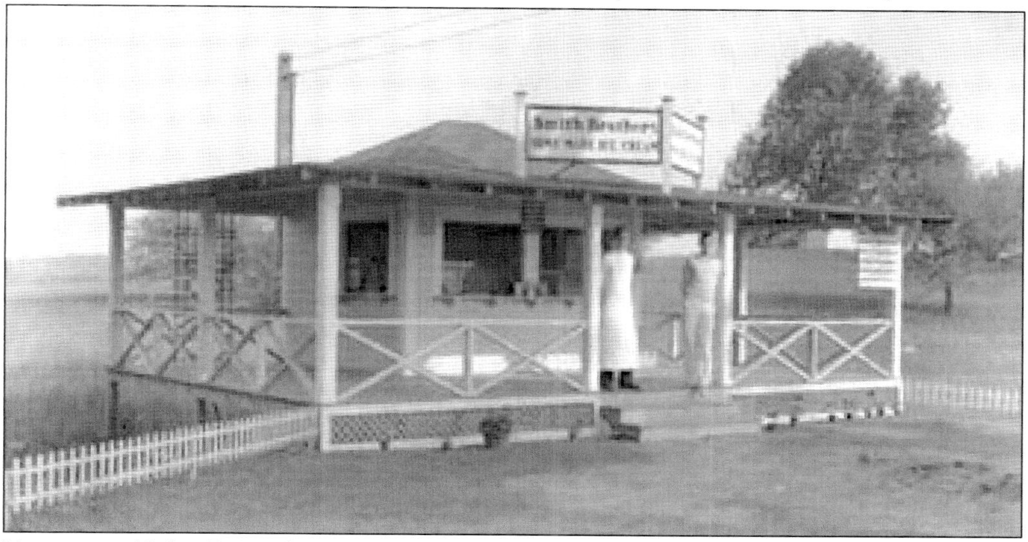

Norman and John E. Smith operated an ice cream stand from 1934 to 1938 at 189 Main Street. They sold 10 flavors of ice cream, which were made by their mother in their house at 196 Main Street. When the stand closed, the building was moved to Smithtown in Seabrook, New Hampshire, right across from the former location of the town hall. (Courtesy of Donald Laing.)

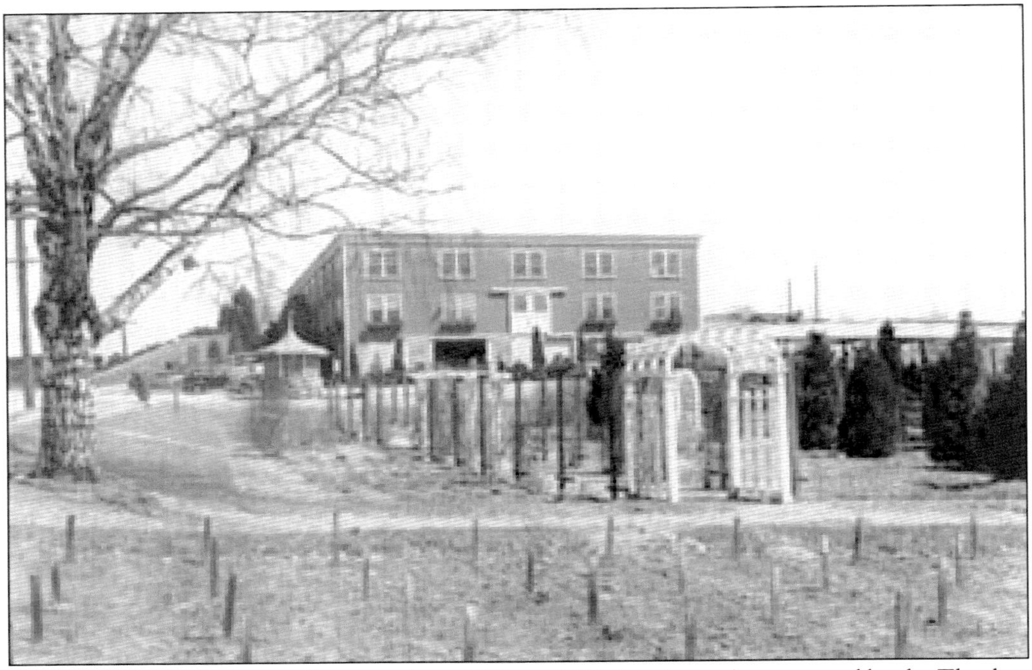

Cherry Hill Nurseries was in business from 1832 until 2000 and was always owned by the Thurlow family. This building, located at 5 Cherry Hill Street, was constructed in 1927–1928. The oak framing was cut and milled on company property off Storey Avenue in Newburyport. The building was unusual in that vehicles could drive into it on all three floors. The nursery was known for its fruit and ornamental trees, peonies, and lilacs. Flower shows all over the country gave highest honors to the Thurlow's exhibits. Their peonies were known all over the world, even as far away as China. Shown below is one of the nursery's advertising postcards. (Above, courtesy of the West Newbury Historical Society; below, courtesy of John Thurlow.)

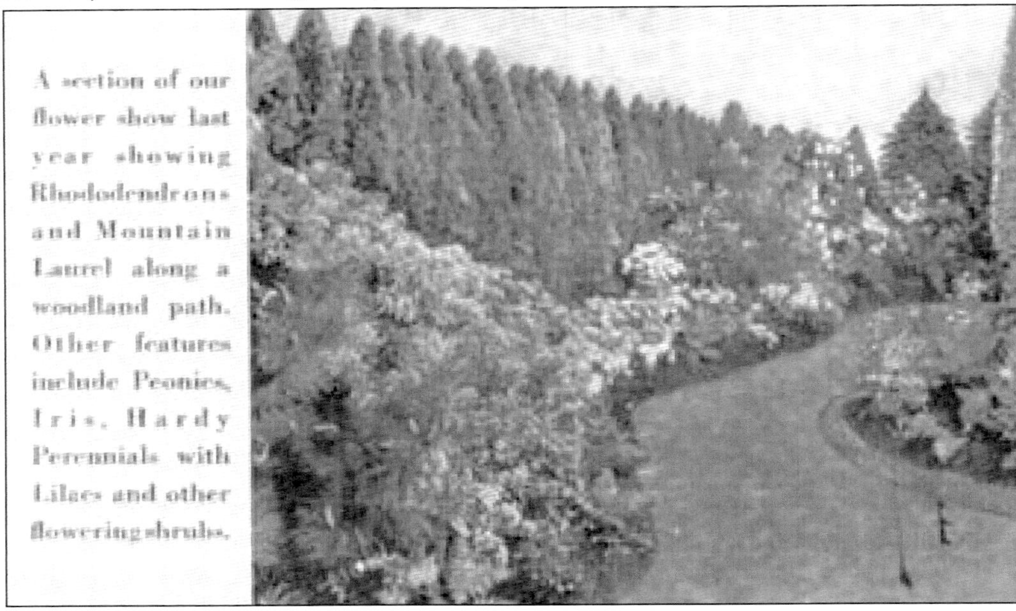

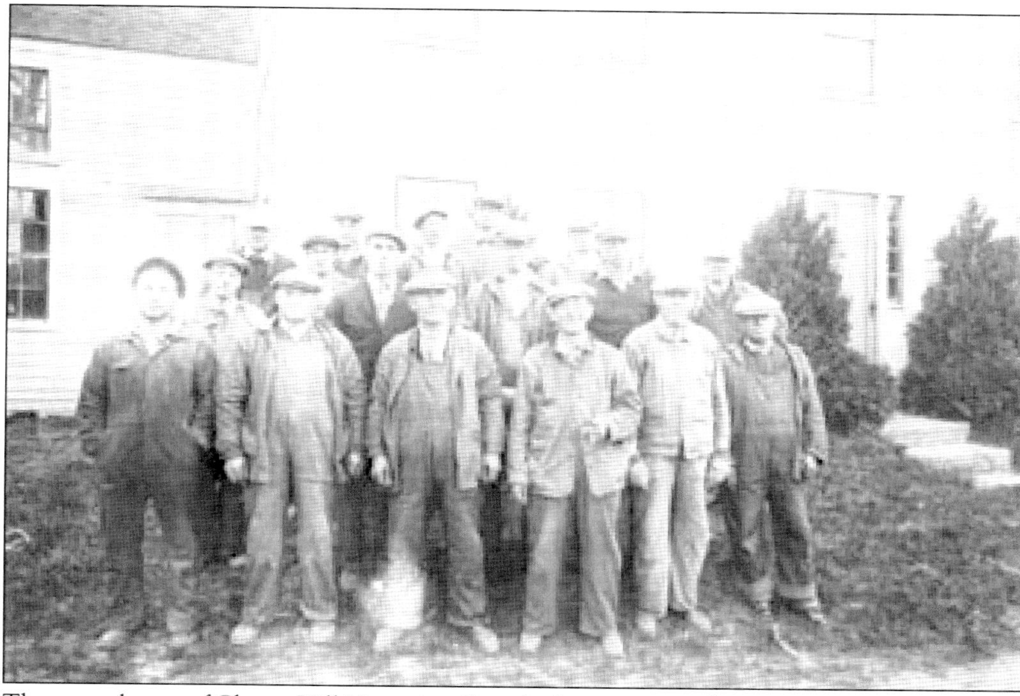

These employees of Cherry Hill Nurseries all worked on a convoy shipment of arborvitae, shown below, which was being trucked to Delhi, New York, in the spring of 1931. The late John Stanley Sawyer drove the first truck, a 1928 Reo. All were residents of either West Newbury or Byfield. Pictured above are, from left to right, (first row) Henry Wheeler, Bill Coffin, Austin Sharples, Joe Marceau, Joe Held, and Howard "Spud" Osborne; (second row) Gene Bradley, Fred Downer, Walter Stranger, Kyle Whiting, Leon Senior, and Murray Coffin; (third row) George Silk, Wilbur Dunn, Bud Sherburne, Malcolm Andrews, and J. Stanley Sawyer. (Both, courtesy of John Thurlow.)

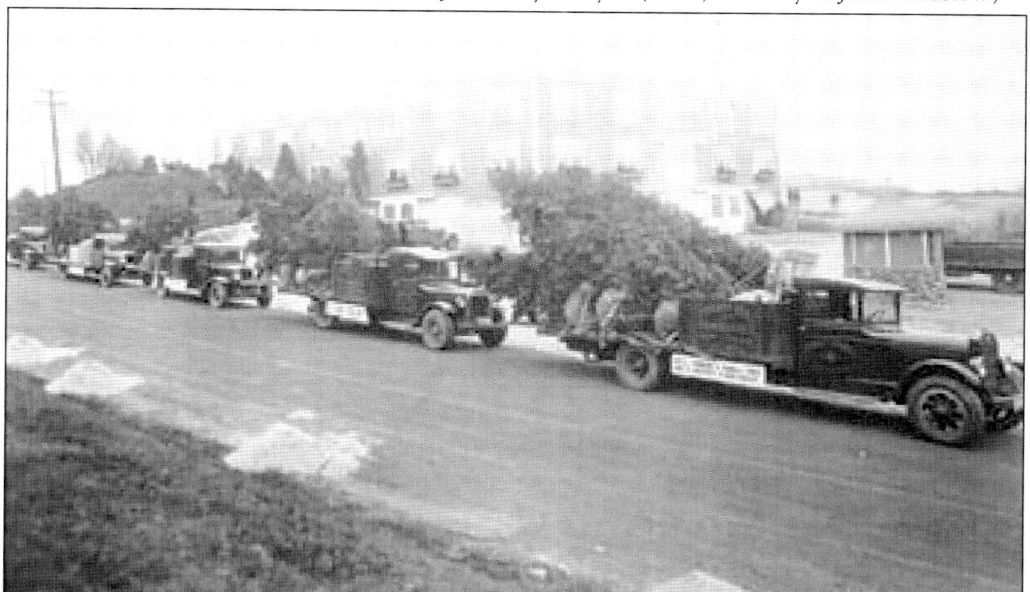

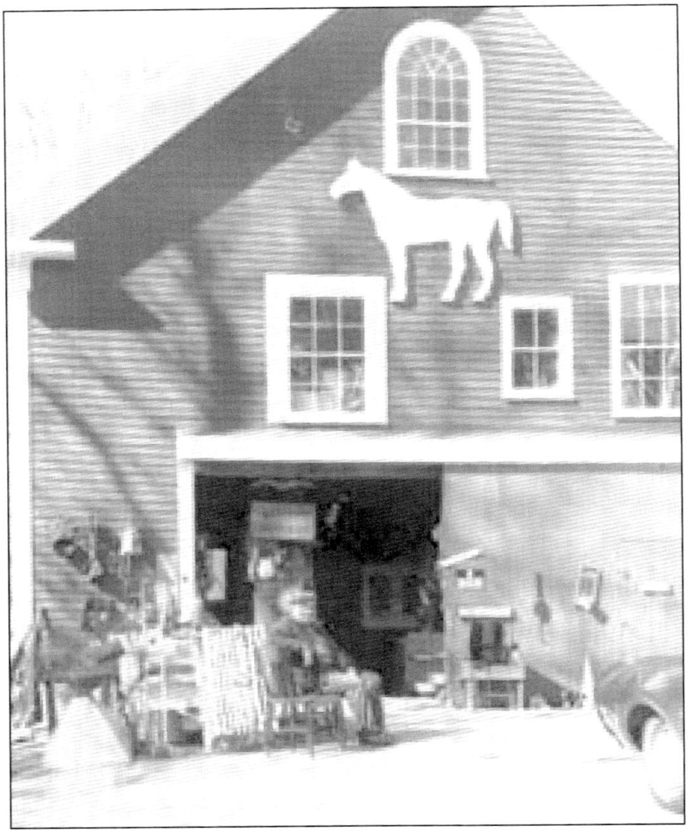

Vernon Burnham is pictured in front of his Antique and Second Hand Barn, which was a fixture at 230 Main Street for many years. The barn had once housed a shoe shop, and the house was the only Victorian in town with gingerbread trim. It was built about 1856. The original owner, Charles Fowler, ran a stage between West Newbury and Haverhill. (Courtesy of Joyce Burnham Dixon.)

John Dawkins ran the store at 192 Main Street, pictured below, in the 1910s or 1920s. Walter Swap had a grocery store here, and Rose Brooks lived in a small apartment on the left side in 1942. In the late 1950s, Wadsworth Burrill lived on the right side and had an office for his printing shop on the left side. (Courtesy of Barbara Hain.)

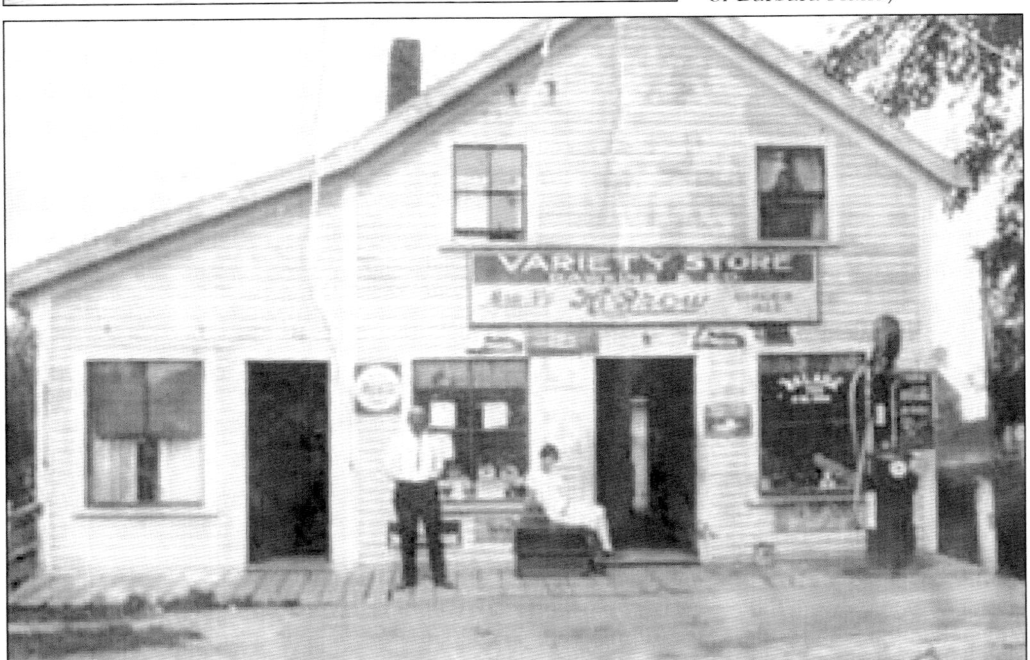

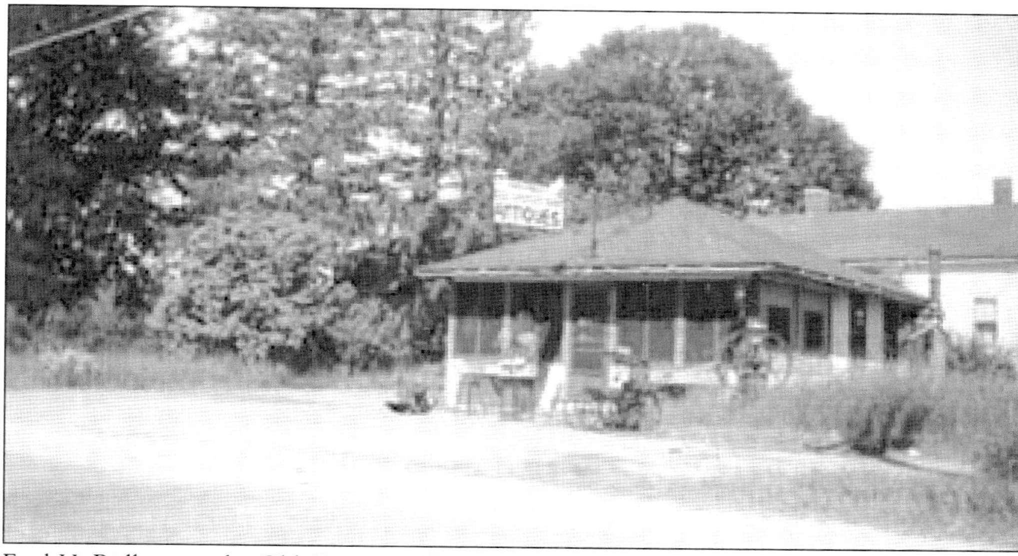

Fred H. Ridley ran the Old Curiosity Shop as an antique and second-hand store at 164 Main Street from sometime after 1930 until about 1960. The Ridleys lived in the house behind the shop. Many children were delighted by the Indian totem pole that stood beside the store. (Courtesy of Joyce Burnham Dixon.)

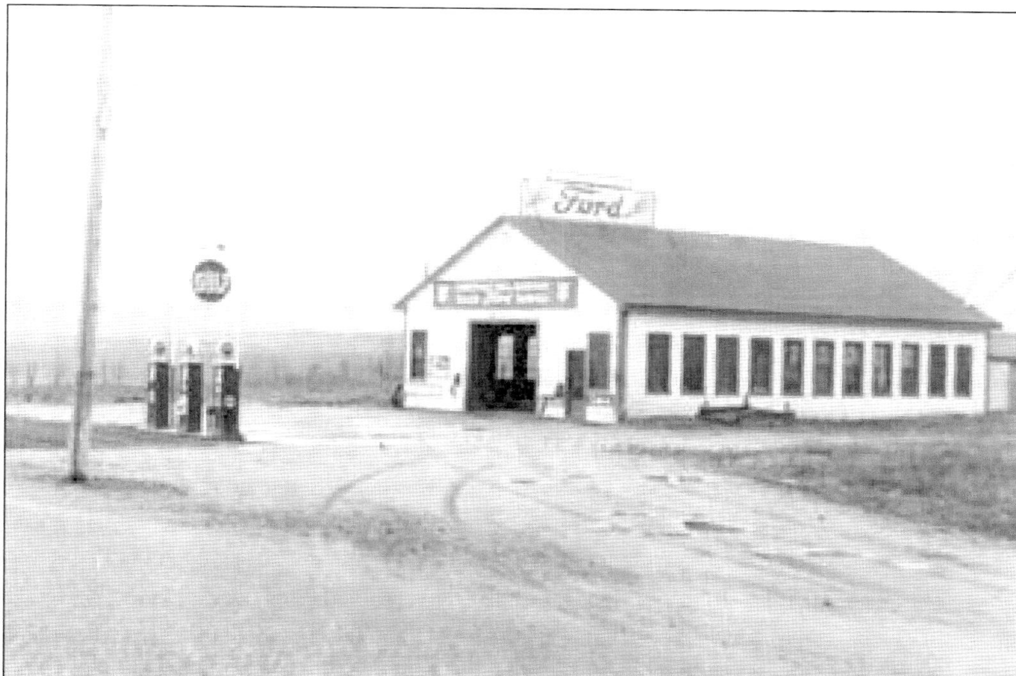

Kenneth Berkenbush, the police chief in the 1930s and a longtime member of the fire department, operated the Chestnut Hill Garage in the 1920s and 1930s. It stood where the Pentucket High School tennis courts are now located. Berkenbush sold the property to Charles Hibbert, and Hibbert stored his carnival equipment there until the school purchased the property. (Courtesy of Sandra Berkenbush.)

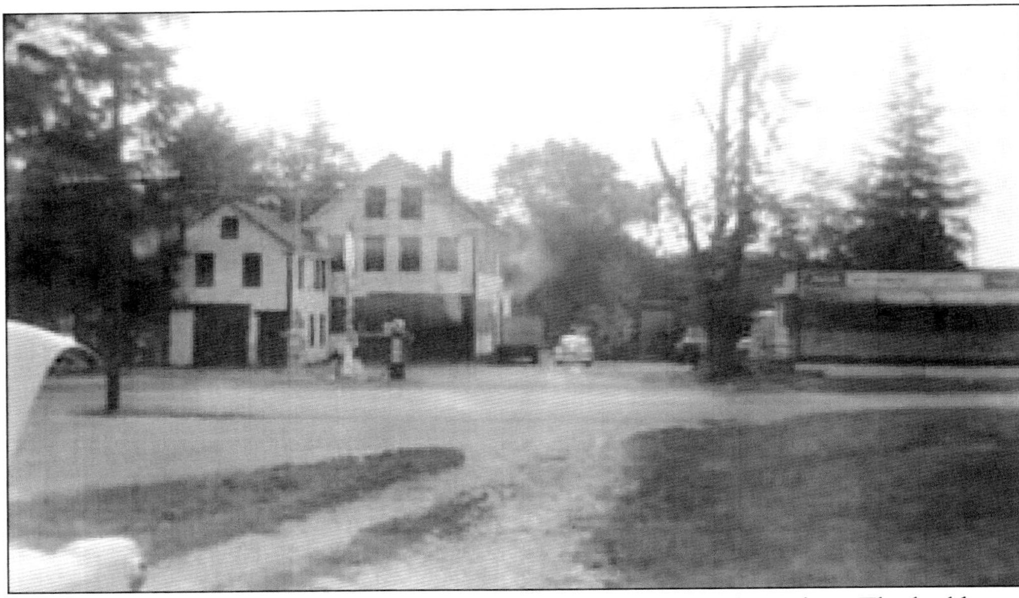

The West Newbury Garage near 275 Main Street was once a machine shop. The building is believed to have been constructed in the 1870s. The West Newbury Food Mart was located in the left side of the first floor of the building, and an electrical manufacturer was in the left side of the second floor. All were heavily damaged by fire in December 1963, and the present Food Mart was built on the site. The diner on the right was brought from Newburyport in 1946 by Walter Swap, who sold it to Bernard and Clayton Woodworth. It had several other owners and was torn down around 1959. Below, Donald Noyes is sitting at the counter, and Clayton Woodworth is waiting for customers. (Above, courtesy of Doris Bailey-Jones; below, courtesy of Joyce Burnham Dixon.)

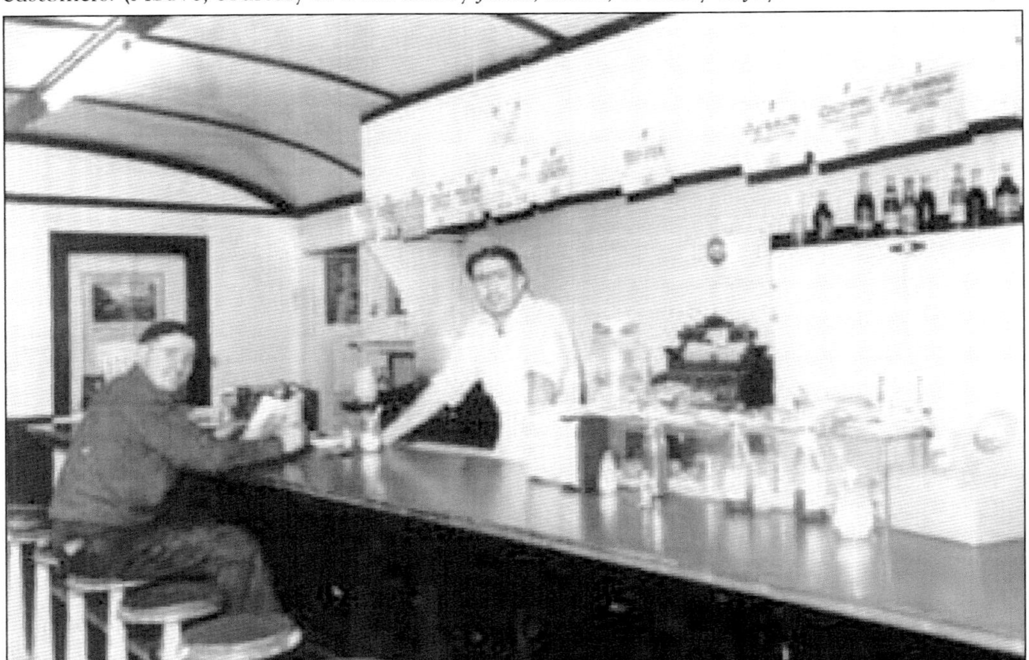

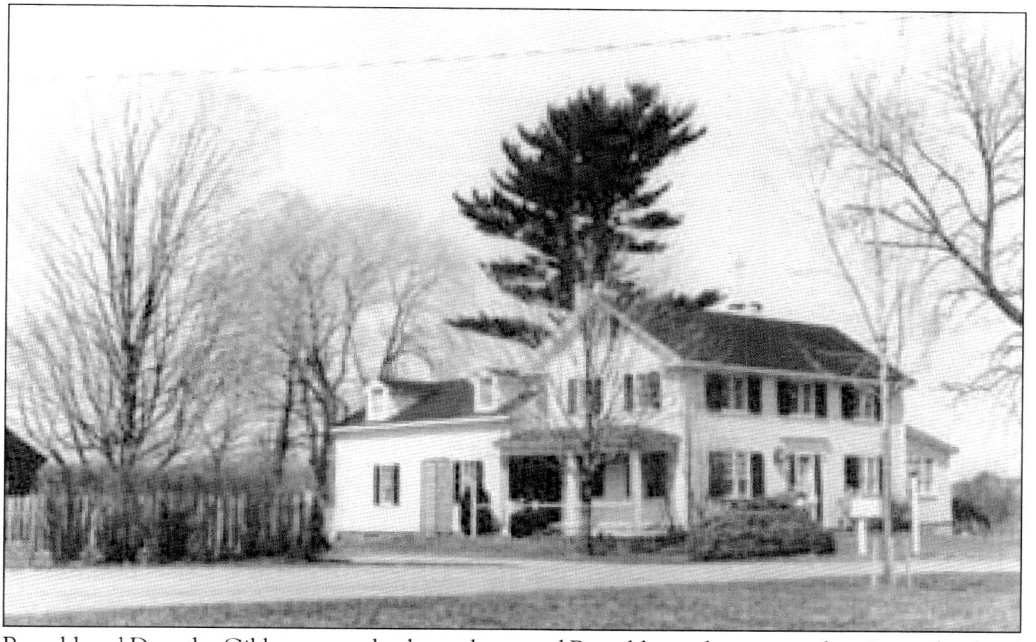

Ronald and Dorothy Gibbons were both teachers, and Ronald was the principal at Central School in West Newbury in the 1940s and 1950s. They opened a candy store in the back room of their house at 10 Training Field Road in 1947, where they sold handmade chocolates for 20 years as a retirement income. These chocolates were highly prized for gift-giving in town. (Courtesy of the West Newbury Historical Commission.)

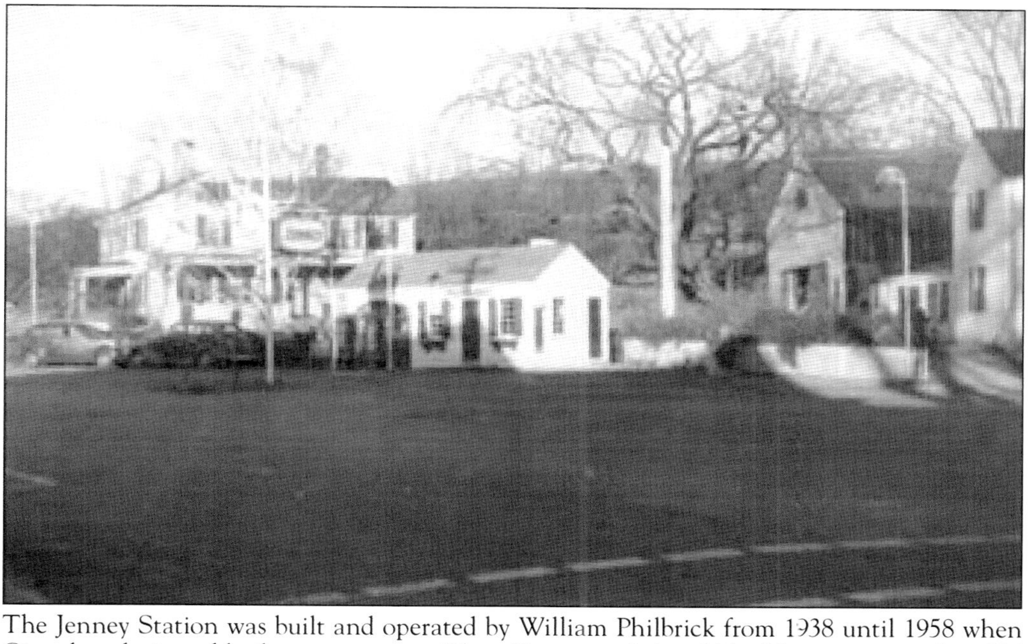

The Jenney Station was built and operated by William Philbrick from 1938 until 1958 when Citgo bought it and built a new station. The office part of the old building was moved to 326 Main Street, and the garage part relocated to 120 Garden Street. (Courtesy of the West Newbury Historical Society.)

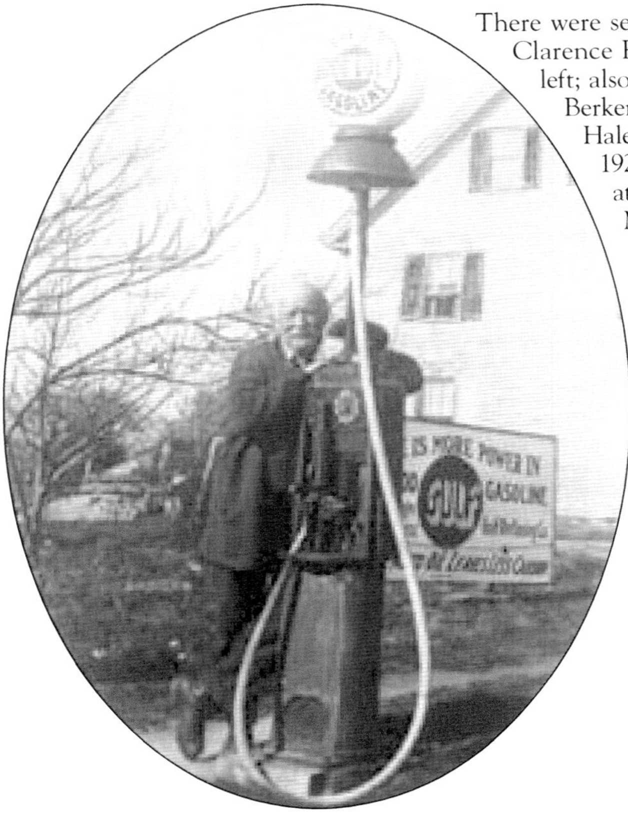

There were several gas pumps in West Newbury: Clarence Rowell's at 820 Main Street, shown left; also Russell Mingo's at 905 Main Street; Berkenbush's near 30 Main Street; George Hale's at 33 Main Street; Walter Swap's at 192 Main Street; West Newbury Garage at 275 Main Street; Bailey's Store at 282 Main Street; Croft's Store at 400 Main Street; and John Ruth's at 529 Main Street. (Courtesy of Rachel Adams.)

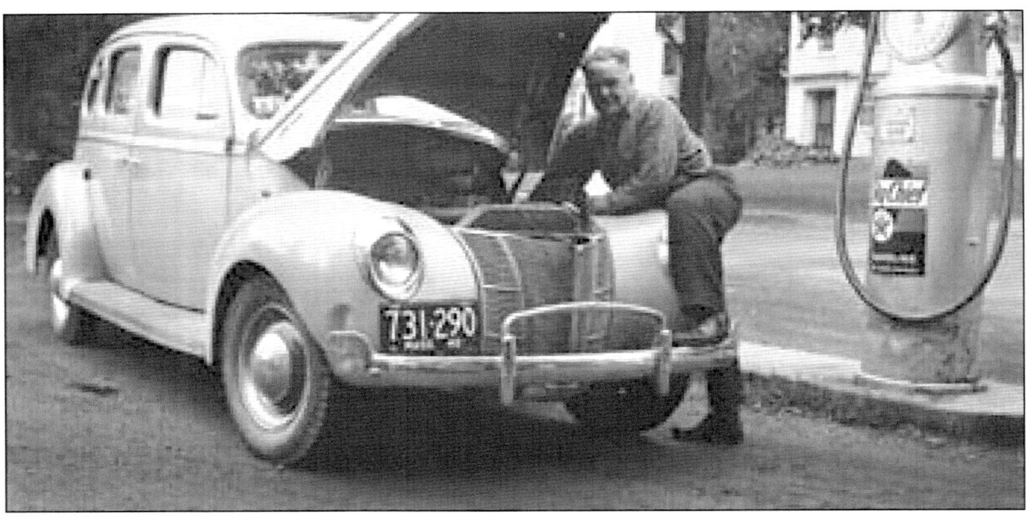

Russell Noyes, owner of the West Newbury Garage along with Horace Brown and Norman Brown, works on a 1940 Ford in front of the garage in 1942. The doorway of the Bailey house at 274 Main Street is visible in the background across the street. Noyes was also the chief of police in West Newbury for a time. (Courtesy of Peter Haack.)

Seven

Transportation
From Buggies to Touring Cars

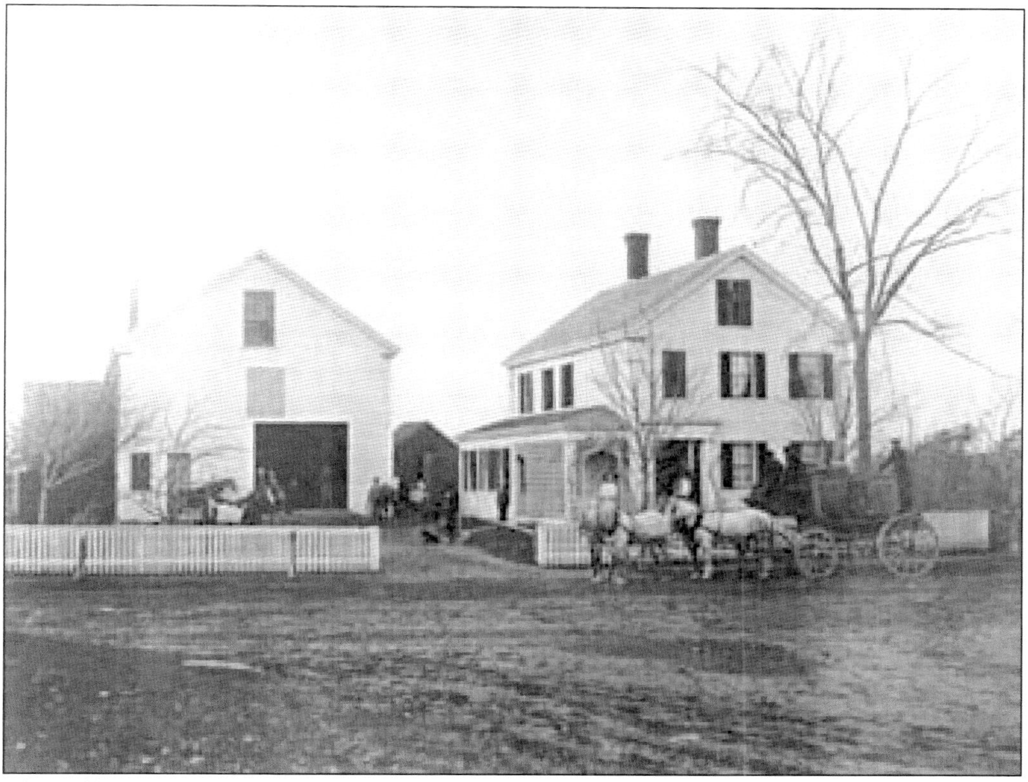

The William P. Bailey Stage, shown here in 1872 in front of Bailey's house at 412 Main Street, was a forerunner of the electric cars. Stagecoaches were the only means of leaving town for those that did not own their own horse and carriage. (Courtesy of the West Newbury Historical Commission.)

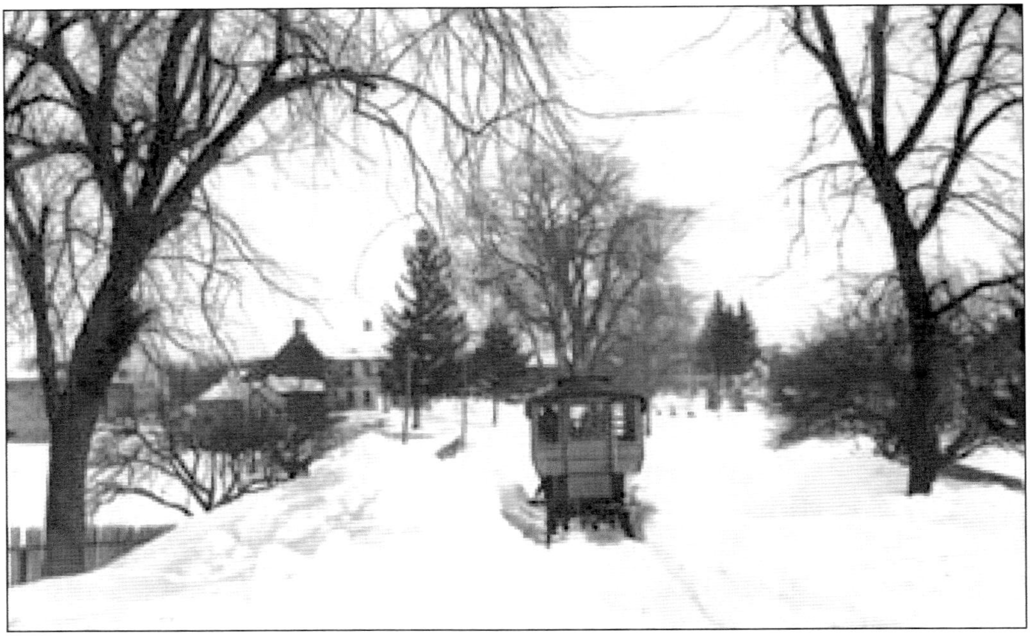

Another horse-drawn conveyance of the late 1800s and early 1900s was the "barge," a sort of closed-in sleigh on runners that was drawn by two horses, such as the one shown here near 152 Main Street in 1893. It went from Newburyport through West Newbury to Haverhill. (Photograph by W.H. Stevens; courtesy of Donald Laing.)

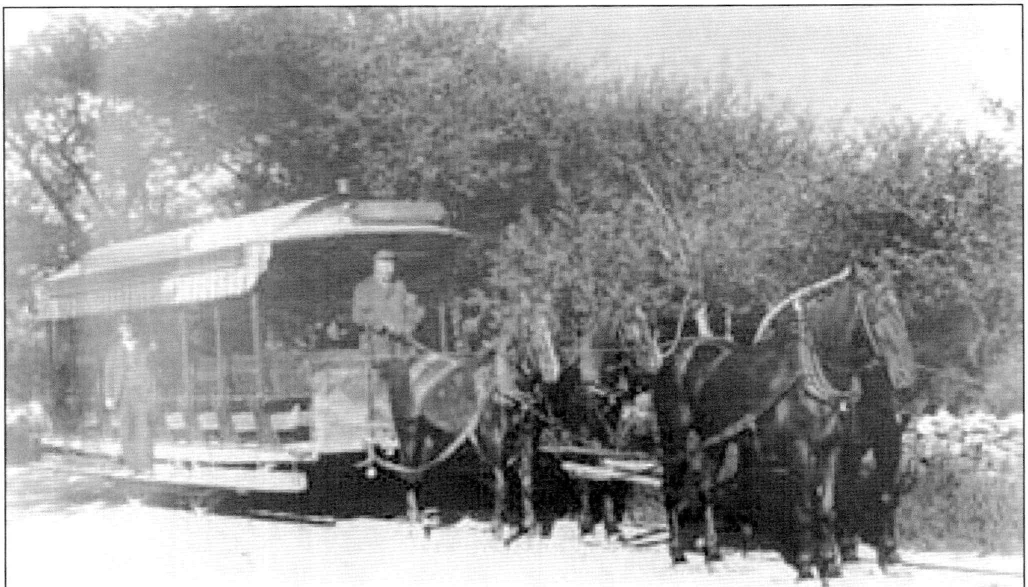

Transportation took a great leap forward in 1886 when tracks were laid, and the horsecar line came from Haverhill to the town hall. The first trip to West Newbury was a momentous occasion. Flags decorated the houses, handkerchiefs waved from the windows, and schoolchildren along Main Street were let out of school to see the sight. (Photograph by William E. Sharples; courtesy of John McGrath.)

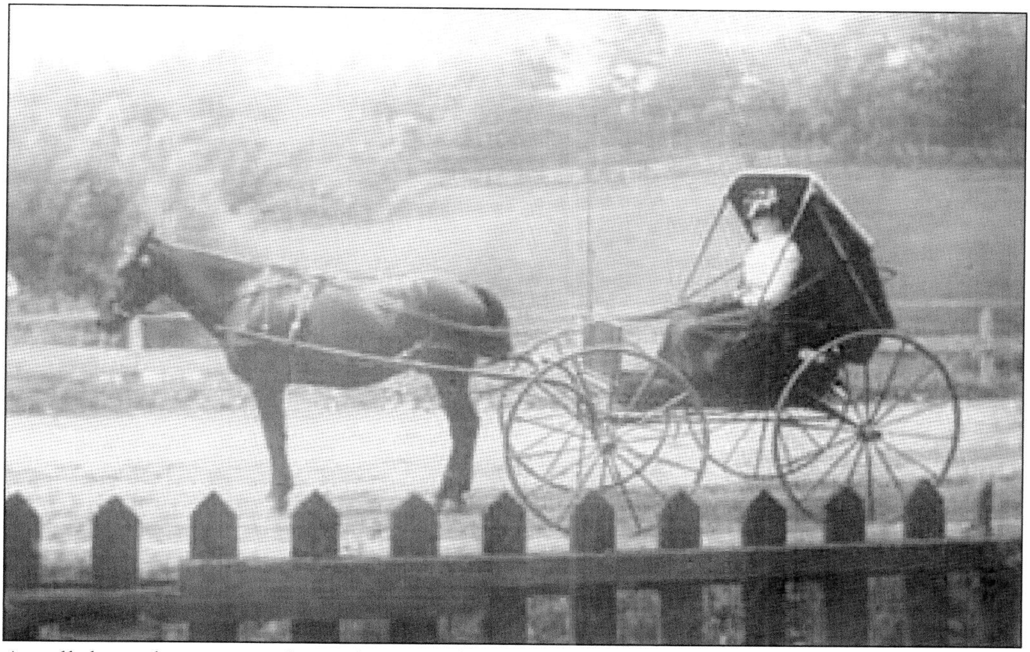

A well-dressed woman is shown here out for a ride on a beautiful, warm day. The carriage is a runabout with bonnet, or a doctor's buggy; they were quite popular around 1900. Carriages like this were made in Merrimac and Amesbury and perhaps also in West Newbury. (Photograph by Jessie Jaques; courtesy of Joyce Burnham Dixon.)

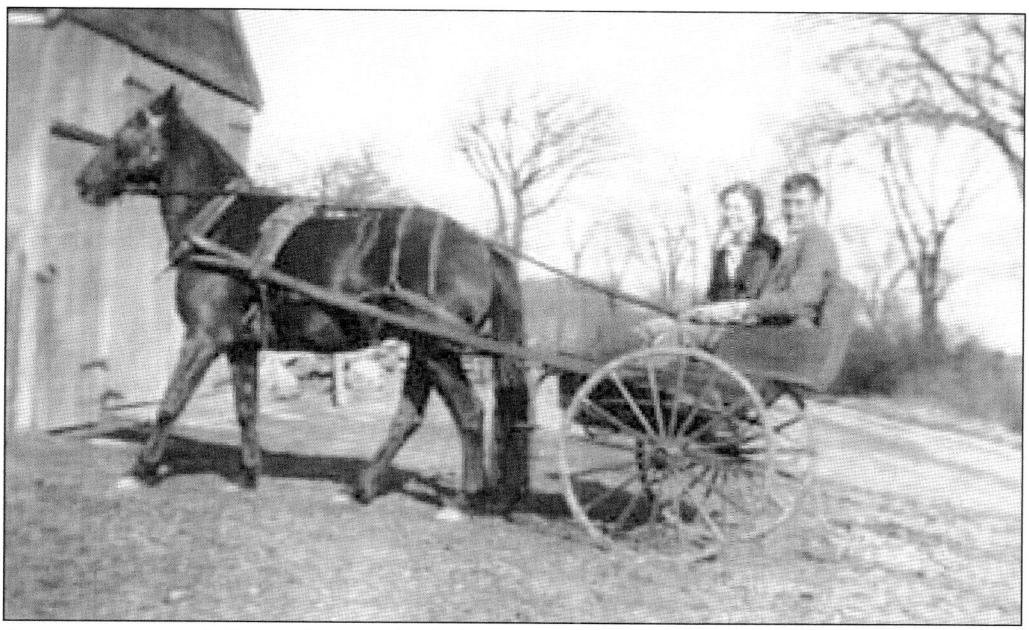

A gig was an open lightweight two-wheeled carriage, the equivalent of a two-seater sports car. A gig with a hood was called a cabriolet, later called a cab. Here, Howard and Mary Poore return to the barn at 406 Middle Street behind Mary's horse Diamond in the early 1930s. (Courtesy of Susan Poore Follansbee.)

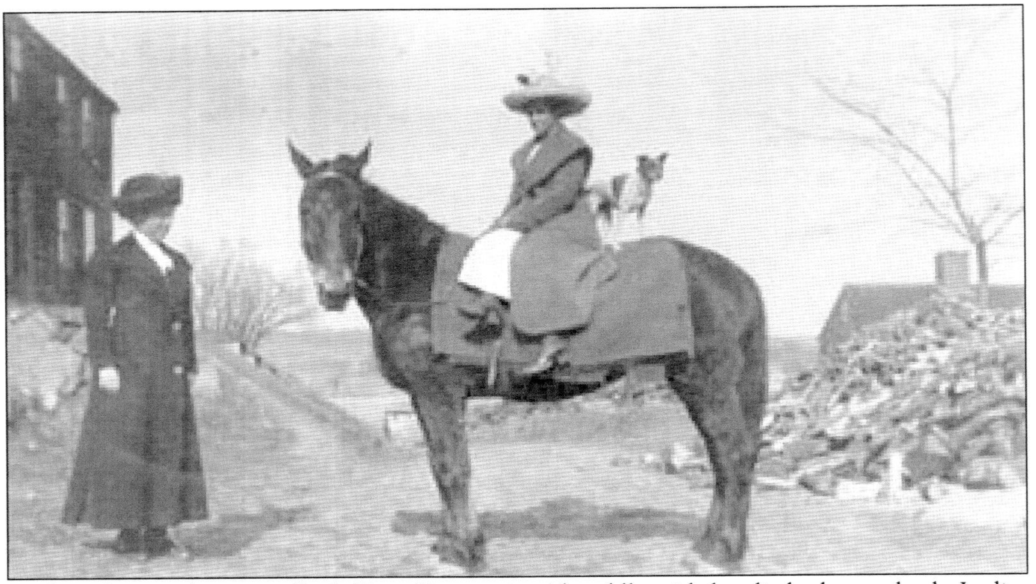

In this whimsical picture, Ruth Trow Brown sits sidesaddle with her little dog on back. Ladies frequently rode sidesaddle, not astride, and there were specially made saddles for this. Many years ago, some of the women riding through town with the Myopia Hunt Club rode sidesaddle. (Courtesy of Elinor Spofford.)

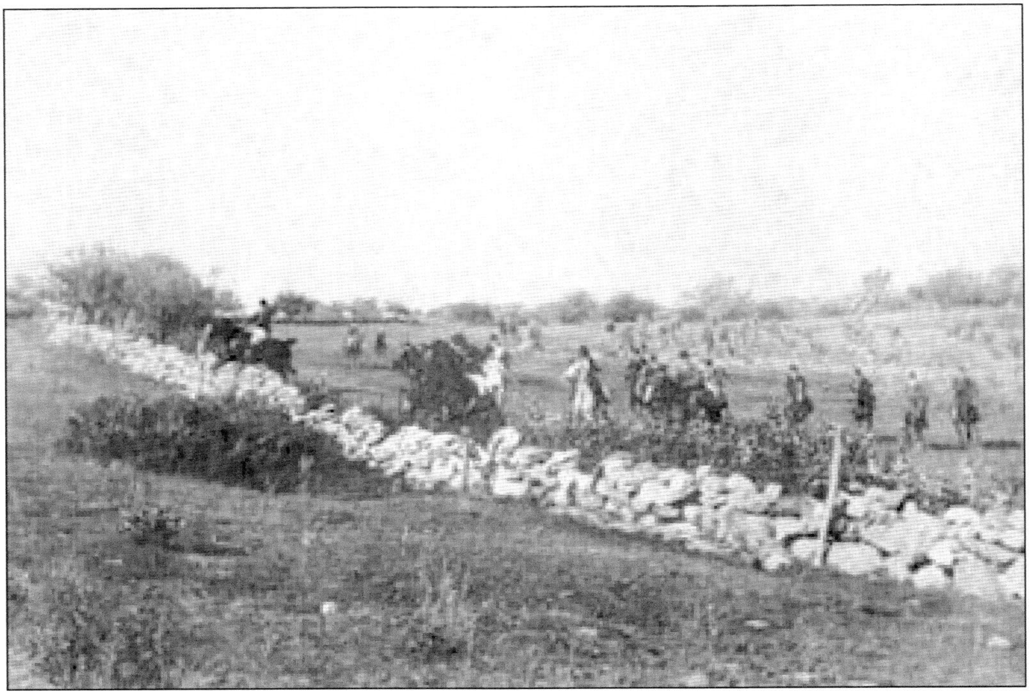

The Myopia Hunt Club, organized in 1882, probably started coming to West Newbury for its hunts in the early 1900s, although the year is uncertain. Traditionally started as a live hunt with a fox, many years ago that changed to a drag hunt, with a rider dragging a bag of scent in advance for the hounds to follow. (Courtesy of the West Newbury Historical Society.)

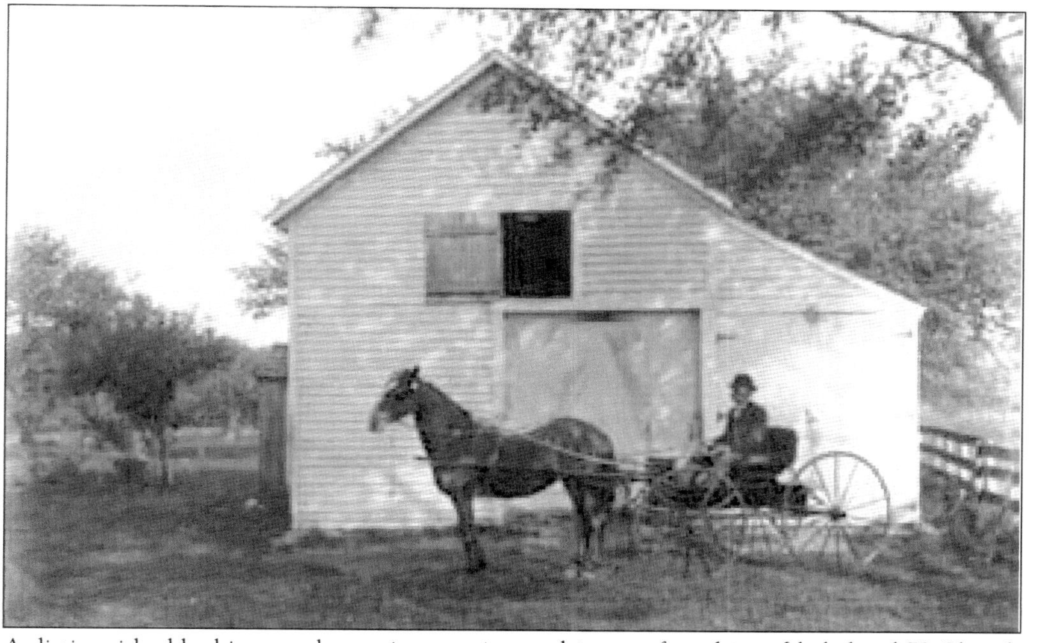

A distinguished-looking gentleman is preparing to drive out from his stable behind 73 Church Street. The carriage is a runabout, a light four-wheeled vehicle that could be easily hitched by one person and pulled over long distances by a single horse. T.W. Lane made many of these carriages in Amesbury. (Courtesy of John McGrath.)

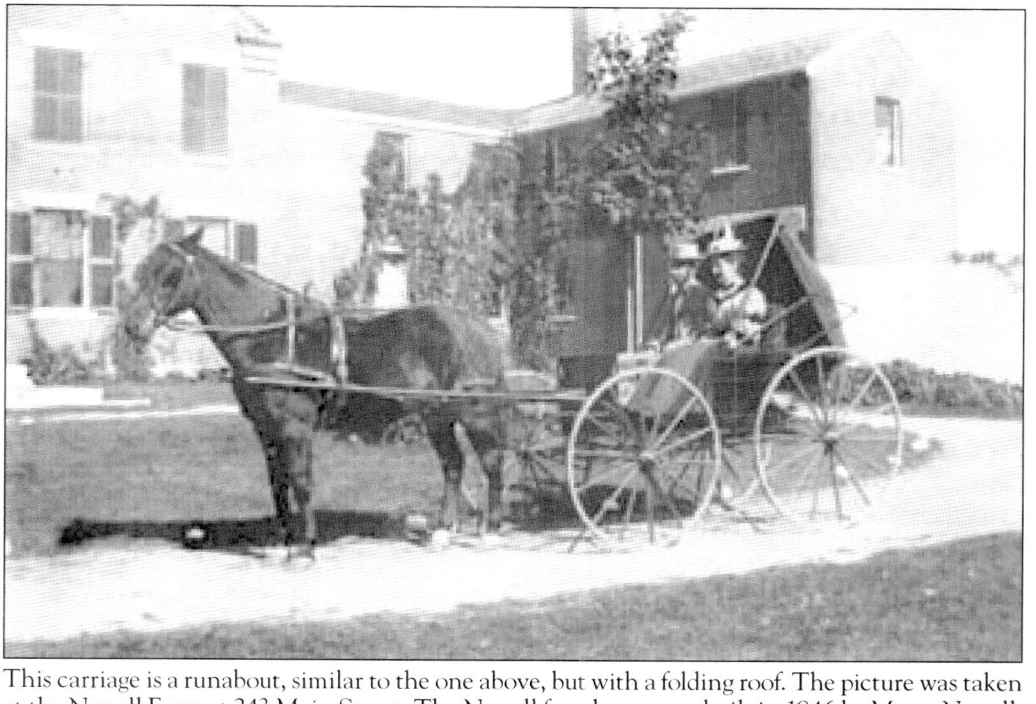

This carriage is a runabout, similar to the one above, but with a folding roof. The picture was taken at the Newell Farm at 243 Main Street. The Newell farmhouse was built in 1846 by Moses Newell; it is now in the National Register of Historic Places. (Courtesy of Joyce Burnham Dixon.)

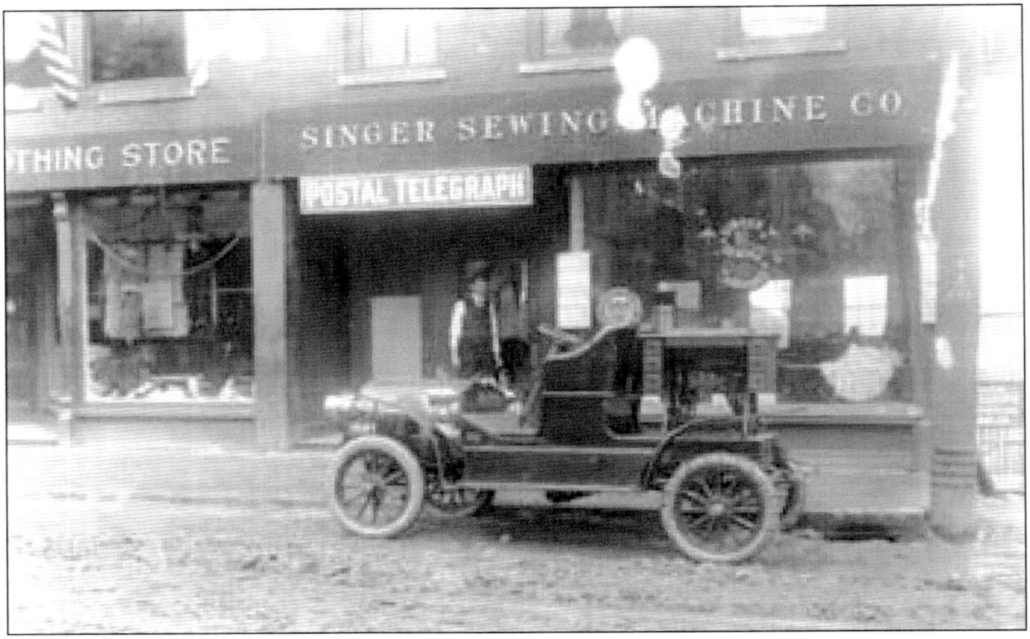

The Hill Motor Car Company of Haverhill was an early manufacturer of touring cars. The first car, which was a sample, was built in West Newbury in Gilman Brown's shop in 1904. It was painted dark maroon and had running boards and splash shields. Ten automobiles were built and sold, but the venture was a financial failure. The car shown above has a sewing machine sitting in back. The car below is a five-passenger touring car with a side-entrance tonneau. Gilman Brown is at the wheel. The engines were 16–18 horsepower with three speeds forward and one reverse. (Above, courtesy of John Poore; below, courtesy of Elinor Spofford.)

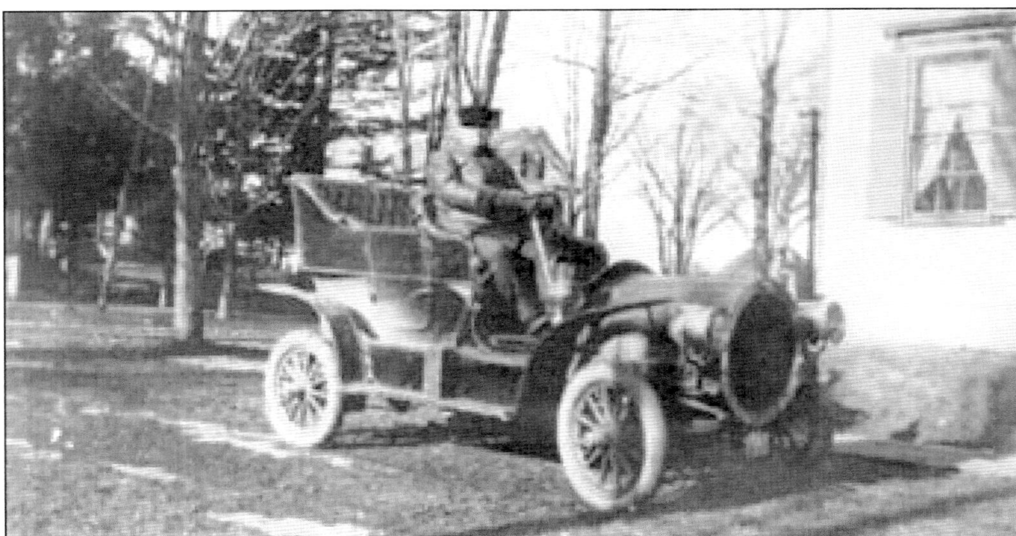

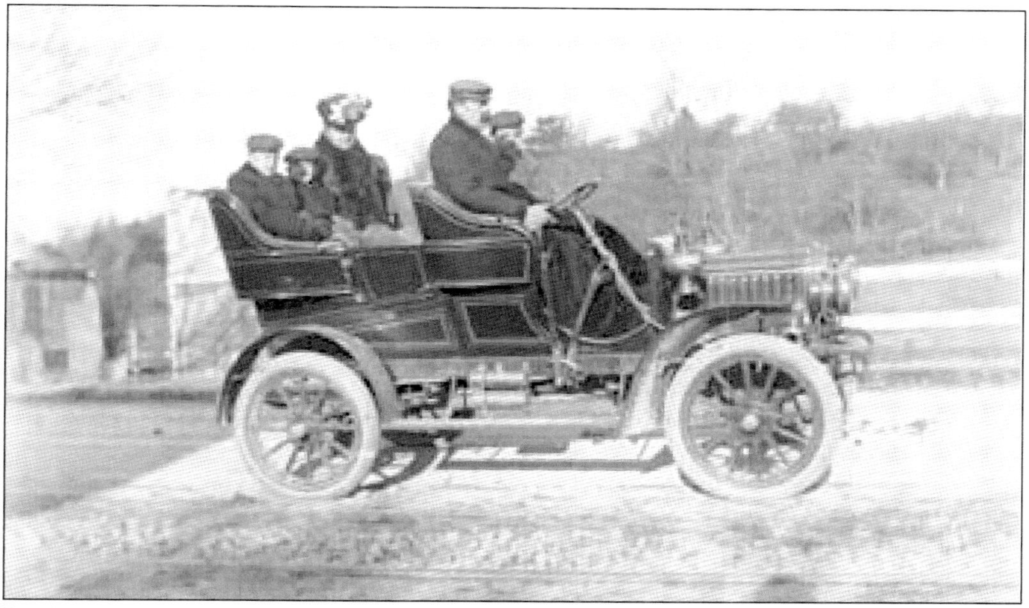

Dr. Amos Peirce takes the family for a ride in his 1908 Maxwell. Shown are, from left to right, Lincoln Peirce, Russell Peirce, Annie Peirce, Dr. Amos Peirce, and John Peirce. The body of the Maxwell was wooden; the radiator, lamps, and hubs were of brass. The headlights were run by carbide gas. (Courtesy of Rachel Adams.)

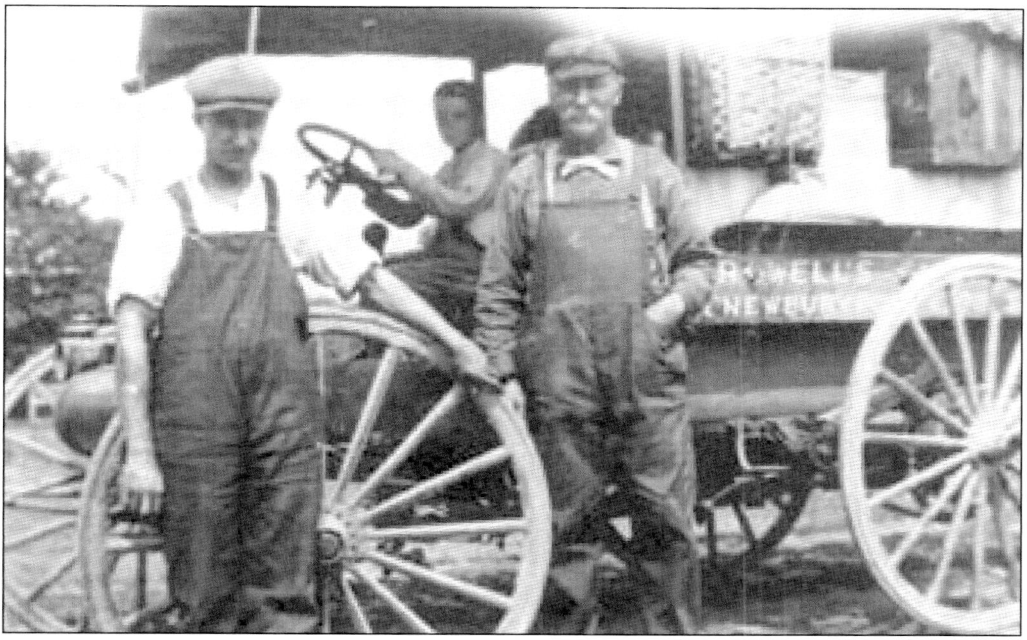

Rowell's Newburyport Express, which was in business around 1910, operated from Clarence Rowell's home at 820 Main Street. In conjunction with this, he also provided a sort of lending library delivery service to residents of the First Parish. His truck may have been a 1911 International. Pictured here are, from left to right, Alan Bradshaw, Harold Rowell, and Clarence Rowell. (Courtesy of Rachel Adams.)

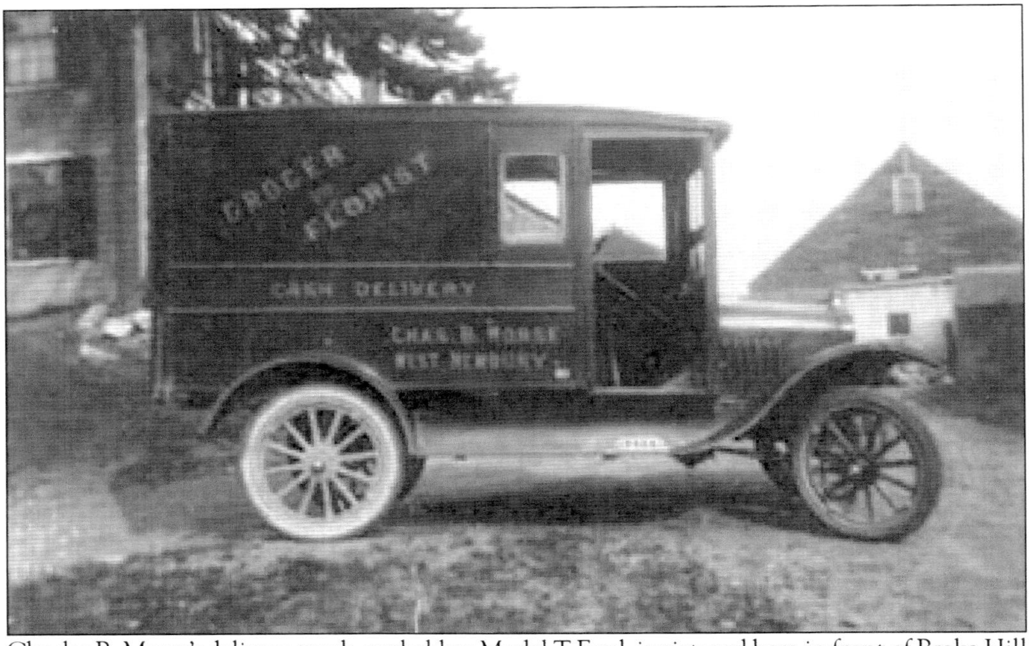

Charles B. Morse's delivery truck, probably a Model T Ford, is pictured here in front of Brake Hill Farm at 117 Main Street. Morse had a greenhouse and small grocery store on Main Street nearly opposite Stewart Street from the 1920s and perhaps up until 1943, when he died. (Courtesy of Donald Fowler.)

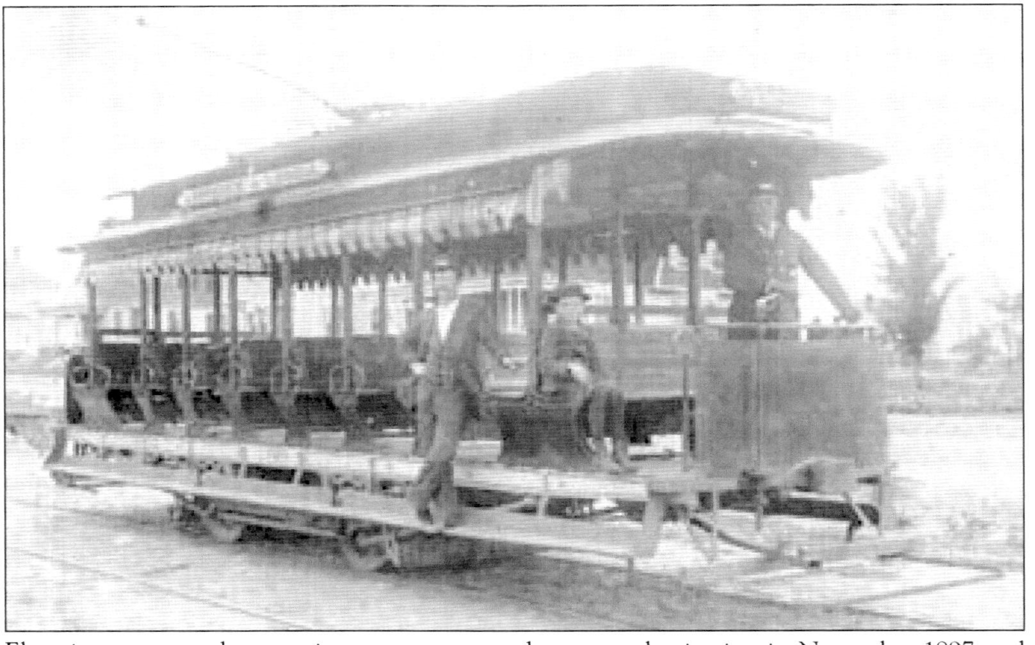

Electric cars were the next improvement over horsecars, beginning in November 1897 and remaining in use until they were replaced with buses in 1930. Cars were open in the summer and enclosed in the winter. Warren M. Dutton, the West Newbury High School principal, is shown here standing on the running board. (Courtesy of the West Newbury Historical Society.)

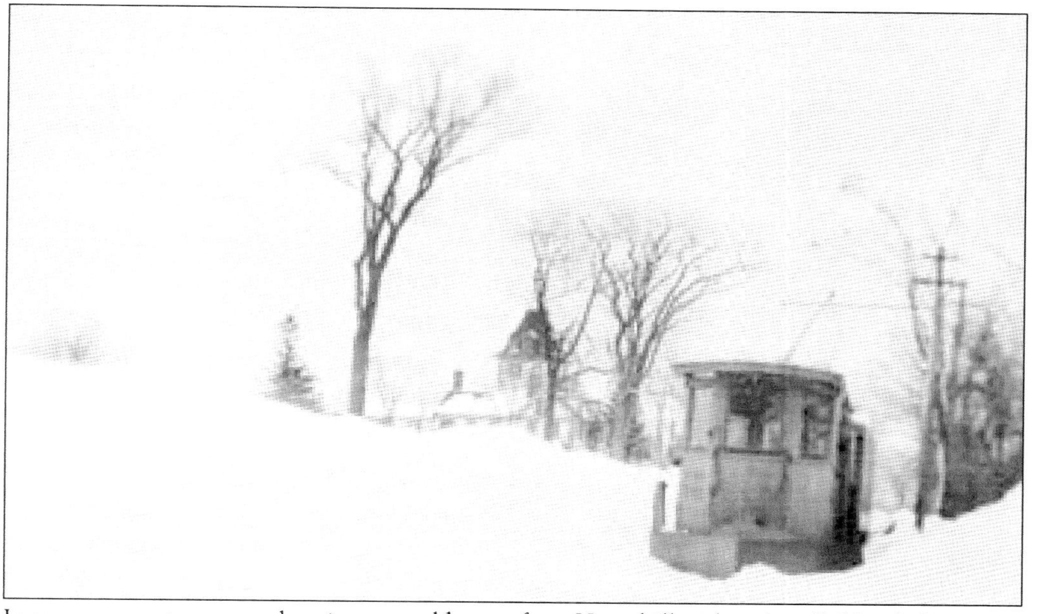

In severe snowstorms, an electric car would come from Haverhill with a plow. E. Moody Boynton's mansion on Pipestave Hill is in the background in this picture. The car line was a single track with turnouts, which allowed cars to pass. There was a turnout at 159 Main Street and another near Long Hill Orchard. (Courtesy of Elinor Spofford.)

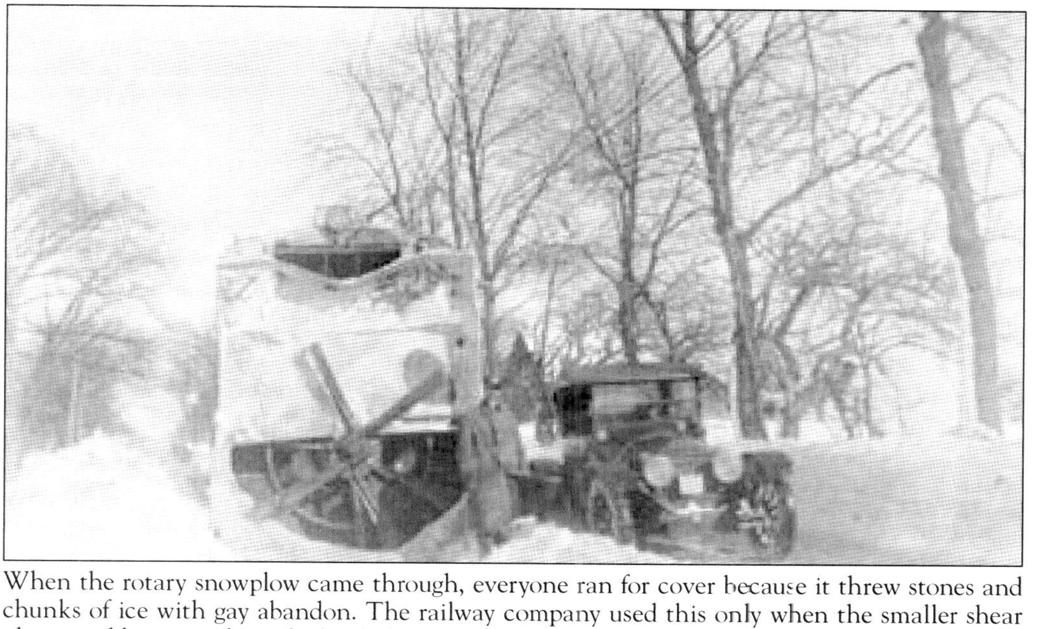

When the rotary snowplow came through, everyone ran for cover because it threw stones and chunks of ice with gay abandon. The railway company used this only when the smaller shear plows could not get through the drifts for the company's plow was always followed by numerous claims of broken windows. (Courtesy of Elinor Spofford.)

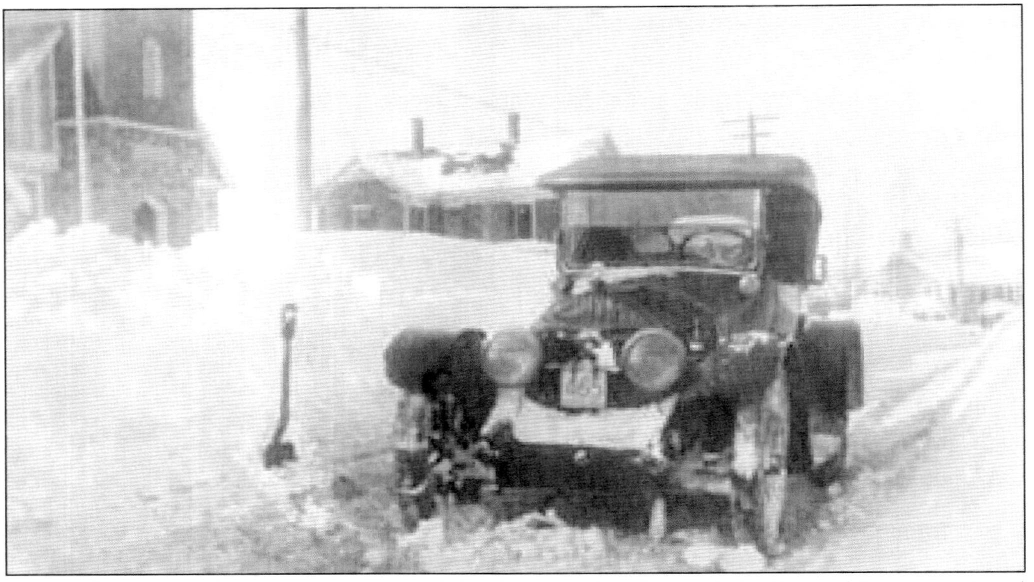

An unidentified old car stops in the middle of the road in front of the Second Congregational Church in 1920. Apparently, Main Street was not heavily traveled then; the road is only cleared about one car wide. Here, a car is parked in the middle of the street. (Courtesy of Elinor Spofford.)

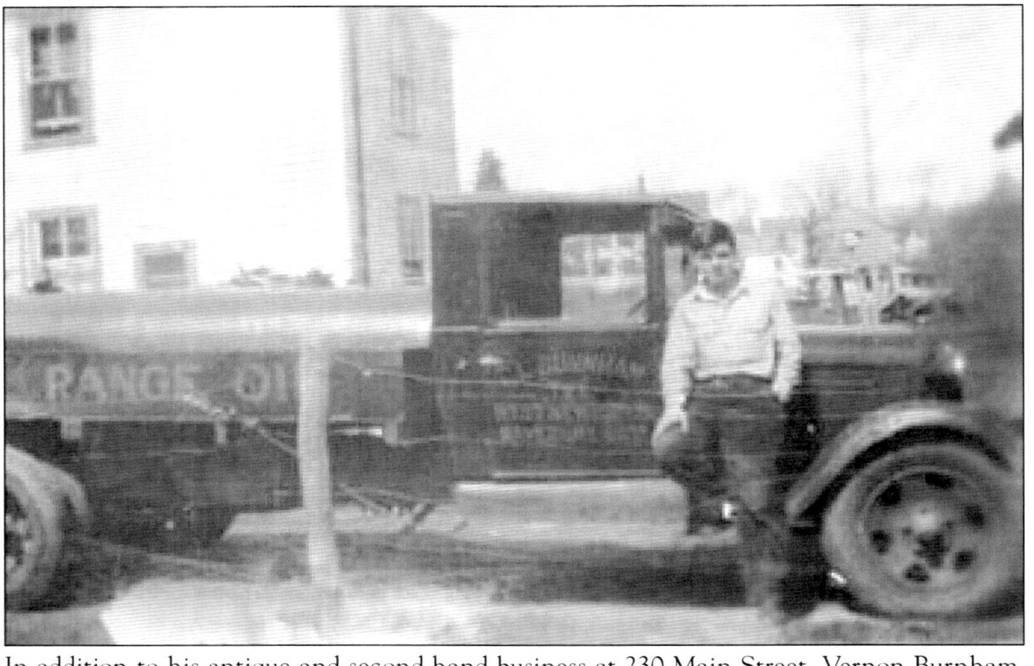

In addition to his antique and second-hand business at 230 Main Street, Vernon Burnham, pictured here beside his 1929 Model A Ford truck, had an oil and wood delivery business and also ran an ice business. He was a police officer, fireman, and school bus driver, and he often served as an auctioneer for local organizations. (Courtesy of Joyce Burnham Dixon.)

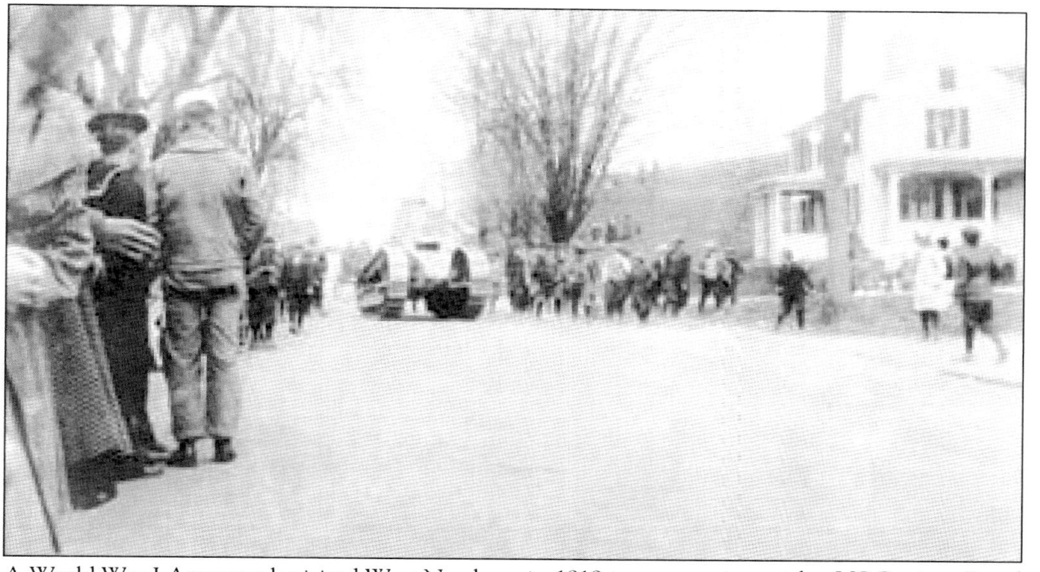

A World War I Army tank visited West Newbury in 1919 in connection with a US Savings Bond drive. Here, it is approaching Post Office Square; the house on the right was later moved to 261 Main Street. Winthrop Thurlow and Lester Kirkpatrick, who had served in a tank corps, drove the tank up the hill opposite St. Ann's Church. (Courtesy of Elinor Spofford.)

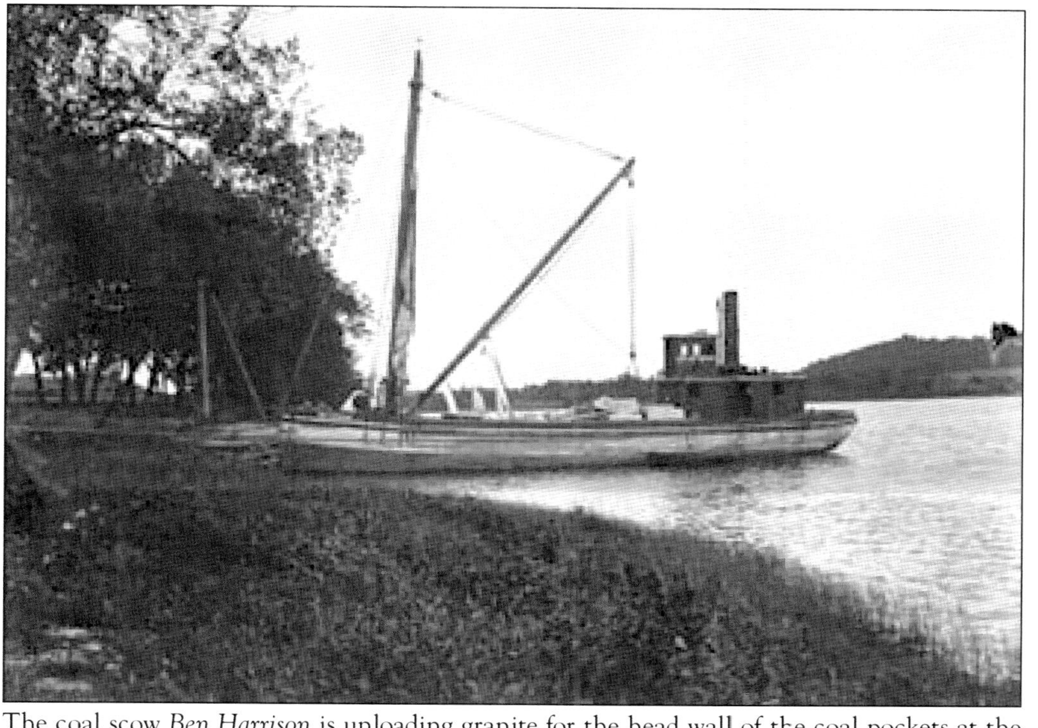

The coal scow *Ben Harrison* is unloading granite for the head wall of the coal pockets at the foot of Whetstone Street around 1890. Coal was brought up the Merrimack River by scows to the coal pockets, where farmers would load it into their tip carts. (Photograph by Jessie Jaques; courtesy of Donald Laing.)

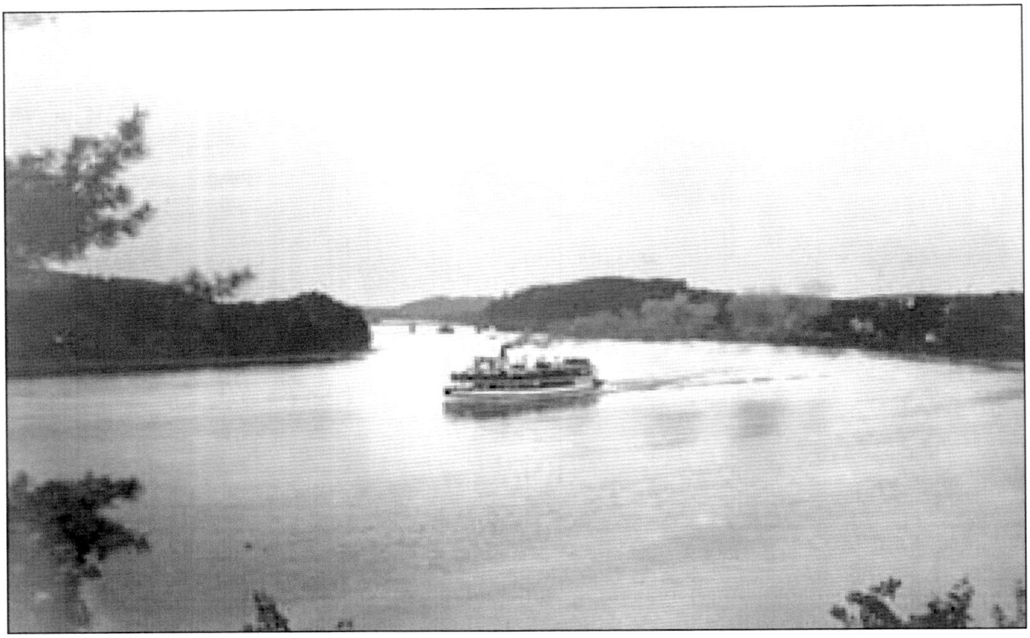

The West Newbury section of the Merrimack River holds some of the most beautiful scenery on the river. Steam transportation on the river began in 1864. As seen in this picture, a stern-wheeler makes its way down the river, loaded with passengers destined for an outing to Salisbury Beach. (Photograph by William E. Sharples; courtesy of John McGrath.)

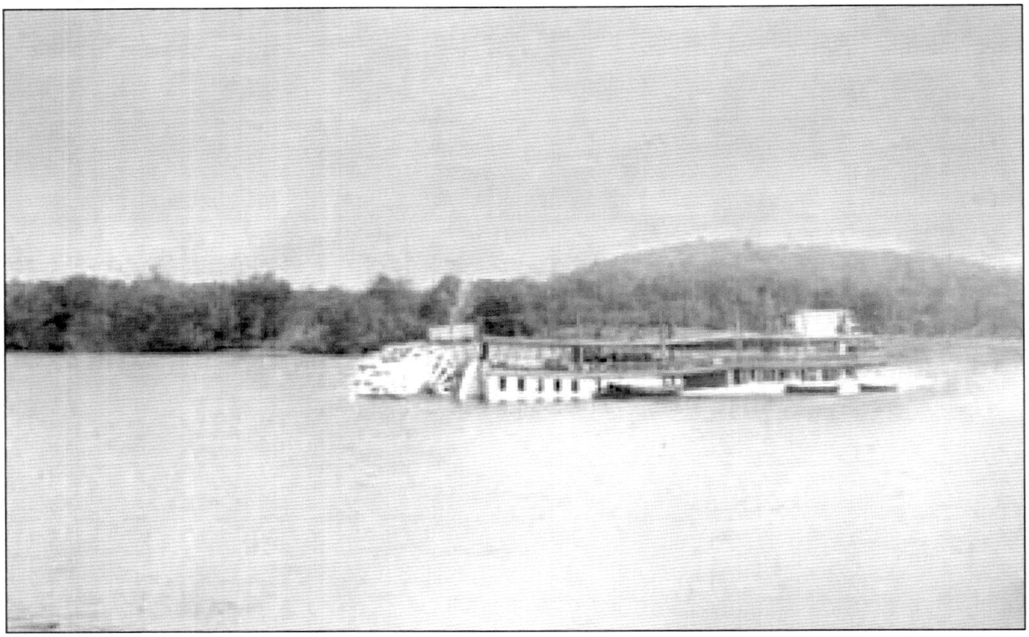

The steamer *City of Haverhill* made her first trip from Haverhill to Black Rocks in Salisbury in 1880. Constructed at Rings Island, the steamer *Merrimack*, which was the largest and fastest boat on the river, replaced it. The *Merrimack*, with 300 persons aboard, struck a rock opposite Huntington Hill in East Haverhill on September 6, 1899. (Courtesy of the GAR Memorial Library.)

Eight

Fire Department

"Ever Ready—Always Willing"

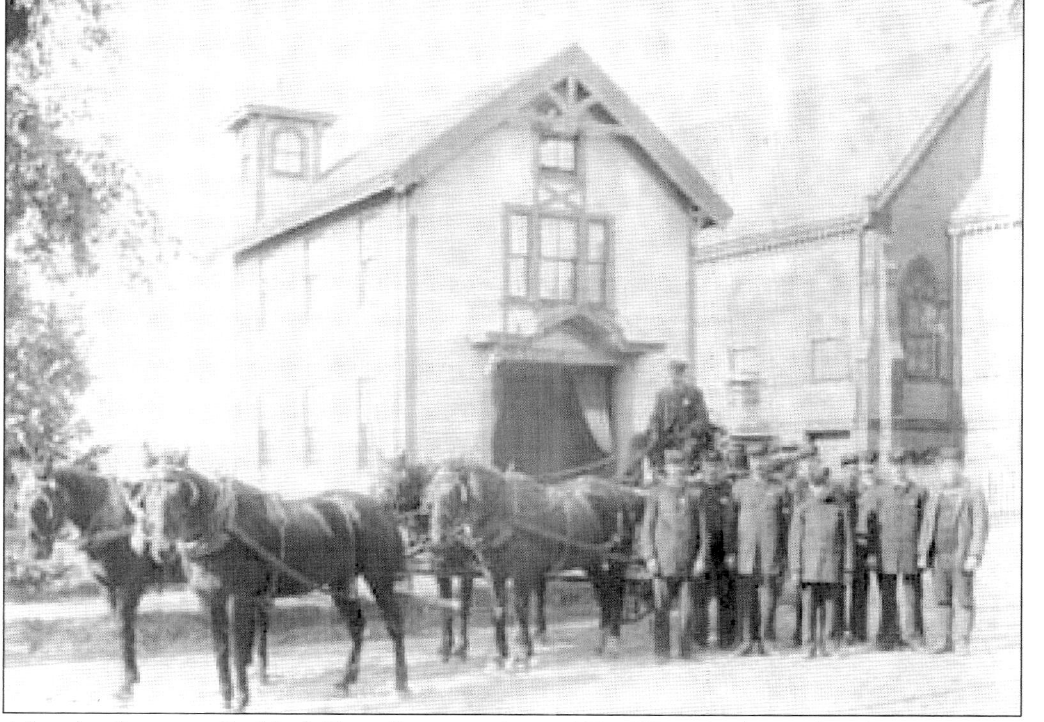

After the disastrous Ruddock Shoe Company fire in 1884, West Newbury's first fire station was built, located on Main Street where the parking lot for St. Ann's Church is now. The building was torn down in 1962. Although a last-minute attempt was made to save the structure for its historic value, the money could not be raised. (Courtesy of Theresa Poore.)

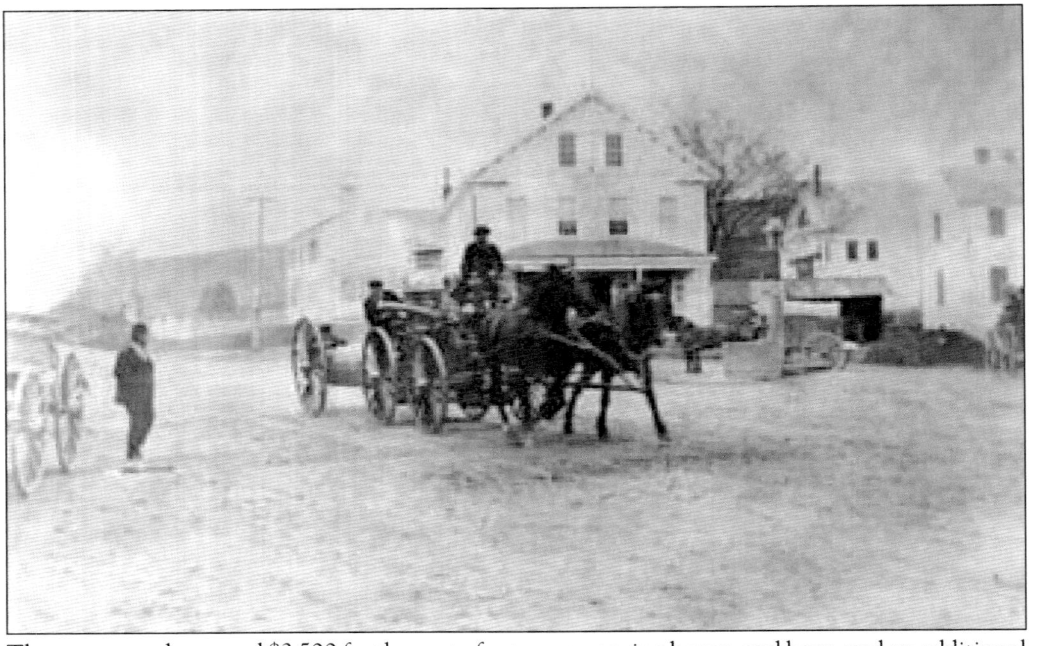

The town voted to spend $3,500 for the cost of a steamer, engine house, and hose, and an additional $2,000 for brick reservoirs that were placed at strategic locations. These reservoirs, which were 12 feet in diameter and 16 feet deep, each held 10,000 gallons of water. The steamer chosen was made by L. Button and Son Company of Waterford, New York, and named the Haydn Brown, shown above, to honor one of the contributors. After it arrived, it was tested and threw a stream of water about 200 feet. Water was thrown over the cross and tower of both St. Ann's Church and the Second Congregational Church. The steamer below is pumping from the reservoir at 117 Main Street. (Picture above by W.H. Stevens, courtesy of Joyce Burnham Dixon; below, courtesy of Sandra Berkenbush.)

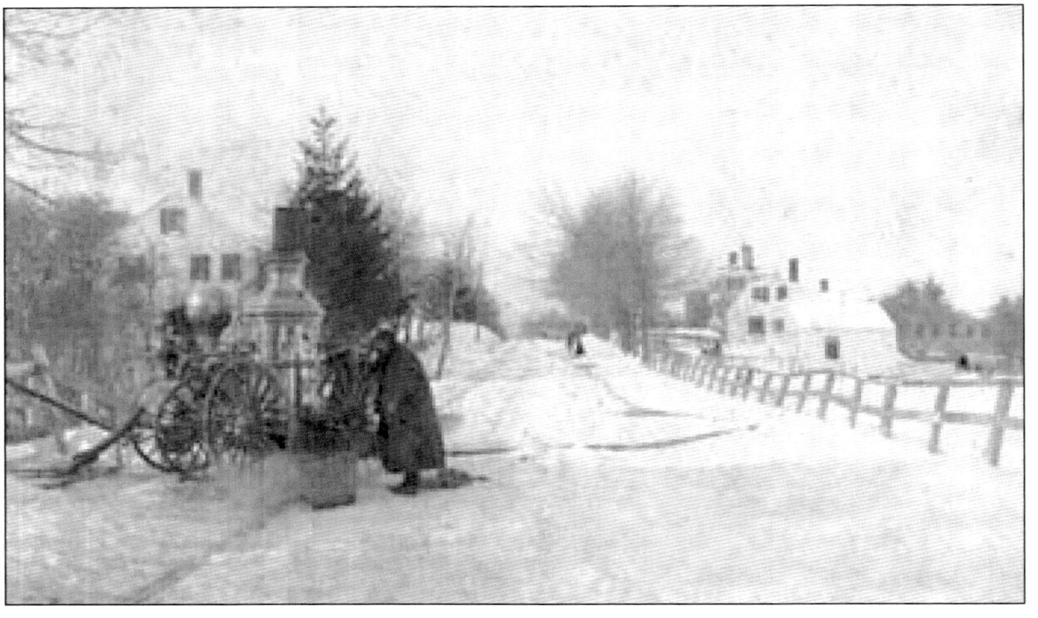

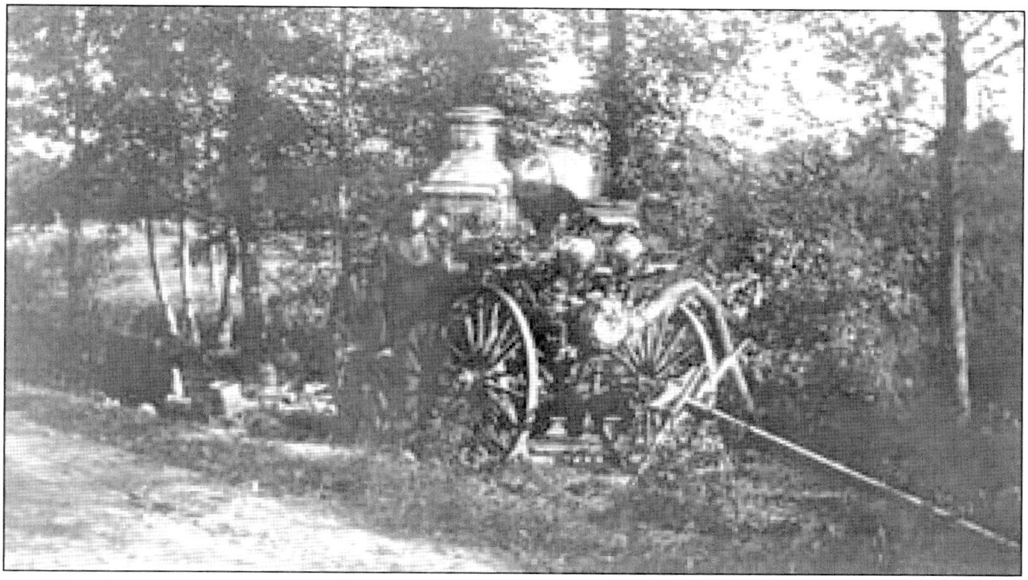

In 1899, the town appropriated $75 to purchase hooks and ladders and a carriage for firefighters to accompany the steamer. The Haydn Brown steamer was used until 1923, when it was retired. In 1929, it was sold to the Henry Ford Museum in Dearborn, Michigan. (Courtesy of Sandra Berkenbush.)

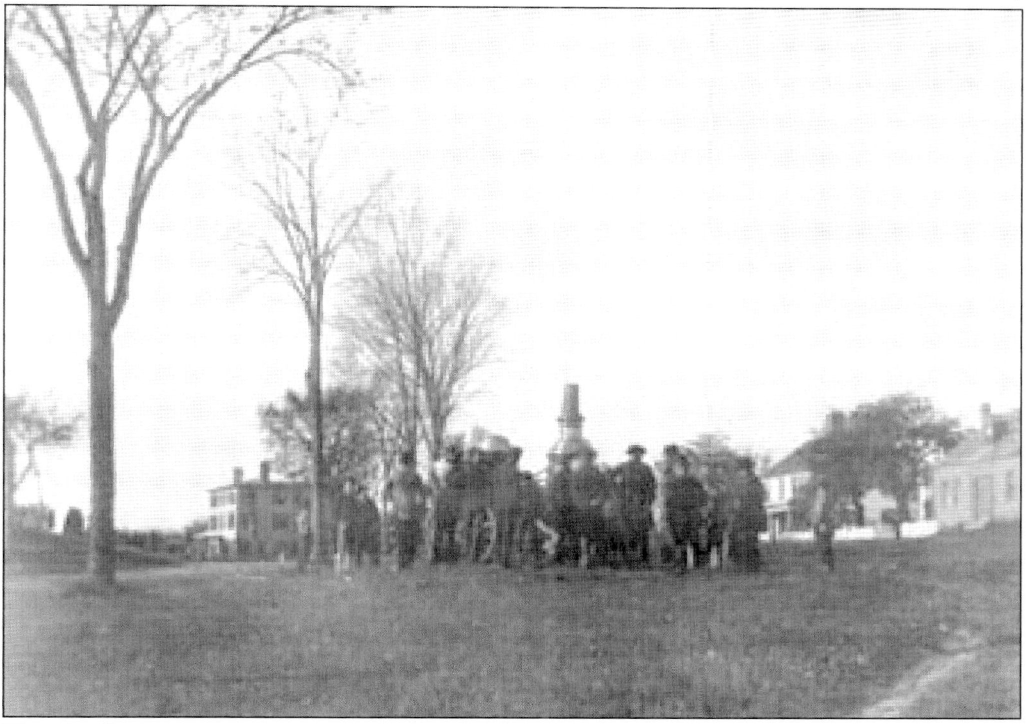

The Haydn Brown steamer is pictured at the fire cistern or reservoir at the easterly end of the Training Field. There were seven reservoirs at various locations in town. The Hotel Albion can be seen in the distance at the left; houses on the Training Field are seen at the right. (Courtesy of Joyce Burnham Dixon.)

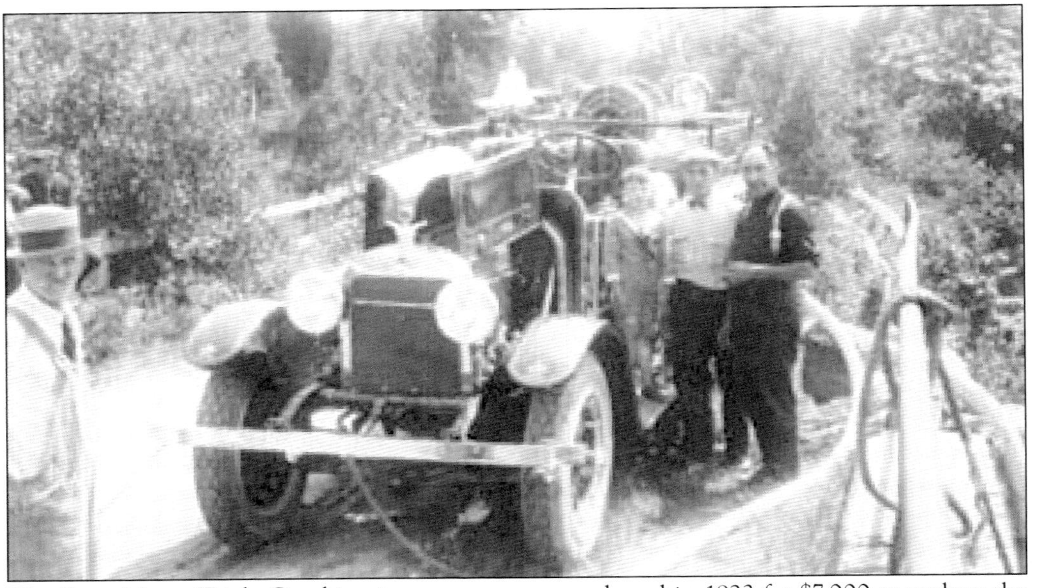

The Stutz Motor Triple Combination pumper was purchased in 1923 for $7,000 to replace the horse-drawn Haydn Brown steam engine. It was shipped in a large double-door railroad car from Indianapolis to the Newburyport railroad freight station on Pond Street and was then driven to West Newbury. Testing the engine on the Middle Street Bridge are, from left to right, unidentified, E. Currier Brown, Horace Brown, and Bradford Swap. (Courtesy of Elinor Spofford.)

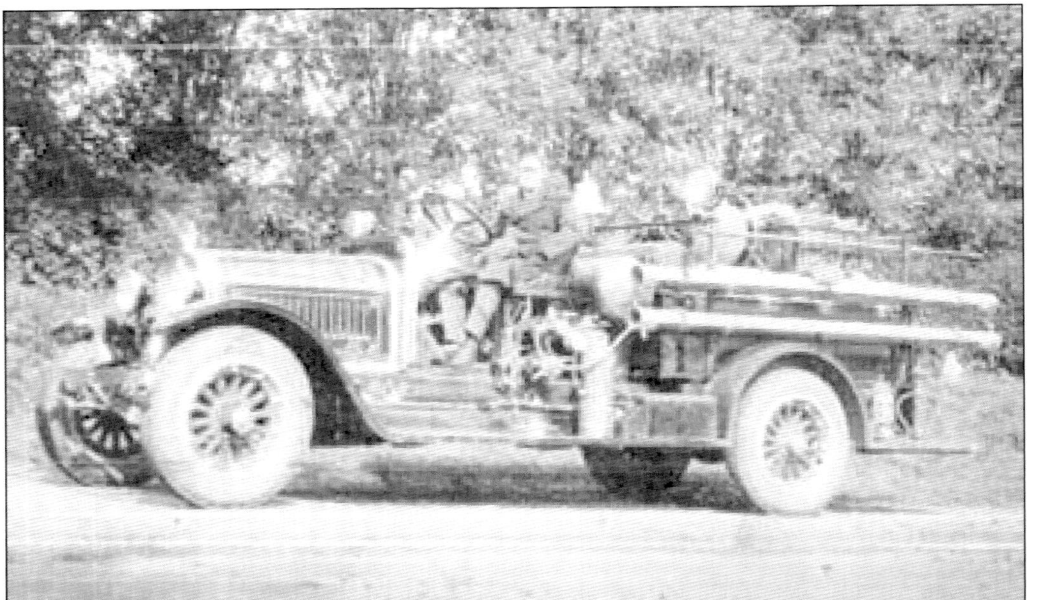

The Stutz fire engine did not come with a windshield, although one was added in 1936. On January 31, 1935, when it was two degrees below zero, Walter Swap drove the Stutz to a house fire at the Cooney farm on Turkey Hill Road and froze his face. (Courtesy of Elinor Spofford.)

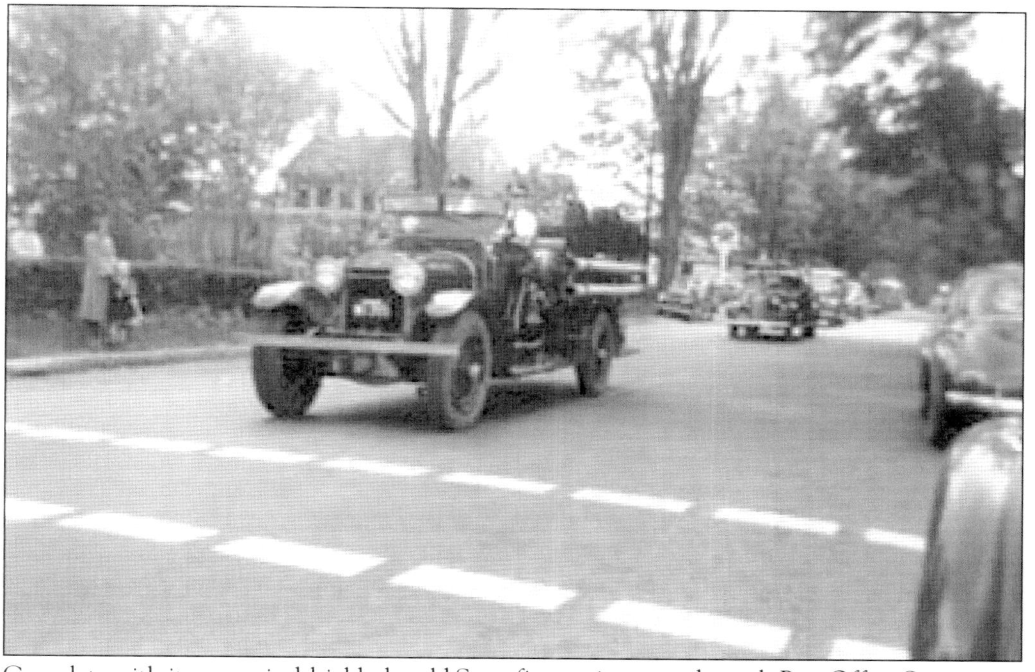

Complete with its new windshield, the old Stutz fire engine goes through Post Office Square in a parade in the 1940s. Visible in the background is the Texaco sign at the West Newbury Garage. The Stutz was retired in 1957 after 34 years of faithful service. (Courtesy of Doris Bailey-Jones.)

The Stutz fire engine was sold to the Tolman family of Georgetown, who lovingly restored it to its former glory, as seen at the right. The new owner's daughter is pictured seated in the passenger seat at a parade venue at Strawbery Banke in Portsmouth, New Hampshire, in 1966. (Courtesy of Scott Berkenbush.)

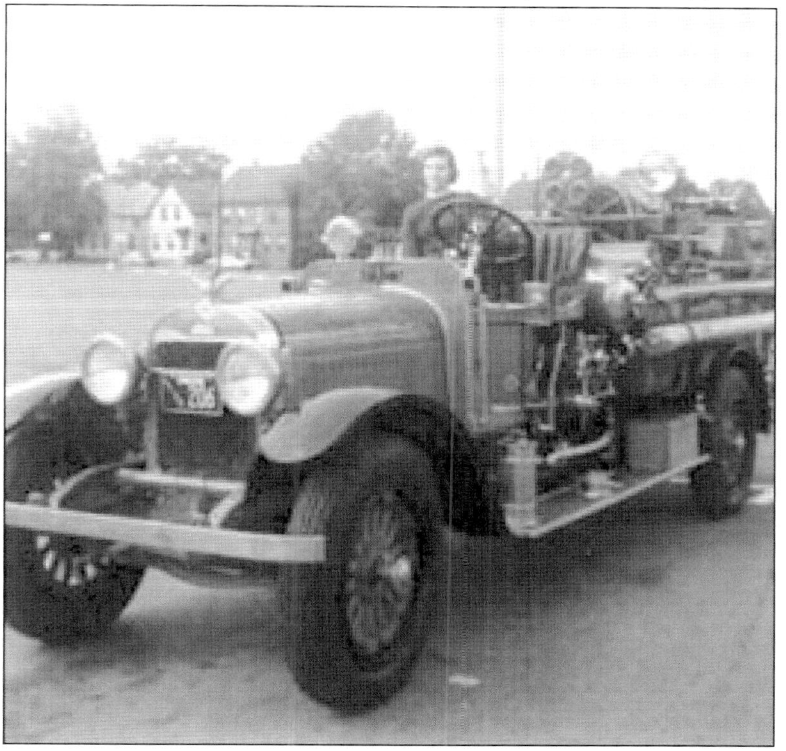

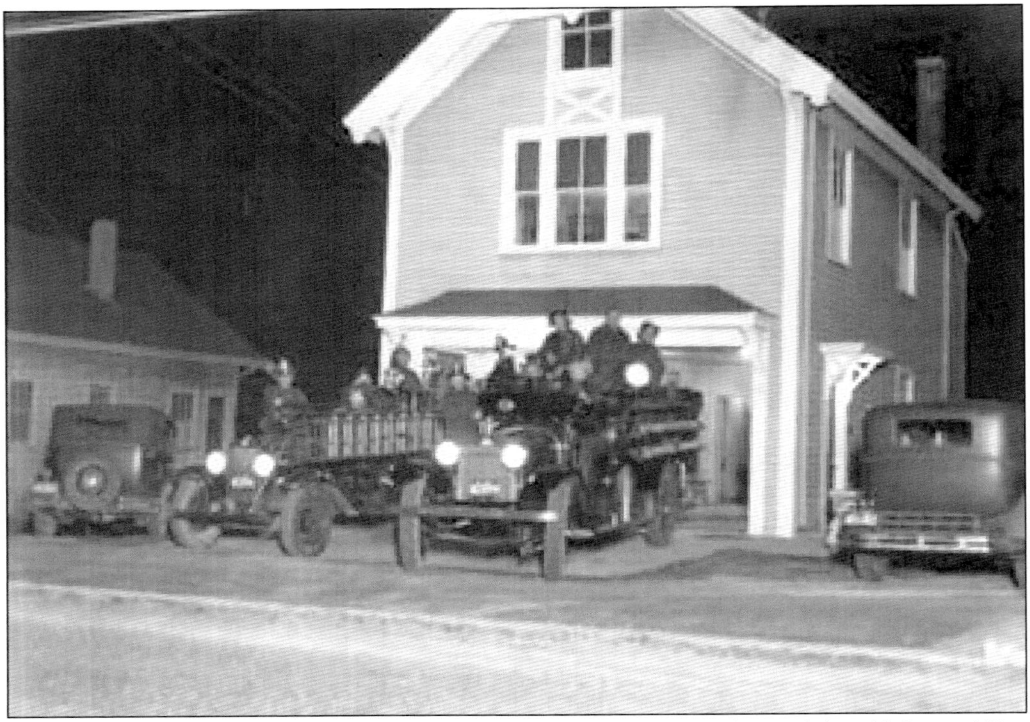

Pictured here are the Kissel fire engine and the Stutz fire engine in front of the old Central Fire Station. The picture was taken about 1936. In 1960, it was determined that the fire station floor was not strong enough for the newer, heavier fire trucks, and a new station was built at a new location. (Courtesy of Scott Berkenbush.)

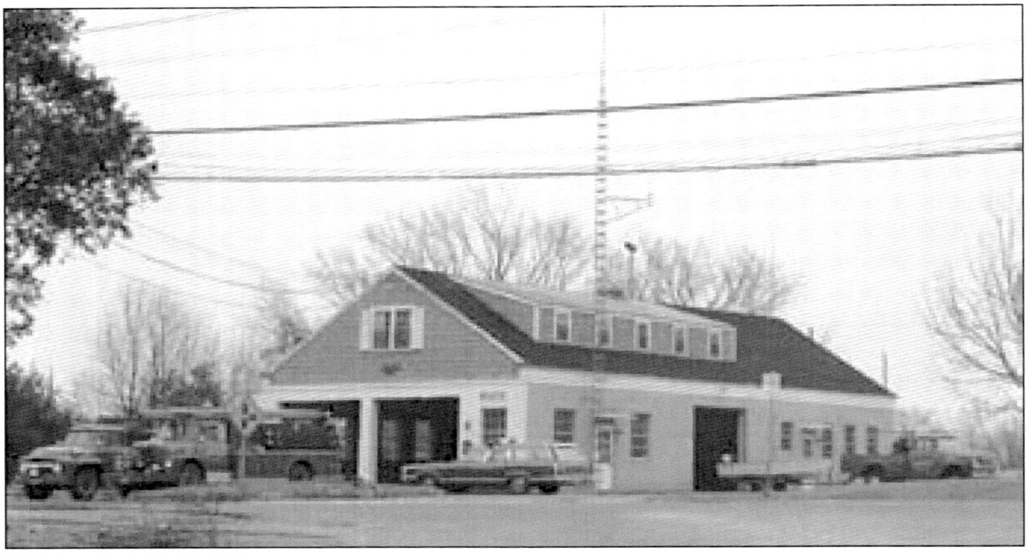

The new Central Fire Station at 399 Main Street was built in 1960. It was torn down in 2004, and a public safety building was erected to house the police and fire departments. Shown here, from left to right, are Engine No. 1, a 1939 Chevrolet; Engine No. 2, a 1956 Ford; and Rescue No. 1. (Courtesy of Sandra Berkenbush.)

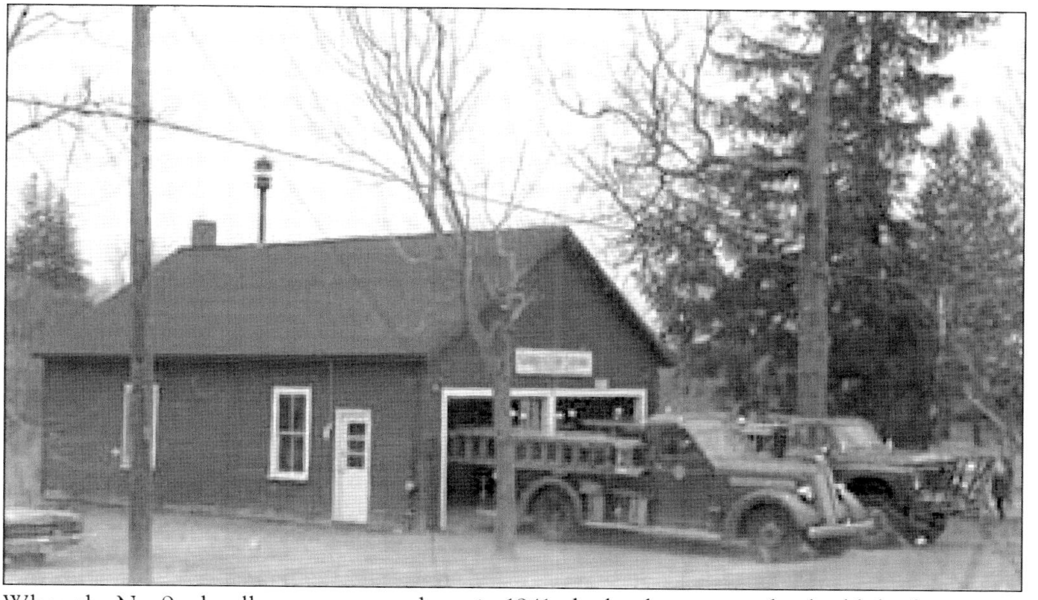

When the No. 9 schoolhouse was torn down in 1941, the lumber was used to build the fire station on Garden Street, pictured above. This building was used until 1976, when newer fire trucks no longer fit inside. At that time, students from Whittier Regional Vocational-Technical High School built a new station, shown below, beside the old one, and Prescott Spalding tore the old one down. (Courtesy of Sandra Berkenbush.)

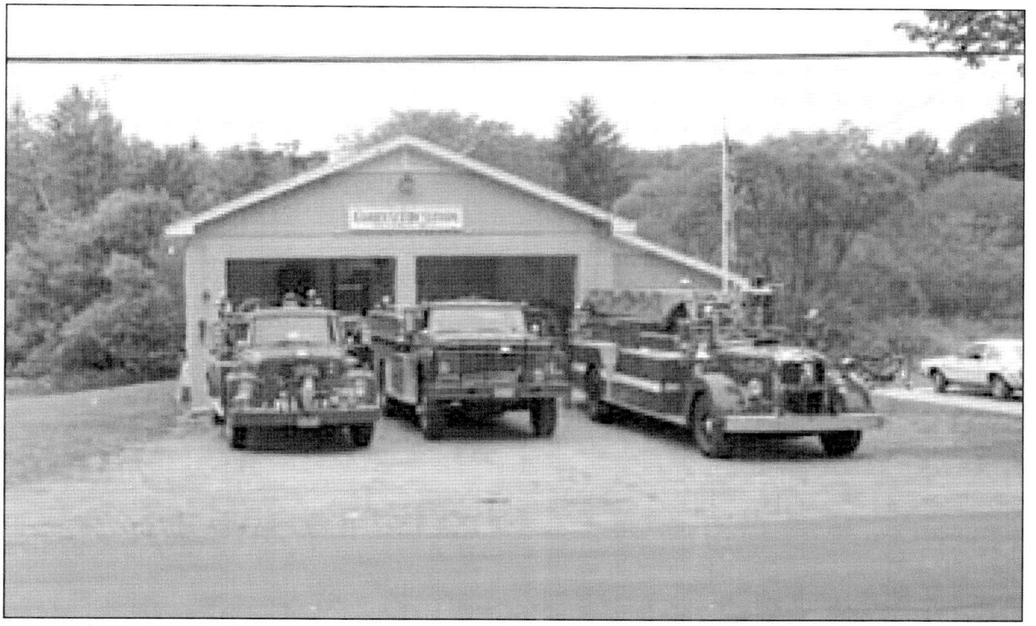

Pictured in front of the new Garden Street station are, from left to right, a 1963 International truck, a 1966 four-wheel drive Ford Forestry truck with a 600-gallon tank capacity, and a 1953 Mack 65-foot aerial ladder truck. The International started as a combination ladder and pumper truck, the first in West Newbury dedicated to the long ladders necessary to protect taller buildings. It was later reconfigured into a pumper. (Courtesy of Scott Berkenbush.)

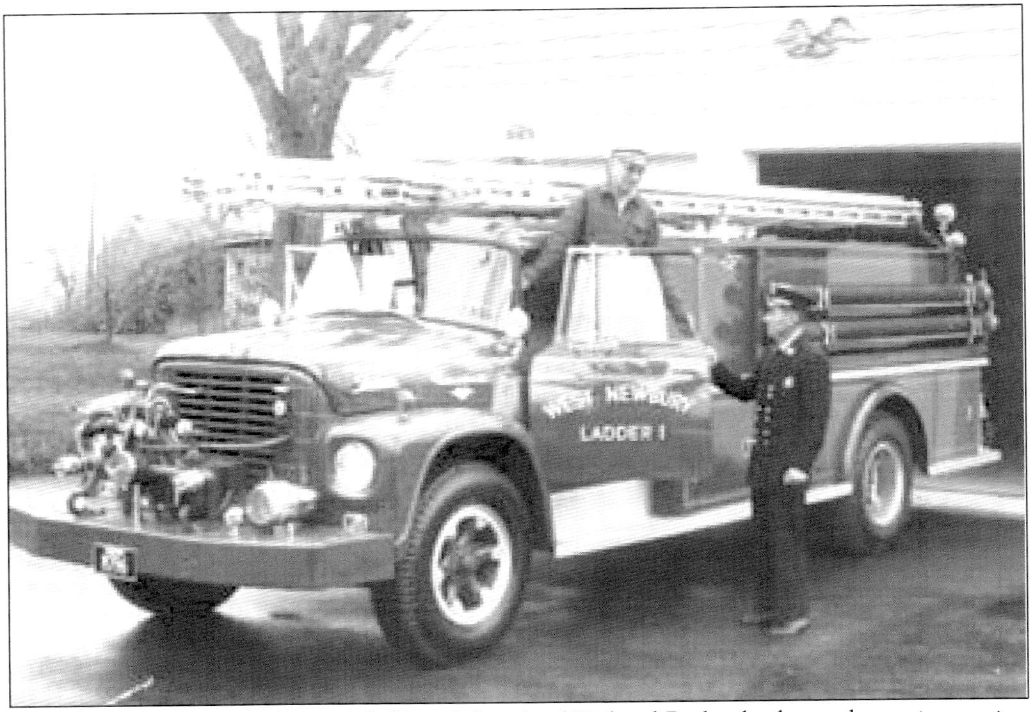

Deputy fire chief Howard Poore (left) and fire chief Richard Berkenbush are shown inspecting the new combination ladder and pumper truck in 1963. At the Gates fire on Dole Place in 1964, a fireman was bemoaning the lack of water pressure from the nearest hydrant. Poore did some rapid calculations and said, "According to the laws of hydraulics and friction loss, you shouldn't be getting any water." (Courtesy of Susan Poore Follansbee.)

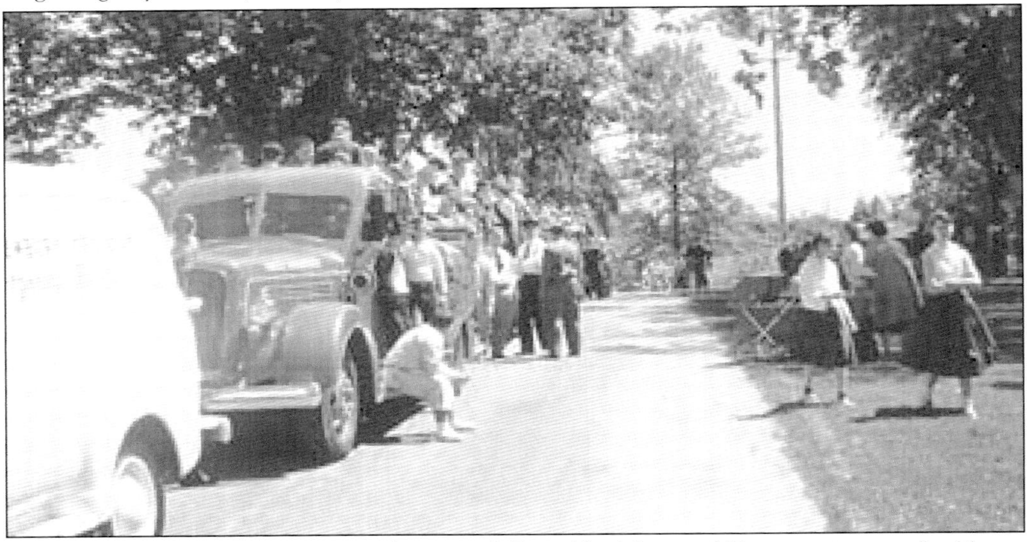

Memorial Day parades in West Newbury are followed by Memorial Day exercises on the library lawn. A highlight of the day for local children for many years has been to ride on fire trucks from the Training Field to the Legion Hall for ice cream and soda after the celebration. Here, children are eagerly awaiting their ride. (Courtesy of Scott Berkenbush.)

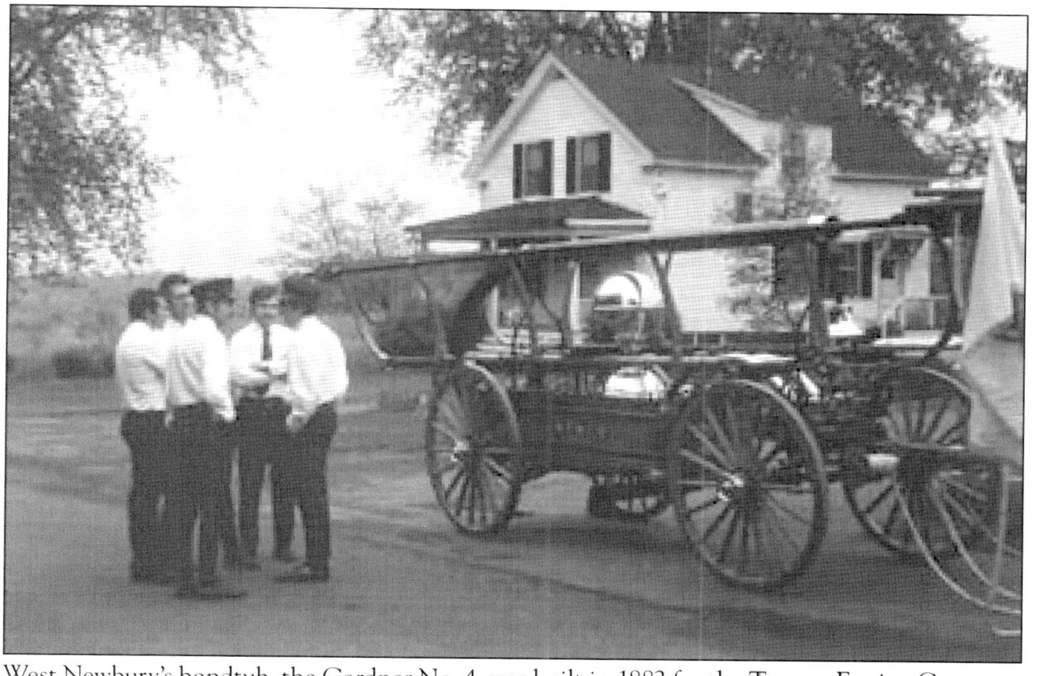

West Newbury's handtub, the Gardner No. 4, was built in 1882 for the Torrent Engine Company in Gardner, Massachusetts. In the early 1960s, the Handtub Association included many young men from town who were also members of the fire department. West Newbury took another handtub, the Edwin A. Whiting, to the New York World's Fair in 1964. (Courtesy of Susan Poore Follansbee.)

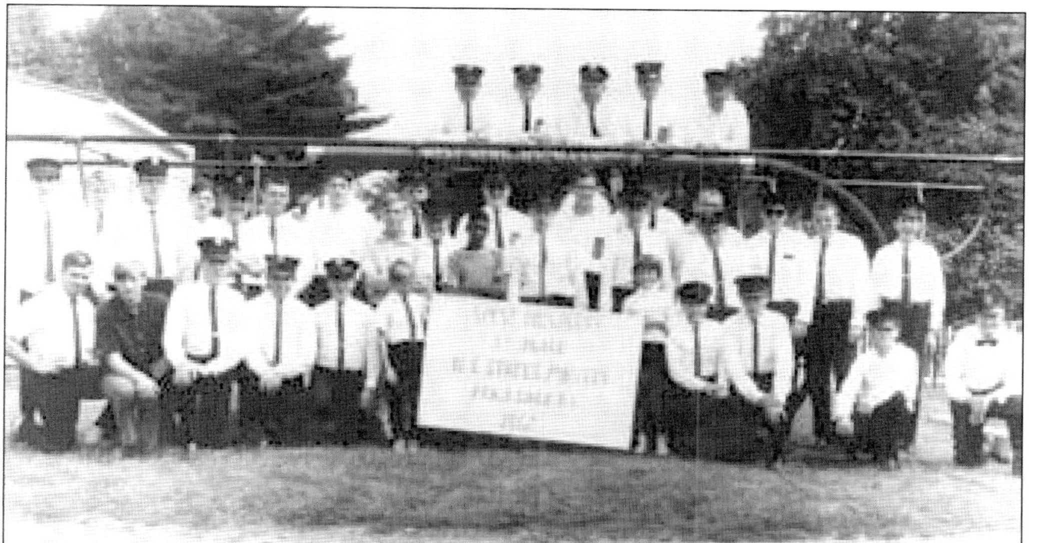

The crew of Gardner No. 4 poses for a celebratory picture after winning the New England States Muster in 1967, the first year West Newbury did so. They went on to win seven consecutive years in a row, a record that has not yet been matched. (Courtesy of the West Newbury Historical Commission.)

Find Your Place in History.

www.arcadiapublishing.com

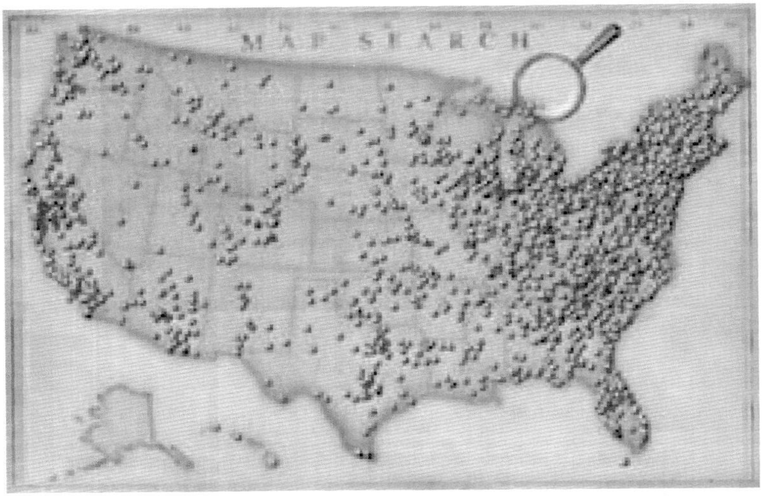

Discover books about the town where you grew up, the cities where your friends and families live, the town where your parents met, or even that retirement spot you've been dreaming about. Our Web site provides history lovers with exclusive deals, advanced notification about new titles, e-mail alerts of author events, and much more.

MADE IN THE USA

Arcadia Publishing, the leading local history publisher in the United States, is committed to making history accessible and meaningful through publishing books that celebrate and preserve the heritage of America's people and places. Consistent with our mission to preserve history on a local level, this book was printed in South Carolina on American-made paper and manufactured entirely in the United States.

This book carries the accredited Forest Stewardship Council (FSC) label and is printed on 100 percent FSC-certified paper. Products carrying the FSC label are independently certified to assure consumers that they come from forests that are managed to meet the social, economic, and ecological needs of present and future generations.

FSC

Mixed Sources

Product group from well-managed forests and other controlled sources

Cert no. SW-COC-001530

www.fsc.org

© 1996 Forest Stewardship Council